ARROW POINTS OF TEXAS AND ITS BORDERLANDS

THE TEXAS EXPERIENCE
*Books made possible by
Sarah '84 and Mark '77 Philpy*

ARROW POINTS

OF TEXAS AND ITS BORDERLANDS

William E. Moore

Foreword by John E. Dockall

Texas A&M University Press
College Station

Copyright © 2025 by William E. Moore
All rights reserved
First edition

♾ This paper meets the requirements of ANSI/NISO Z39.48-1992
(Permanence of Paper).
Binding materials have been chosen for durability.
Manufactured in the United States of America.

Library of Congress Cataloging-in-Publication Data

Names: Moore, William E., 1943– author | Dockall, John E. author of
    introduction, etc.
Title: Arrow points of Texas and its borderlands / William E. Moore ;
    foreword by John E. Dockall.
Other titles: Texas experience (Texas A & M University. Press)
Description: First edition. | College Station : Texas A&M University Press,
    [2025] | Series: The Texas experience | Includes bibliographical
    references and index.
Identifiers: LCCN 2024059265 (print) | LCCN 2024059266 (ebook) | ISBN
    9781648432972 | ISBN 9781648432989 ebook
Subjects: LCSH: Arrowheads—Texas | Arrowheads—Southwest, Old | Indians of
    North America—Implements—Southwest, Old | Indians of North
    America—Southwest, Old—Antiquities | Texas—Antiquities
Classification: LCC E78.T4 .M677 2025 (print) | LCC E78.T4 (ebook) | DDC
    976—dc23/eng/20250311
LC record available at https://lccn.loc.gov/2024059265
LC ebook record available at https://lccn.loc.gov/2024059266

I am fortunate to have worked with and been mentored by some great people to whom I credit my success as a professional archaeologist. During the formative years of my interest in archaeology, Doris L. Olds was the Curator of Records at the Texas Archeological Research Laboratory (TARL) on the campus of the University of Texas at Austin. She taught me how to record sites and label artifacts and, along with the rest of the staff, was a constant source of encouragement. After retirement, she gave me her personal library, and I consider myself only the curator because I plan to pass it on some day. This book is dedicated to her memory.

Contents

Foreword, by John E. Dockall ix

Preface xiii

Acknowledgments xv

Introduction 1

CHAPTER 1. What is an Arrowhead? 13

CHAPTER 2. Raw Materials 25

CHAPTER 3. Projectile Point Typologies 49

CHAPTER 4. Archaeological Planning Regions 59

CHAPTER 5. Relevant Literature 69

CHAPTER 6. Arrow Points 75

CHAPTER 7. Final Thoughts 239

Epilogue 243

Appendix A. County Abbreviations 245

Appendix B. Texas Arrow Points Found
in Other States and Mexico 251

Appendix C. Shapes of Arrow Points 253

Appendix D. Sites with Manning Fused Glass 255

Appendix E. Counties in the Planning Regions 257

References Cited 259

Index 301

Foreword

John E. Dockall

WHEN I FIRST ENTERED graduate school at Texas A&M University in 1986, I was fortunate to study archaeology and anthropology with Harry J. Shafer and to participate in several seasons of fieldwork at the NAN Ranch in New Mexico. My master's thesis focused on the chipped stone technology at the NAN Ranch and provided my first real experience in dealing with the multiple typological conundrums of projectile points and gave me the opportunity to take a lithic analysis from start to finish. It was a simultaneously terrifying and exhilarating experience that follows me to this day, 37 years later, as a professional archaeologist working in the Cultural Resource Management (CRM) field in Texas. For many reasons, every lithic assemblage I have had the opportunity to study starts as a huge knot in the pit of my stomach and ends in great satisfaction as I have finished the last sentence of the last paragraph of one of many "just so stories" in prehistoric technology and archaeology: a story that likely will be much better written by future archaeologists who get to stand on the shoulders of those who trod the same research ground decades earlier.

Through my years at Texas A&M and later, I had the distinct pleasure of working shoulder to shoulder with, or at least getting to swap ideas and discussion of "all things lithic" with, many folks I consider to be my mentors and colleagues in Texas archaeology. I equally include degreed professionals and avocational archaeologists in that list because they all shaped my present approach to lithic technology and interpretation.

I want to acknowledge that it was Bill Moore who provided my first "paid gig" in CRM and my first "paid gig" in lithic analysis. On several occasions, I was fortunate enough to get to do lithic analysis and reporting for some of his projects at Brazos Valley Research Associates (BVRA) and

x | Foreword

participate in survey projects that were relatively close to College Station, Texas. While small compared to what I have done since, those were some of the most memorable and meaningful projects I have participated in. It is for this reason, among others, that I am happy to produce this foreword to the present volume *Arrow Points of Texas and Its Borderlands*. I have always been happy to consider Bill a valuable colleague and friend.

True to Bill's penchant for detail and thoroughness, this volume presents a very welcome addition to the literature on Texas prehistory and lithic technology. It does not supplant and replace anything gone before but rather is a coherent and much needed addition that builds on previous efforts to present the "knot" of Texas point typology in a coherent manner. This volume includes updated information on many of the known arrow point types in Texas and provides much needed synthesis of regional and chronological data that will be useful to professional and avocational archaeologists alike.

Bill's volume on arrow points makes no judgments regarding the validity of some types that have been brought into question by various archaeologists in recent decades, as those type names still appear in the literature from time to time. What this volume does is provide enough background history and geographic range for each point type, dimensional information where available, and coherent presentation of chronological range and cultural associations. Enough information is included with each type so that the reader can evaluate the veracity of previous information. Even so, the volume provides an extensive and useful bibliography of available literature for each type included. Trinomial information and common-usage site names are included as part of the available information for each type. This information is almost always difficult to track down.

In my thirty-plus years in doing archaeology and CRM archaeology, tracking down references with illustrated examples, detailed descriptions, metric data, raw materials, and sufficient chronological and geographic information for projectile points has typically involved multiple references and editions of works by Turner and Hester, Bell, Perino, Prewitt, and others. Much of the usually needed information to make judicious assessments of arrow point styles and types is presented succinctly in this volume.

I am pleased to see another volume devoted to projectile points in Texas, especially one that takes on arrow points as a class of data by themselves. It will be a welcome and well-used reference for years to come. I firmly believe that it will be regarded as a useful resource for professional and avocational archaeologists alike as it brings together much useful, but very thinly published, material in one handy location and format.

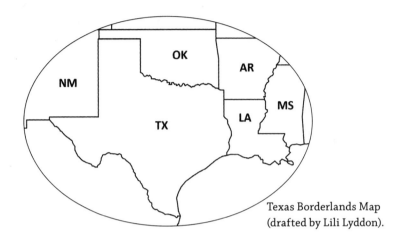

Texas Borderlands Map (drafted by Lili Lyddon).

Preface

THE TEXAS BORDERLANDS REGION is defined as the state of Texas, adjacent states Arkansas, Louisiana, New Mexico, and Oklahoma, and the northern regions of Mexico. *Arrow Points of Texas and Its Borderlands* provides in-depth discussions of all arrow points native to Texas that have been typed with names that are considered defensible by most archaeologists. This includes points from neighboring states that have also been reported as occurring in Texas. Mississippi is not a border state, but it is included because some Texas types have been reported in that state. The purpose of this inclusivity is to provide the reader with as much information as possible regarding each of the known types. One criterion for naming a point is its unique shape or configuration. Since some points are very similar in form to other types, other criteria such as context and provenience are used to differentiate between the two sometimes barely indistinguishable examples. Variation and disconformity occur in all known types due to such factors as quality of raw material, skill of the knapper, reworking following breakage, and such. Those illustrated here are considered good to excellent examples of each type. Sources are provided where more depictions of each type are presented. Some types may not be recognized by some researchers as valid types, and the author does not assume responsibility for their authenticity.

Acknowledgments

THIS PROJECT could not have been completed without the help of a great many people, and any omissions are completely accidental. Factual errors in this book are solely mine. I would not be in the position to have conducted this level of research without encouragement from other archaeologists when I was much younger. My formal introduction to archaeology was in 1959 when I attended a meeting of the newly formed Houston Archeological Society and became a charter member. Wayne Neyland, Alan R. Duke, and Hubert Mewhinney were always supportive, and it was with this society that I participated in my first excavation that took place at the Jamison site (41LB1) under the supervision of Lawrence E. Aten. Neyland introduced me to the Texas Archeological Research Laboratory (TARL) on the campus of the University of Texas at Austin and stressed the importance of recording sites. At the time, Dee Ann Story was the director, Doris Olds was the curator of artifacts and records, and Carolyn Spock was a graduate student employed by the university. I made frequent trips to TARL to document newly found sites, and Mrs. Olds was very patient with me. She showed me how to calculate Universal Transverse Mercator (UTM) coordinates the old way using a pencil, yardstick, and a transparent UTM coordinate grid. These visits were often the highlight of my day. Mrs. Olds was succeeded by Carolyn Spock, whose knowledge of the records at TARL will probably never be surpassed. The accumulation of data for this book was a very exhausting venture, and I doubt I could have finished this project without the help of key people at TARL. Associate director Jonathan Jarvis and TexSite coordinator Jean Hughes spent many hours matching site numbers with names and copying articles for me. Stephen Bales is a former Humanities and Social Sciences Librarian in the Texas A&M University Libraries System who helped me to obtain reference materials from other universities.

xvi | **Acknowledgments**

Professional archaeologists who took time from their busy schedules to discuss this project with me or help in other ways include Jeffrey Alvey, Fernando Arias, George Avery, Stephen Black, Roger Boren, Robert L. Brooks, Ken Brown, Andy Cloud, Peter Condon, E. Mott Davis, Julie Densmore, William A. Dickens, John E. Dockall, H. Blaine Ensor, Mary Jo Galindo, John Greer, Lorraine Heartfield, Thomas R. Hester, Jonathan Jarvis, David Keller, Leonard Kemp, Christopher Lintz, Dan McGregor, Robert J. Mallouf, Mickey Miller, Roger G. Moore, Timothy K. Perttula, Harry J. Shafer, Ross Skowronek, Michael J. Shott, Bob Skiles, Dee Ann Story, Jesse Todd, Mary Beth Trubitt, Solveig A. Turpin, Jim Warren, and Richard Weinstein. I would like to close by personally thanking Edward B. Jelks for his assistance and support, especially his recounting of the methods employed during the production of *An Introductory Handbook of Texas Archeology* as well as reading the first draft of the manuscript.

Laura Nightengale, former director of collections at TARL, photographed specimens housed at that facility. Brian Wootan, Tanner Singleton, and Maggie Bailey are professional photographers who participated in this project. Permission to use illustrations from publications was granted by Ken Brown and Richard J. McReynolds. Lili G. Lyddon drafted certain figures and created the scales for artifacts. I'm appreciative of those who allowed access to their collections, some pieces of which are included in this book. They include Troy Adler, George Avery, Jack C. Bates, Jr., Michael Boutwell, Ken Brown, William Dickens, Brady Epperson, Adrien Fauchois, John Fish, Trent Jackson, Sam Johnson, Chris Merriam, Heath Neyland, Thomas Oakes, Jason Pearson, Timothy K. Perttula, Dwayne Rogers, Matt Soultz, and Brandon Wilson. Sallie Cotter Andrews and Mary Jo Gallindo edited the manuscript prior to submission to the university press. Computer and formatting assistance was provided by Rodney Hermes of Mobile Wiseguy Solutions. Terry Sherrell converted the color images to grayscale to comply with the requirements of Texas A&M University Press.

In 1985, Thomas R. Hester realized the need for a current book on point typology as it had been twenty-three years since the Texas Archeological Society and the Texas Memorial Museum collaborated to publish *Handbook of Texas Archeology: Type Descriptions* in 1962. His hunch was right

Acknowledgments | xvii

on when he, along with Ellen Sue Turner and artist Kathy Roemer, published *A Field Guide to Stone Artifacts* with successive volumes in 1993 and 1999. These sought-after publications were followed by an expanded and improved *Stone Artifacts of Texas Indians* in 2011. This time, Richard L. McReynolds was responsible for the illustrations. Hester is acknowledged for inspiring me to follow up his work with this volume.

ARROW POINTS
OF TEXAS AND
ITS BORDERLANDS

INTRODUCTION

THE EXCITEMENT one gets from finding his or her first "arrowhead" is an experience that can only be understood by those who have held a stone object that was made and used by people hundreds, if not thousands, of years ago. Similar seminal events have been the catalyst that helped transform many casual collectors into professional archaeologists who have made significant contributions to the discipline of archaeology. My first introduction to projectile point typology—the assignment of names as a method of identification—was at a young age when an employee at Garner State Park let me borrow his copy of the highly collectible volume 25 of the *Bulletin of the Texas Archeological Society* titled "An Introductory Handbook of Texas Archeology." The authors were Dee Ann Suhm and Alex D. Krieger (who collaborated with Edward B. Jelks who is often cited as a third author). Suhm and Krieger (1954:1) argued for the utility of handbooks when they wrote "Archeology has never developed the handbook principal, except in the case of guides to individual museum collections." This breakthrough handbook was not without its problems, as data were often sparse or nonexistent in some areas of Texas. For example, Suhm and Krieger (1954:Figure 4) referred to much of Texas as "undefined" in terms of known culture complexes in the Archaic and Neo-American stages of Texas prehistory.

Their work represents the first large-scale attempt at creating a useful system of typology for Texas projectile points. The catalyst for this publication was an absence of articles submitted to the Texas Archeological Society (TAS) for its annual bulletin (Suhm and Krieger 1954:5). Therefore, the editors decided to publish the 1954 bulletin as a comprehensive compilation of what was known about projectile points and ceramics in

2 | Introduction

Texas at the time as well as an overview of Texas archaeology. It was a very ambitious project that required the examination of thousands of specimens and an exhaustive data search for the entire state. Krieger writes in the introduction: "The actual writing of this Handbook would not have been too difficult if all the typological research had been set beforehand. However, it was necessary to re-examine every pottery and projectile point type set up by all those who have created them in the state, including the re-examination of those of the authors themselves" (Suhm and Krieger 1954:12–13). The authors examined more than 25,000 specimens and held in reserve an additional 20,000, "which were then examined to see whether the types could readily be recognized in consistent form and variation" (Suhm and Krieger 1954:5). They only assigned type names if there was a minimum of 100 examples. A few types were scantily represented, but most were based on samples of several hundred, and in some cases 3,000 pieces were available.

Alex D. Krieger and J. Charles Kelley were pioneer Texas archaeologists credited with early attempts at typing points. Krieger (1944:271–288) described the purpose of a type in archaeology as "an organizational tool which will enable the investigator to group specimens into bodies which have demonstrable historical meaning in terms of behavior patterns." He favored names that described the physical appearance of points such as *Alba Barbed* and *Bassett Pointed Stem*. The authors of the 1954 bulletin relied heavily on the work of these predecessors, but they shortened the names of some types. Their reasoning is explained in the following: "All qualifying terms have been dropped from projectile point names, even from those which have previously been published. Qualifying terms give too restrictive an idea of what variations may occur within a type" (Suhm and Krieger 1954:16). Thus, the arrow point *Bassett Pointed Stem* simply became *Bassett*.

Suhm and Krieger (1954:5) wrote that a major problem in the process of establishing new types is the desire by some to "make every specimen to fit into some kind of a type. The obvious result is an inordinate number of new types proposed to account for a few divergent specimens." The authors posited that it was impossible to type every known artifact. The final shape of an arrow point is some variation of a triangle, with a finite number of possibilities. This fact complicates the separation of types according to their physical appearance. It is only natural that overlap and controversy can (and does) occur. Some *Catahoula* and *Sabinal* arrow points, for example, are similar in general outline, but they are found in vastly different regions of Texas. *Catahoula* is a common type in East Texas and Louisiana, while *Sabinal* points are only known to occur in a portion of the Edwards Plateau in the Texas Hill Country.

Another area of disagreement occurs among archaeologists who call themselves "lumpers" and "splitters." Lumpers consider some differences too minor to be more than broad distinctions. Suhm and Krieger (1954:4) wrote that, "In practice, very rough typing of the 'lumper' variety is often quite useless for strict comparisons." "Conversely, 'splitters' believe even minor differences in the shape of an individual specimen can sometimes justify creating a new type." Suhm and Krieger (1954:3) described splitters as preferring "to set up types of great refinement, so that the smallest differences are considered to designate typological distinction, and a collection will be sorted into innumerable small groups of rigid uniformity."

Clarence H. Webb was an early member of the Louisiana Archaeological Society and one of the premier avocational archaeologists whose interest in Louisiana and Texas archaeology began in the 1940s. His approach to typing artifacts is explained in the following: "The reader should know that lithic types are not sacrosanct. They are developed by a person or a group of people who study examples from a site, a cultural group or a given area, who attach a name or names to perceived groups of objects in order to develop a tool for study and comparison" (Webb 2000:1). Volume 19 of the *Bulletin of the Louisiana Archaeological Society*, edited by Jon L. Gibson and Hiram F. Gregory Jr. (1992), is dedicated to Webb's memory. Included with various accolades and tributes is a complete bibliography of his works.

Point Typing Methods

A type is based on much more than its physical appearance. Major factors to be considered are the region of the state where it was found and its association with other artifacts and features (a.k.a. context). When a new type is identified, it is given a name as a matter of convenience for communication between archaeologists and other interested parties. Not all names,

4 | Introduction

however, are readily recognizable. The *Perdiz* point is found throughout Texas. As a result of its widespread distribution, it is well known by most archaeologists and collectors as an example of a Late Prehistoric (a.k.a. Neo-American) arrow point. In contrast, there is less familiarity with regional types such as *Caracara*, *Homan*, and *Moran*, even among some professionals. Suhm and Krieger (1954) argued for a systematic method of evaluating points being considered as types. The need for such a method in Texas was formally presented to the Texas Archeological Society by Jimmy Mitchell thirty years after publication of the influential 1954 bulletin. A typology committee was organized to study the process of recording new types. In November 1984, the committee presented its findings for discussion at a TAS Board meeting. Elton R. Prewitt and Jimmy Mitchell explained the necessity for guidelines and criteria for determining new types. They mentioned the confusion that had arisen about new types that had already been named. Norman Flaigg moved the report be accepted and a committee be appointed. The motion was seconded and carried. The typology committee dissolved in 1995 without crafting a systematic methodology. Apparently, there were some formal meetings, but the members were not interested in continuing. Thomas R. Hester (personal communication, February 8, 2020) related to me that some archaeologists believed it was "ill-conceived and a waste of time."

Today, anyone can proclaim that they have identified a new type. There is no supreme authority to make the final decision, no minimum sample size, and no empirical data such as context or relative and absolute data are required. For these reasons, a proposed type should not appear in the literature without some supporting evidence, a credible number of specimens, serious research that involves discussions with colleagues familiar with the area of the find, and a review of published literature from that area. Disagreement exists between some professional archaeologists as to the validity of certain types. Once a type name appears in the literature it is virtually impossible to eliminate it. One example that deserves mention is the recording of a "typical" *Scottsbluff* point at 41SJ160 in San Jacinto County, Texas (Keller and Weir 1979:23, Figure 12). Although this type has been reported over much of Texas, my personal examination concluded that a large, stemmed biface would have been a better classification.

Another option would be a point that bears resemblance to *Scottsbluff*, such as the designation "*Scottsbluff*-like."

The resulting confusion is obvious and is a detriment to arriving at a consensus regarding age and distribution of a particular type. In the past, type names were primarily based on place names such as nearby towns (*Maud*), counties (*Rockwall*), or geographical features (*Mount Livermore*). On rare occasions, the type names of arrow points have honored landowners such as *Lott* and *Means*. As mentioned, the sample size on which each type is based varies, but larger numbers would definitely add to the validity of a proposed type. When Hester (1977) named the *Guerrero* type, it was based on a sample of around 200 specimens found in and around the missions of *Guerrero* in Coahuila, Mexico. Campbell (1979) studied the known Indian groups who lived in around the Guerrero missions.

Ultimately, the real judge of a type's validity is rendered by other archaeologists who evaluate its merits based on the evidence presented by the person proposing the type. Unfortunately, the appearance of the groundbreaking handbook by Suhm and Krieger (1954) and the reprint (sans overview of Texas' archaeology) by Suhm and Jelks (1962) was misused by archaeologists and collectors in other states that had not conducted a systematic study of the point types where they live. Although it's true that types are not restricted by artificial borders, the claim that certain Texas points were fashioned and used in states as distant as Alabama and Mississippi is not well founded. Examples can be found in the typologies for these states by Cambron and Hulse (1964, 1975) for Alabama and McGahey (2000) for Mississippi. I experienced this unfortunate misrepresentation of types during the writing of a report for a large survey in Mississippi. The person hired to conduct the lithic analysis was a resident archaeologist in that state who classified several types as the same types found only in Texas. Arkansas, Louisiana, New Mexico, and Oklahoma have overlap, but since they are contiguous states, their occurrence in Texas is more believable.

Type Sites

The identification of archaeological sites where the various types have been found is an important piece of an artifact's provenience. The term

6 | Introduction

"type site" refers to the location where a new type was first identified, and they are mentioned when known. The number of sites listed in this book for each type varies according to available information and frequency of each type. *Scallorn* points, for example, are found virtually statewide. Therefore, no attempt was made to list every known site. On the other hand, efforts were made to list as many valid sites as feasible for those types considered to be especially significant or rarely found, such as the *Haskell* type reported by Prewitt (1995:Figure 24), which had fewer than 11 known examples at the time his article was published.

Archaeological sites can be identified by names and/or unique trinomials, with the latter being more specific as multiple sites can have the same or similar names. With few exceptions, only those sites with trinomials issued by TARL appear in the discussion of known sites where types have been documented. In the 1930s and 1940s, the Smithsonian Institution created the trinomial system still used today. It consists of three parts that represent the alphabetical position of the state, the county abbreviation, and the unique site number. An example is 41WA55. This trinomial lets one know that this site is found in Texas (the 41st state alphabetically before the admission of Alaska and Hawaii to the Union), specifically in Walker County as indicated by the abbreviation "WA," and the number 55 indicates that this site is the 55th recorded site in Walker County barring gaps in the records. Appendix A contains a list of the abbreviations for all 254 Texas counties.

Often, sites are assigned names that have no meaning to anyone but those who named them. Two examples are "Tonto's Workbench" and "Not Quite a Site Site." These names are fine for laughter around the campfire, but not suitable for inclusion in permanent documents. They, and others like them, have been deleted from the site forms.

Organization and Resources Used

The information presented in this book was taken from primary sources, including projectile point typology books, contract reports, articles in journals and newsletters, bulletins published by archaeological societies, unpublished manuscripts, special publications, artifact collections, site forms

Introduction | 7

at TARL, and discussions with professional and avocational archaeologists. Not surprisingly, I was exposed to numerous sources that I had not been aware of. In some cases, my opinion on certain aspects of Texas archaeology and the arrow point types I present here was changed based on new information. I was aware of the overlap of some points in adjacent states, but I had never given any thought to those other than those I was most familiar with, such as *Catahoula, Perdiz,* and *Scallorn.* Appendix B lists those types that have been reported in adjacent states as well as in Texas.

My purpose in writing this book was to compile as much information as possible regarding any named arrow point that appears in the scientific literature. I make no judgment as to the validity of the types discussed herein. Most archaeologists only describe and illustrate examples that they believe are valid types. This practice may exclude projectile point types that are accepted by other archaeologists, and those that have been named by nonprofessionals. The most recent book on artifact typology (Turner et al. 2011) focuses solely on stone points. It excludes 13 types in this volume that are recognized by others as justifiable. As time passes, some types have been discarded and new ones added. Some points have more than one example. Unfortunately, I was not able to obtain illustrations for each type, and not all images have scales. Many of the types are illustrated by only one photo, and every attempt was made to feature classic examples. Ideally, the variation of each type would be depicted, but this was not possible. Turner and others (2011) did an excellent job of portraying the various forms of individual types.

I was only able to get a single *Lozenge* point, while 12 examples were presented by Turner and others (2011:192). Therefore, this source is a must for those interested in the different forms a single type can take. Some points portrayed herein may not be the best example of that type. The likeness of some is so close that variations of a particular type can closely resemble other types. Other sources that depict numerous examples of a single type include Davis (1995), Duncan and others (2007), Suhm and Krieger (1954), Suhm and Jelks (1962), Turner and Hester (1985, 1993, and 1990), and Turner and others (2011). The points illustrated by Duncan and others (2007), are housed at the Gilcrease Museum in Tulsa, Oklahoma; Sam Noble Museum of Natural History in Norman, Oklahoma, Museum of the

8 | Introduction

Red River in Idabel, Oklahoma, the Panhandle-Plains Museum in Canyon, Texas; TARL; and private collections. Those described and illustrated by Suhm and Krieger (1954) and Suhm and Jelks (1962) are curated at TARL, on the campus of the University of Texas at Austin. The maps depicting the suspected distribution of each type are estimates taken from various sources. In some cases, types known primarily in areas such as Northeast Texas are believed to extend into states as far north as Illinois.

The writing of this book used a combination of accepted styles. When I began writing reports and other documents on archaeological subjects, the convention was to follow the style guide adopted by *American Antiquity*. There was a problem with this method, as it was written for peer-reviewed articles in a national magazine. Writing contract reports, however, required some deviation, and it was recommended that the *Chicago Manual of Style* be used to address instances not covered by *American Antiquity* (incorporated into the Society for American Archaeology [SAA] style guide). Other disciplines, such as biology and chemistry, have vastly different style guides. I use my preferred version that adheres in part to *American Antiquity* (SAA) and the *Chicago Manual of Style* as well as personal choice. In the past, projectile point types were written in italics (e.g., Hall 1981) and/or underlined for emphasis. Currently, this practice is seldom (if ever) used. I use it here because it is my opinion that it makes it easier to differentiate between projectile points and similar terms in the text. The acronyms used regarding time (past and present) adhere to those cited by the authors and as listed in the SAA guide. They include BC and B.C. (years before Christ), A.D. and AD (years after the death of Christ), B.P. and BP (Before Present—1950), B.C.E. and BCE (Before Current Era—Year 1), and C.E. and CE (Current Era—Year 1). It was my intention to use as many primary sources as possible. Major sources that contributed to this publication are listed below.

Books

Athanase de Mezieres and the Louisiana-Texas Frontier, 1768–1780 (Bolton 1970); *Digging into South Texas Prehistory* (Hester 1980); *Traces of History: Archeological Evidence of the Past 450 Years* (Fox 1983); *Indians of the*

Upper Texas Coast (Aten 1983); *A Field Guide to Stone Artifacts of Texas Indians* (Turner and Hester 1985, 1993, 1999); *Historical Dictionary of North American Archaeology* (Jelks and Jelks 1988); *Stone Age Spear and Arrow Points of the Midcontinental and Eastern United States* (Justice 1987, 2002); *Prehistoric Artifacts of the Texas Indians* (Davis 1995); *Selected Preforms, Points, and Knives of the North American Indians* (Perino 1985, 1991, and 2002); *The Prehistory of Texas* (Perttula 2004); *Stone Artifacts of Texas Indians* (Turner et al. 2011); and *Pioneering Archaeology in the Texas Coastal Bend: The Pape-Tunnell Collection* (Tunnell and Tunnell 2015).

Contract Reports

By far, one of the most used sources was contract reports prepared by archaeological contractors documenting their findings. The information sought was types of arrow points found and their provenience. Sometimes these reports provided additional information not related to field investigations. One such example is the report by Prewitt & Associates Inc., titled *Cultural Resources Investigations along Whiteoak Bayou, Harris County, Texas* (Fields 1988). Chapter 9, "Analysis of Previous Collections," described six typed points from 19 sites (Bailey et al. 1988).

Bulletins

Bulletin of the Texas Archeological Society (formerly the Texas Archeological and Paleontological Society); *Bulletin of the Lower Plains Archeological Society*; *Bulletin of the South Plains Archeological Society*; *Central Texas Archeologist* (published by the Central Texas Archeological Society); *The Steward* (Potter and Simons, editors); and bulletins of the Oklahoma Anthropological Society.

Journals

Panhandle-Plains Historical Review (Panhandle-Plains Historical Society, Canyon, Texas); *The Cache* (a publication of the Texas Archeological Stewardship Network); *La Tierra* (Journal of the Southern Texas Archaeological

Introduction

Association); *Journal of the Houston Archeological Society* (published by the Houston Archaeological Society); *Louisiana Archaeology* (published by the Louisiana Archaeological Society); *Ancient Echoes* (Journal of the Hill Country Archeological Association; *Journal of Big Bend Studies* (published by the Center for Big Bend Studies); *Plains Anthropologist* (Journal of the Plains Conference); *American Antiquity* (Society for American Archaeology); *Notes on Northeast Texas Archaeology* (published by Friends of Northeast Texas Archaeology, Austin and Pittsburg); *Journal of Northeast Texas Archaeology* (published by Friends of Northeast Texas Archaeology, Austin and Pittsburg); *The Artifact* (publication of the El Paso Archaeological Society); *Transactions of the Regional Archeological Symposium for Southeastern New Mexico and Western Texas* (each issue published by the organization that sponsored the event); and *Archeological Journal of the Texas Prairie-Savannah* (an AJ Consulting Publication, Jesse Todd, editor).

Abstracts in Texas Contract Archeology

This project began with abstracts for cultural resource management (CRM) reports published in 1987 and was terminated for those published in 1992. *Abstracts in Texas Contract Archeology, 1987* (Moore 1991a); *Abstracts in Texas Contract Archeology, 1988* (Moore 1990); *Abstracts in Texas Contract Archeology*, 1990 (Moore 1992a); *Abstracts in Texas Contract Archeology*, 1991 (Moore 1992b); *Abstracts in Texas Contract Archeology*, 1989 (Moore 1993a); and *Abstracts in Texas Contract Archeology, 1992* (Moore 1994).

Special Publications

Handbook of Texas Archeology: Type Descriptions (Suhm and Jelks 1962); *Stone Points and Tools of Northwestern Louisiana* (Webb, 1981, 2000); *Southern Plains Lithics: The Small Points* (Duncan et al. 2007); *Some New and Revised Projectile Point Classifications for the Eastern Trans-Pecos and Big Bend Region of Texas* (Mallouf 2013); *A Collection of Papers Reviewing the Archeology of Southeast Texas* (Wheat and Gregg 1988); *The Native History of the Caddo: Their Place in Southeastern Archeology and Ethnohistory*

(Perttula and Bruseth 1998); and *A Catalog of Texas Properties in the National Register of Historic Places* (Steely 1984).

Bibliographies

An Annotated Bibliography of Texas Related Articles in the Plains Anthropologist (1947–1981) (Moore and Moore 1982); *Archeological Bibliography of the Southern Coastal Corridor Region of Texas* (Bailey 1987); *Archeological Bibliography for the Northern Panhandle Region of Texas* (Simons 1988); *A Bibliography of Archaeological Reports Prepared by the Contract Laboratory, Texas A&M University* (Moore 1988b); *Archeological Bibliography for the Southeastern Region of Texas* (Moore and Simons 1989); *Bibliography for the Prehistory of the Upper Texas Coast* (Patterson 1989b); *Archeological Bibliography for the Northeastern Region of Texas* (Martin 1990); *The Technical Series, published by the Texas Archeological Research Laboratory 1971–1987: A Bibliography* (Moore 1993b); *Historical Archaeology in Texas* (Moore and Moore 1986); and *Archeological Bibliography for the Central Region of Texas* (Simons and Moore 1997).

Indexes

An Annotated Index of La Tierra (1974–1983) (Mitchell and Moore 1984); Louisiana Archaeology: An Index to the First Ten Years (Moore 1986); and An Annotated Index to the First Ten Volumes of the Bulletin of the Central Texas (Moore and Bradle 1986).

Newsletters

"Typical Projectile Points." *Newsletter of the Louisiana Archaeological Society* 3(2):4–5. Authored by Clarence H. Webb (1976).

Databases

An Archeological Data Base for the Southeastern Texas Coastal Margin. Houston Archeological Society Report 7 (Patterson 1989a) and A Data

12 | Introduction

Base for Inland South Texas Archeology, Houston Archeological Society Report 6 (Patterson 1989c).

Internet

This vast repository of facts contains numerous articles about the prehistory of Texas written by experts in various fields. Sources consulted include "Texas Beyond History," "Archeology FAQs," and "Unstemmed Point Tradition" as well as the Texas State Historical Association's (TSHA), "Prehistory" (updated June 28, 2021).

Visual Aids (Posters)

The Community Historical Archaeology Project with Schools (CHAPS) program at the University of Texas, Rio Grande Valley, created an "augmented reality projectile point poster" that it uses for research, education, and community engagement. Most of the points can be viewed in 3D, and there is information on where they were found and their material makeup, including metal and glass. Additionally, there are short 90-second films embedded in the poster for teaching purposes. www.dropbox.com/s/6kni 0yeaht703vj/Lower%20RGV%20Projectile%20Point%20Types.pdf?dl=0.

CHAPTER 1

What is an Arrowhead?

THE COMMONLY used term "arrowhead" is usually a misnomer because those using it are often referring to a broad category of chipped stone objects that may or may not have ever been part of the weapon system associated with Late Prehistoric–era people in Texas and the rest of the country—the bow and arrow. The artifacts featured in this book are considered to be arrow points because of their size, shape, and acceptance by professional archaeologists. It should be noted, however, that even what appears to have been fashioned to function as the tip of an arrow might have in reality served a different purpose.

When a person says he or she is going "arrowhead hunting," they usually mean that they are looking for any artifacts associated with Indigenous peoples. Archaeologists prefer the designation "arrow point" when describing the object attached to the tip of a wooden shaft that was propelled with a bow. This term is meant to distinguish arrow points from larger projectile points associated with hand-held spears used for throwing or thrusting and the tips associated with the ancient spear thrower called the *atlatl*. The tipped shafts used with the atlatl are called darts, and the stone objects that perform the same function as arrow points are "dart points." A collector may be proud of his or her collection of "Indian arrowheads," even though only a percentage may have functioned as arrow points.

There is no hard and fast rule regarding the minimum or maximum size for an arrow point, but arrows with points attached (a.k.a. hafted) have been found in archaeological sites, and they are typically small. The weight of an arrow point is crucial because those that are too light or too heavy will negatively affect the flight of the arrow. So, how do people know

14 | CHAPTER 1

if their recent find is an actual arrow point or something else? Oren F. Evans (1961:159–162) discusses this topic in his article "The Development of the Atlatl and the Bow." There are several factors to consider before one can reach a logical conclusion. Size and weight are often referred to as the primary determinants that can affect the accuracy of flight. Fenega (1953) reached the conclusion that "weight differences best documented dart and arrow points." Blitz (1988:126) writes that "experiments with bow and atlatl reproductions have claimed that both large and small projectile points prove adequate when used with either weapon." He cites Browne (1938, 1940); Evans (1957); and Fenega (1953) as his sources for this and other statements. Hamilton (1982:27) writes that "arrow shaft diameter limits the thickness of the point base which can be mounted into the notched or split shaft end." "Haft area thickness of actual mounted arrow point specimens was generally no more than 3/16 of an inch."

Evans (1957) argues that the invention of the bow and arrow combination was the result of "an evolutionary period that was preceded by the use of wooden clubs, throwing stones, spears, and finally the atlatl." The discovery of the bow also involved change. He (Evans 1961:161) discusses some of the advantages that the bow possessed that the atlatl lacked. "It is quite evident that the bow is much superior when shooting at an object in a tree or on the side of a cliff. Also, arrows are more accurate and, although lighter, they have two or three times the effective range of a spear." "Also, the bow can be used with less effort than the spear and can be shot with less body exposure."

Mallouf (1985b:150) conducted a synthesis of Eastern Trans-Pecos prehistory. He writes that "the bow and arrow was a more effective weapon than the atlatl and was therefore assimilated easily." The bow and arrow served a variety of purposes, such as hunting, warfare, and, in miniature form, as a method of teaching children how to become proficient with its use.

The transition from the atlatl was made easier by the production of stone points used as part of that weapon system. "Dart points 3 or 4 inches long and weighing 1.5 to 2 ounces were already in use" (Evans 1961:161). He implies that the first arrows may not have been fletched. If so, he argues, a heavy point would have been required to create the proper balance between the size of the bow and the arrow. "If the center of gravity of the arrow with point attached is not correct, the weight of the point becomes so great that the increase in the trajectory interferes with accuracy." He states that arrows are typically 2 to 3 feet long and ⁵⁄₁₆ to ⅜ of an inch in diameter. Experiments have shown that points from 2 to 3 ounces in weight work well in this situation. He believes that larger points were effective on featherless arrows as long as the weight was comparable. The change in the size of the typical arrow point occurred when the benefits of attaching feathers to the shaft became known. It was discovered that "lighter arrow heads would give just as true a flight, a good penetration, and a flatter trajectory than the heavier ones" (Evans 1961:162). Regarding the size of arrow and dart points, he writes: "I suggest that our classification of projectile points could well be changed. I believe it is now usual to consider points up to one and one-half inches long as arrow points and all above that as dart or spear points. Perhaps, considering their probable use, it would be more logical to consider points up to two inches in length (50 mm) as arrow points, from two to four and one-half inches (114.3 mm) as either arrow or dart points, and above four and one-half inches as spear points" (Evans 1961:162). It seems reasonable to assume that some types may have retained their classic form but became smaller as the transition was made from dart points to arrow points. Four points from Walker County that adhere to the accepted shape of *Gary* points are illustrated here: "a" and "b" measure 2 inches [5.08 cm] and 1.6 inches [4.064 cm] in length respectively and likely functioned as dart points. Conversely, specimen "c" measures 1.37 inches [3.48 cm] and "d" measures 1 inch [2.54 cm]. These fall well with the range of arrow points based on the criteria established by Evans (1961).

Keller and Weir (1979:37) mention the evolution of *Gary* points in their discussion of projectile points from 41SJ160. They write that "if one compares the *Gary*, Variety I with *Gary*, Variety III, as to morphology and distribution, there is a deduction to be made. The *Gary*, Variety III, is small, thin and by many standards could be considered an arrowpoint type. If so, it probably evolved from a larger *Gary* type such as *Gary*, Variety I." Their conclusions were that Gary, Variety III clustered in levels 2 and 3, below the "arrowpoint bearing zones." They postulate that "*Gary*, Variety III evolved as an early arrowpoint form that gave way to types common to

Figure 1.1. Gary points from Walker County (photo courtesy of Bryan Wootan).

the area such as *Catahoula* and *Perdiz*. If so, then the atlatl and dart were never completely replaced by the bow and arrow."

Duffeld's (1961:72) comments about the frequency of small *Gary* points at the Limerick site adds support to the theory that the bow and arrow were contemporaneous and that small *Gary* points also functioned as arrow points: "no one form dominated the arrow point category as the small forms did the dart point category." Julie Densmore (2007:9) relates the continued use of this point as extending into the Late Prehistoric. "They are most abundant during the Transitional Archaic time period in Texas (2250 BP–1250 BP), in which a number of important cultural changes took place: the transition from the atlatl to the bow and arrow, increases in population, the introduction of pottery, and the start of sedentary lifestyles." "The projectile transition occurred at different times, and at different rates, throughout the world. Atlatls and bows and arrows were used in tandem in the recent past in the Arctic, the North American Southeast, and parts of Mesoamerica" (Yu 2006:201).

Hildebrandt and King (2012) proposed a new method for differentiating atlatl darts from arrow points by means of a "dart-arrow index." They analyzed 1,601 projectile points from the Great Basin and discuss how neck width, maximum thickness, and other factors can be used to differentiate between arrow points and dart points. They (Hildebrandt and King 2012:794) write that, "Strictly speaking, we cannot know the answer to this question [darts or arrows] without reference to collections of hafted projectile points." The term "hafted" describes points attached to wooden shafts and held in place with materials such as sinew or asphaltum. This term is used incorrectly by some archaeologists who describe points with stems as being hafted even though they are unattached. This hypothesis is shared by Newell and Krieger (1949:161). The possibility of a particular point being used effectively in both weapons systems, the atlatl and bow and arrow, is reasonable. The assignment of a point to only one of these platforms places the artifact in one of the two major cultural periods, Archaic and Late Prehistoric. Dockall (personal communication, 2022) cites this possibility in the following quote: "One thing I have always thought about *Gary* points, while some points I could clearly tell had been resharpened until quite small, many of the smaller ones just couldn't be argued to be the result of resharpening and clearly were made small. Same for the larger ones . . . meaning that there always seemed to me to be deliberate size differences among *Gary* points." The use of *Gary* points as arrow points creates a problem that I have not seen addressed in the literature. That is, are they variants of *Gary* or a similar form yet to be typed? It should not be overlooked that the smaller size of some *Gary* points is probably a result of resharpening as suggested by Dockall (2022, personal communication).

Not every artifact shaped like an arrow point is an arrow point. One truism that has stayed with me was imparted by Texas A&M University professor Harry J. Shafer, who said, "Form does not dictate function." What appears to be a real arrow or dart point, based on its shape, could have been created for a variety of purposes. Microscopic analysis of wear patterns on the edges of artifacts that resemble projectile points may show that some specimens were used for cutting or scraping. This could mean it was created for a purpose other than as a projectile and served multiple functions including trade or ceremony as well as a projectile point. A cache of 151 complete *Alba* points associated with one of the burials at the George C. Davis site (Shafer 1973:Figure 17) may be an example of ceremonial use. Shafer (1973:197) reports that "their position suggests that they were stored

18 | CHAPTER 1

in a basket-like container." "Their post-mortem use can only be speculated, but it's possible that they were intended for use in the afterlife."

The diminutive size of most arrow points has resulted in them being called "bird points" by collectors. Although archaeologists seldom use that term, Dr. Cyrus N. Ray (1929:12) did as early as 1929 when he described arrow points belonging to the "Sand Dune Culture" in the "Abilene Section" of Texas as "slender, thin, keen bird points representing the ultimate in artistic designs." He does not define "bird point" as a descriptor for size or type of game hunted. In his discussion of additional research in the Abilene Section, Ray (1930:37) continues the use of the term in the following when describing "the larger portion of a small bird point which was flat on one side [probably made on a flake] and of exactly the same culture type as the one later found in the soil taken from the graves of two flat headed deolichocephalic skeletons found by the author in Shackelford County." Doris Olds (1965:148) used the term "bird point" for specimens from Brawley's Cave in Bosque County. "There are many variations of forms which may be grouped with classes B and C and vary in size from a tiny 'bird point' up to a spear 5 inches long." This term is used today by collectors to include all arrow points. Michael J. Shott is professor emeritus of archaeology at the University of Akron. When asked if he was aware of the etymology of the term "bird point," he replied, "I know of no specific research on the question of the function or target of 'bird points' compared to other points."

The size of an effective arrow point is commensurate with the size and pull of the bow. Metcalf (1963:111) writes that metal arrow points made by the Plains Indians became bigger and heavier through time. He speculated that this change may have been due, in part, to the use of larger bows. The image of an Indian shooting arrows at great distances while hunting or in warfare is a myth. Closeness to the target was always the objective. Per Cattelain (1997:227), "preferred throwing distances with bow and arrow are about 9–25 m, beyond which accuracy is compromised."

During my participation in the testing of site 41MQ41 on Lake Conroe, I found what surely was a projectile point. Later analysis revealed I was wrong. Shafer and Stearns (1975:21) describe this artifact: "Formwise, this would appear to represent an expanding stem dart point of tan flint."

"However, microscopic examination of all lateral edges shows moderate smoothing, and the flake scar ridges near the edges and tip show faint smoothing and polish. No striations could be discerned, but the character of the wear plus the edge retouch (beveling) suggests that this stemmed biface functioned as a cutting tool, perhaps a knife. This illustrates how any artifact, including an arrow point, could have its function misinterpreted based on shape."

Hildebrandt and King (2012:795) observed an increase in the size of arrow points following historic contact. They posit two reasons for this change, including a "widespread loss of traditional archery technology" and a "change in their intended use." They hypothesized that the latter was due to some specimens being made as collector's items. The celebrated Yahi Indian Ishi made numerous replicas for the University of California museum, and his functional arrows were significantly smaller than those made for other purposes (Pope 1918). Pope (1923) wrote that the larger arrows made by Ishi seem to have been made more for show, ceremonies, or as presents. Other studies cited by Hildebrandt and King relevant to this discussion are Christenson (1986); Shott (1993, 1997); and Thomas (1978).

The creation of an arrow point can be a very time-consuming and delicate process, or a suitable product can be created very quickly and function as well as those that require more skill. Patterson (1982, 1992, 1994b) discusses unifacial arrow points and their transition to bifacial points. He (Patterson 1994b:21) proposes that "recognized bifacial point types represent the standardization of technology after earlier use of unifacial arrow points." He illustrates examples of unifacial points from sites 41HR5, 41HR185, 41HR210, 41HR315, 41WH19, and 41WH73 in figures 1–5 (Patterson 1994b:23–24). Arrow points often break after one or more uses. Persons knowledgeable with lithic manufacture can usually identify breaks caused during manufacturing or on impact (a.k.a. impact fracture [see Dockall 1997]). Broken points are not always discarded as they can be used for various tasks. When a point loses its edge, it can be resharpened. John Wesley Powell visited Numic-speaking groups in the Great Basin and Colorado Plateau during the period 1867–1880 and obtained an impressive collection of material culture that included numerous hafted arrow points of stone, metal, and glass (Fowler and Matley 1979:151–153).

20 | CHAPTER 1

In the absence of actual points at a site, the presence of flakes is evidence of stone tool manufacture. However, small flakes cannot always confidently be described as the result of arrow point production, as they could be the result of pressure flaking associated with the reduction of stone to create a variety of tools. Some nonprofessionals have argued that points can be created by droplets of water on heated pieces of chert, but that has been debunked. It has, however, been substantiated that a hafted point or tool can be sharpened or reworked without removing it from the haft. Arrow points were made in a variety of shapes and sizes with some specimens not conforming to standard terminology (Appendix C).

David Hurst Thomas (1978) used the dimensions of 142 ethnographic and archaeological examples of dart points (n = 10) and arrow points (n = 132) from collections throughout North America that were preserved in a hafted state to explore the difference between and darts and arrow points. Using the dimensional data, he developed two mathematical equations to discriminate between them. Of the 142 specimens, 20 were incorrectly assigned to a category based on Thomas' equations, for an overall accuracy rate of 86 percent (Carpenter et al. 2013:325). Michael J. Shott (1997) refined Thomas's discriminate analysis by increasing the size of the sample and, subsequently, the rate of successful classification by evaluating and eliminating some variables. Shott's (1997:89) analysis only included specimens "if: (1) they were hafted to a shaft or foreshaft; (2) all attributes could be measured; (3) they were undoubtedly authentic; and (4) they were not known to be designed for use in marine hunting."

In his analysis of the metric variables, he systematically reduced the number of significant variables from four (length, shoulder width, thickness, and neck width) to one (shoulder width). Ultimately, one-variable and two-variable solutions were found to exceed the successful classification rate of a four-variable solution. The one-variable and two-variable approaches are applicable to a wider range of archaeological specimens, including those that have been resharpened or damaged during use (Carpenter et al. 2013:325–327). A metric discrimination study using all projectile points recovered from the testing and data recovery at 41WM1226 indicated that the conventional means used to type prehistoric projectiles in Texas (morphology and comparative study) into dart or arrow categories is relatively accurate (Carpenter et al. 2013:336).

The actual preference for stone arrow points versus sharpened wooden arrows is unknown. Nicole M. Waguespack and colleagues (2009:786), write that the use of sharpened wooden arrows is well documented ethnographically. "Their use by foraging populations from throughout the world suggests that common knowledge explanations of projectile point superiority over wooden tips cannot be assumed in all hunting contexts. In fact, the abundance of wooden hunting implements in the ethnographic record suggests that their prehistoric paucity is largely a function of preservation as opposed to technological and/or economic reasons." Evidence of preservation is discussed in "new insights on the wooden weapons from the Paleolithic site of Schöningen in Germany" (Schoch et al. 2015). Mardith Schuetz discusses perishable objects that have preserved in Val Verde County shelters. In addition to sandals, basketry, and other artifacts made from plants, she describes hafted knives (Schuetz 1956:150), grooved arrow foreshafts (Schuetz 1961:173), and scrapers (Schuetz 1963:162). She illustrates a hafted stone point but does not identify it as a dart or arrow point (Schuetz 1961:Specimen B, p. 174) and what appears to be a hafted arrow point (Specimen E, p. 174). Thomas C. Kelly (1963:221) discusses a probable arrow foreshaft from Roark Cave (41BS3) in Brewster County. "A section of cut reed is probably part of a projectile main shaft [possibly an arrow]. A pointed stick (6 cm long) found in a nearby level fits snugly into the cut end of this reed and is possibly the companion foreshaft."

Examples of the use and effectiveness of sharpened and fire-hardened wooden points are cited in the following. When referring to the Apache of New Mexico, Opler (1941:389) writes, "More commonly, however, no flint is used; the wooden tip of the arrow is simply sharpened and fire hardened." Spier (1978:134), referring to the Yuma of Arizona, writes, "Other arrows lacked stone points, the end merely sharpened and hardened in some fashion."

Arrows lacking a point for balance will not travel as far and with the same speed as those with properly weighted points. One often-cited argument for the advantage of stone over metal points is better penetration.

22 | CHAPTER 1

Waguespack and colleagues (2009:786) provide evidence that disputes this theory: "In a series of well-controlled experiments, the authors show that stone arrow-heads achieve barely 10 per cent extra penetration over wood." The Mbuti of the Congo provide an example: "It has been argued that the Mbuti hunt is dependent upon metal arrow points, spear blades, and knife blades. It is not. We shall see that the Mbuti frequently prefer to use the poisoned arrows that have only a fire-hardened tip.... Old Mbuti assert that fire-hardened spears are effective even against the largest game" (Turnbull 1965:36).

As stated, there are variations in most, if not all, point types. Arrow points are no exception, and this makes accurate typing difficult, if not impossible, in some cases. These variations can be the result of knapping errors, faulty material, expediency, and/or personal taste. I have found no ethnographic evidence that certain tribal members were responsible for making all arrow points or even specific types. My assumption is that it could have been a shared task that may or may not have been assigned to status or sex. Studies aimed at determining gender-based tasks are numerous. Fumiyasu Arakawa (2013) discussed this subject in his analysis of lithics in the central Mesa Verde region. He writes that "both men and women created lithic debitage and stone tools." However, it is his belief that women created and used tools associated with residential sites, while men were responsible for projectile point production, and this occurred away from the village. Although interesting, I would hesitate to extrapolate his findings to the Indigenous populations of Texas.

The procurement of larger game such as deer and buffalo with bows and arrows is well documented. George Catlin (1796–1872) was a famous artist who captured North American Indians on canvas in the 1830s before widespread acculturation. More paintings by Catlin involving the Indians' dependence on buffalo are encapsuled in *George Catlin's American Buffalo* (Harris 2013).

Two sources of food that are not commonly discussed are birds and fish. Lintz (2009) provides an excellent in-depth discussion of species selected for food and ornamentation as well as methods of hunting them. He (Lintz 2009:122) writes that "it may have to be acknowledged that bird hunting occasionally used chipped stone projectile tips." Examples of blunt wooden

What is an Arrowhead? | 23

tips to stun birds and small game have been found in the dry shelters at Kenton Caves in the Oklahoma Panhandle (Lintz 1981; Lintz and Zabawa 1984).

Waguespack and colleagues (2009:789) cite Ellis (1997) in the following quote: "It should be noted that there are numerous examples of hunter-gatherers who prefer the use of metal- or stone-tipped weapons for the hunting of large game, and reserve wood-tipped weapons for small mammals and birds, particularly in North America and Africa."

The use of the bow and arrow as a means of obtaining fish was also practiced. In Kilman's (1959) book about the coastal Texas Karankawa titled *Cannibal Coast*, he writes, "They found their food principally in the bays adjoining the Gulf of Mexico and spent much of their time in the tidewaters. They swam like porpoises and were amazingly skilled at spitting fish in the water with bow-and-arrow or spear." Their marksmanship was excellent. "The Karankawa, standing motionless in shallow bay water, arrow strung to bow, could detect the position of a submerged fish by the slightest rolling of the water and, with an arrow, unerringly spit the fish which a white man wouldn't even know was there" (Kilman 1959:215).

An additional source of the use of wood for arrow point manufacture is provided by Greenville Goodwin, who wrote about the Western Apache making points of wood, stone, and steel (Basso 1971:232). "A section of cut reed is probably part of a projectile main shaft [possibly an arrow]. A pointed stick (6 cm long) found in a nearby level fits snugly into the cut end of this reed and is possibly the companion foreshaft." Examples of the use and effectiveness of sharpened and fire-hardened wooden points are cited in the following: When referring to the Apache of New Mexico, Opler (1941:389) writes, "More commonly, however, no flint is used; the wooden tip of the arrow is simply sharpened and fire hardened." Spier (1978:134), referring to the Yuma of Arizona, writes, "Other arrows lacked stone points, the end merely sharpened and hardened in some fashion."

The use of the bow and arrow persisted in some parts of the country well into the twentieth century among certain isolated groups. When Bennett and Zingg (1976) published their definitive history of the Tarahumara, *The Tarahumara: An Indian Tribe of Northern Mexico*, in 1935, they wrote that this weapon system was obsolete except among those who lived in the Rio Conchos area who "commonly carried them." Tarahumara arrow

24 | CHAPTER 1

points were typically fashioned from obsidian and hafted to hollow reed shafts before metal was available as a replacement for stone. The main reason for the disappearance of the bow and arrow was the availability of the Mauser rifles that were readily available during the numerous Mexican revolutions. Other sources relevant to the discussion of projectile points, that include arrow points, include "Adoption of the Bow in Prehistoric North America" (Blitz 1988); "Antiquity of the Bow" (Browne 1938); *Neck Width of Projectile Points: An Index of Continuity and Change* (Corliss 1972); "Probable Use of Projectile Points" (Evans 1957); "The Weights of Chipped Stone Tools: A Clue to Their Functions" (Fenenga 1953); "Spears, Darts, and Arrows: Late Woodland Hunting Techniques in the Ohio Valley" (Shott 1993); and "Hunting during the Upper Paleolithic: Bow, Spearthrower, or Both" (Cattelain 1997).

CHAPTER 2

Raw Materials

NDIGENOUS GROUPS in Texas were exposed to a variety of raw materials that they relied on to make arrow points and other stone tools. These sources include, but are not limited to, agate, agatized alligator gastroliths, basalt, chalcedony, chert, dolomite, flint, gar scales, hornstone, jasper, Manning Fused Glass, novaculite, obsidian, quartzite, rhyolite, and silicified wood. In historic times, glass and metal were available, and these materials gradually replaced stone as the preferred medium for arrow point manufacture. Geologists prefer the term chert in lieu of flint, while collectors and some archaeologists tend to identify these materials collectively as flint. In Texas, chert/flint is arguably the most cited material used to make arrow points. It exists primarily in two forms—nodules and strata in sedimentary rocks. In Starr County two bedrock outcrops contain a chert known as *El Sauz* that is believed to have been formed *in situ* in a terrestrial setting. Chert nodules are found on eroded upland ridgetops and lag deposits of rivers and major streams. At site 41RE53, chert nodules are embedded in the rear wall of a rockshelter. Ledge chert refers to a relatively thick impermeable layer of chert beneath or between permeable layers of less erosion resistant rocks such as chalk or limestone.

One might argue that arrow points found at campsites were probably made from local materials. While this appears to be the case at many sites, there are aberrations. It is well documented that points fashioned from distinct materials such as Alibates chert, Georgetown chert, and obsidian occur at sites far from their known source. Often, these specimens are few in number and believed by archaeologists to be intrusive, perhaps objects

Figure 2.1. Chert nodules at 41RE53 (photo by the author).

of trade. The Upper Farmersville site (41COL34) presents a different scenario. Crook (2008–2009:36) discusses this in the following: "While some local material is present in the arrow point assemblage, cherts of clearly foreign origin comprise two-thirds of the points found in the test unit. These include both typical Edwards Plateau root beer–colored chert as well as more exotic red and red-orange cherts like those found in Arkansas and northeastern Oklahoma. In contradiction, the vast majority (85%) of the debitage found in association with the points is of local origin. Few flakes corresponding to the non-local cherts were recovered, lending support to the supposition that most of the arrow points were made elsewhere and brought into the site."

There are some problems inherent in the identification of various types of cherts that must be addressed. "Not all of the chert recovered [at Fort Hood] can be placed in exact type categories" (Dickens 1997:46). The color of certain cherts cannot always be tied to a local source. Additionally, a wide range of colors and textures can be found within individual chert types. Archaeologists were only able to isolate individual types at Fort

Hood after examining several thousand examples of chert and over 5,000 bifacially flaked tools (Dickens 1993b, 1993c; Dickens and Dockall 1993). The results of these studies identified seven types of chert present. They are Owl Creek Black, Fort Hood Gray, Gray/Brown/Green Mottled, Fort Hood Tan, Texas Novaculite, Heiner Lake, and Cowhouse White. These are described by Dickens (1997:46–48). There are two later studies of chert types at Fort Hood that built on and refined Dickens's basic chert types to include descriptive properties like UV fluorescence, surface patination, heat treatment effects, and instrumental neutron activation analysis (INAA) (see Frederick and Ringstaff 1994). It is not uncommon for a variety of chert that appears to be unique to be given a name by nonprofessionals and for this name to be adopted by professional archaeologists and appear in the literature. Two examples are Texas Novaculite and Owl Creek Black. Per William A. Dickens (1997:46), Texas Novaculite is a variety of chert and not a true novaculite. The name was coined by local flintknappers because, once heat altered, it looks and acts much like true Arkansas novaculite. This chert occurs at Fort Hood in Bell and Coryell Counties.

Our overall knowledge of arrow points (their manufacture, use, and distribution) is limited and sometimes inconclusive. There are parts of the state, for example, that have received little attention by archaeologists compared to the more densely populated areas where archaeological survey is more often required for various construction projects. "Prior to 2009, South Texas was essentially an archaeological *tabula rasa*, largely unknown in the academic, public, or grey literature due to its location far from research universities, the state historic preservation office, and cultural resource management firms" (Bacha-Garza et al. 2022:169). Much of the void in this area has been filled by a consortium of researchers involved with CHAPS at the University of Texas Rio Grande Valley who published "Characteristics and Genesis of *El Sauz* chert, an Important Prehistoric Lithic Resource in South Texas" (Kumpe and Kryzwonski 2009) and "Lithic Raw Materials in the Lower Rio Grande Valley, Southeast Texas and Northeast Mexico" (Reger et al. 2020). Although credible information regarding the various types of chert found in Texas can be obtained through the internet, a major source of information from an

28 | CHAPTER 2

archaeologist's perspective is Larry Banks's (1990) report titled "From Mountain Peaks to Alligator Stomachs." Turner and colleagues (2011:10) consider it to be the "only comprehensive study of stone tool resources in Texas and adjacent states." Banks lists 137 chert-bearing formations within Texas, and a map by Turner and colleagues (2011:Figure 2–4) depicts the location of some of the major sources of chert within the state. Barbara Luedtke (1978) discusses chert sources and trace element analysis in an issue of *American Antiquity.*

Quarries Outcrops, and Lithic Procurement Areas

Chert and other usable materials for making stone tools were procured from various geological settings such as nodules and pebbles on deflated surfaces, cobbles embedded in limestone strata, and pebbles and cobbles on lag deposits of certain rivers and streams. Archaeologists refer to these locales as lithic procurement sites or quarries and often assign a site number based on the trinomial system created by the Smithsonian Institution.

Located within Big Bend National Park in the Trans-Pecos area of Texas is the Burro Mesa quarry (41BS220), which Native Americans frequented to collect chert for the manufacture of stone tools. Burro Mesa chert is technically a silicified tuff that creates a stone of excellent quality that varies tremendously in color and texture. Every shade of the spectrum is represented as solid colors or mottled or banded patterns. Deposits of the chert are underlain by tuff beds within which are veins of kaolinite, a relatively soft, white claystone that was used by prehistoric peoples to make ornaments such as beads and pendants. This quarry is listed in the National Register of Historic Places (NRHP) as part of the Burro Mesa Archeological District. It is located in the foothills of the Chisos Mountains and covers an area of over 40 acres. It is considered one of the most important sites in the park. Chipped stone tools and debitage from this site have been found as far as 50 miles to the north and west of the Chisos Mountains. Banks (1990:84) describes it as a "colorful chert with variegated red, brown, and white colors often striped or mottled." Most of this information was taken from Wikipedia at https://en.wikipedia.org/wiki /Burro_Mesa_Archeological_District.

Cloud and Mallouf (1996:173–175) discuss other areas of Big Bend National Park where raw materials suitable for the manufacture of stone tools exist. "Siliceous stones suitable for the manufacture of chipped-stone artifacts, such as chert, chalcedony, agate, and rhyolite, occur in abundance in the park, as well as in adjacent areas" Cloud and Mallouf (1996:173). Riebeckite rhyolite is also found in abundance in the northwest portion of the park. This fine-grained stone is exposed in the intrusive igneous rocks that comprise the Cienega Mountains and their foothills. "A massive outcrop of Perdiz Conglomerate, a formation that contains a wealth of siliceous stone," is also exposed in the park (Cloud and Mallouf 1996:174; Mallouf 1993). It is present in the area between the flanks of the Cienega Mountains and Alamito Creek. "Contained within this conglomerate are large to small cobbles of various stone types, including chert, rhyolite, chalcedony, and agate" (Cloud and Mallouf 1996:173–175). Other formations mentioned include Rawls (Cloud and Mallouf 1996:175) and Morita Ranch (Barnes 1979).

"The diverse nature of siliceous materials on sites in the area suggests that numerous discrete outcrops are present" (Cloud and Mallouf 1996:173). The authors discuss Santa Elena limestone, Del Carmen limestone, and Shafter limestone as chert-bearing limestones. Quarries, outcrops, and lithic procurement areas in the park that have been recorded with trinomials are 41PS480, 41PS570, 41PS572, 41PS573, 41PS584, 41PS591, 41PS597, and 41PS599.

Chandler and Lopez (1992) documented a quarry as part of site 41DV133 in Duval County. At the time, this county was in one of the least known regions in the state in terms of archaeological resources (Hester 1980). It is situated on the crest of a low ridge in the Goliad Sands formation, a Pliocene depositional system 300–600 feet thick made up of clay, sand, sandstone, marl, caliche, limestone, and conglomerate (Sellards et al. 1954). They (Chandler and Lopez 1992:12) write: "The quarry material appears as an exposed surface outcrop of large, embedded boulders on the upper slope of the ridge." The boulders exhibit "considerable evidence of quarrying activities with numerous flakes and chunks on the ground surface." The quarry is described on the site form as a "mass of lithic debris with tools in all stages of production, primary and secondary flakes, tested raw material, primary and secondary biface reduction" and an "extensive lithic procurement and lithic workshop." It has been identified as quartz arenite with specimens that are light gray and brownish yellow in color.

A survey of southern Culberson County encountered a quarry that Hedrick (1989:135) refers to as the Purple Tan Chert Quarry (41CU449). "It covers about 390,000 square meters on the ridge and slopes of a range of cretaceous limestone hills in the eastern part of the Plateau Complex." He describes it in the following: "The chert, exposed in nodules, is extremely dense and has a fine, glossy texture that produces an excellent conchoidal fracture and thin translucent flakes." "Predominate colors are grayish orange (10YR 7/4), very pale orange (10YR 8/2), grayish red purple (5RP 4/2), pale red (5P 6/2), and pinkish gray (5RP 8/1)." These colors were taken from the Rock Color-Chart Committee (1984). "The entire area of the quarry is densely covered with evidence of removal from matrix, testing, and trimming of the chert" (Hedrick 1989:135).

Hedrick (1989:135) also mentions three white chert quarries (41CU42, 41CU72, and 41CU79) located on ridges and slopes of three separate cretaceous limestone hills in his Plateau Complex Study Area. These sites are large and range from 4,800 to 78,000 square meters. "The colors range from white (N9) and medium light gray (N6)—some have fossil inclusions— and pinkish gray (5YR 8/1)" (Rock Color Chart Committee 1984). "The chert is coarse to fine grained and has good conchoidal fracture" (Hedrick 1989:139). These sites are littered with debris from testing and preparation.

Felsite quarries in Culberson and Hudspeth Counties with trinomials are 41CU441, 41CU443, and 41HZ397. "Pebbles and boulders of felsite quarry 41HZ397 are scattered among the pediment gravels in Study Area 6, Carrizo Mountains, Area 2. The coarse-grained to fine-grained material is extremely hard and dense. Colors are dark reddish brown (10YR 3/4), dark red (5YR 3/4), moderate red (5YR 5/4) and grayish red (5YR 4/1 and 5R 4/3) (Hedrick 1989:135)." The remnants of pebbles and boulders that exhibit the early stages of reduction are indicators of activity areas. "Tumbled fragments of agate, jasper, and chalcedony are found in the gravels which are identical to felsite quarries" (Hedrick 1989:135).

Another quarry recorded by Hedrick (1989) is dubbed the Van Horn Mountain quarry (41CU389) on a mesa in his Study Area 4 in the Van Horn

Mountains. The material is scattered over an area of about 9,000 square meters and consists of broken nodules that have eroded out of the limestone cap. The area is littered with debris resulting from testing and preparation. "The raw material is spotted and/or marbled combinations of moderate red (5R 5/4) to grayish red (5R 4/2) and very pale orange (10YR 8.2). It has a medium- to fine-grained matte texture and excellent conchoidal fracture. Debris from testing and preparation of material is scattered over the area" (Hedrjck 1989:135 and Rock Color Chart Committee 1984).

Charles K. Chandler (1984a) discusses lithic resources in the Texas Coastal Bend, Jim Wells and Nueces Counties. The most promising locality is known as Piedras Crossing (a.k.a. De Leon's Crossing). Pebbles considered to be large enough for knapping are found in the riverbank of the Nueces River. Chandler (1984a:27) writes the following: "The heavy concentration of large cobbles extends along the riverbed and up the east bank for 250 to 300 feet. They appear to be coming from a buried Pleistocene terrace, and while they do not appear to be of adequate quantity for a modern commercial aggregate operation, this lithic deposit does appear to be of sufficient size and quantity to be considered a major lithic source for the prehistoric inhabitants of the area." A random collection was donated to the Center for Archaeological Research at the University of Texas at San Antonio to serve as reference material. The collection contains a "fairly high percentage" of silicified wood. Quartzite was absent. Chandler (1984a) regards the distances of these sources "to be well within the range of lithic procurement of much of the Lower Nueces River area and definitely establish the existence of source materials for the manufacturing of lithic tools by the prehistoric inhabitants of the Texas Coastal Bend."

In 1993, archaeologists from Texas A&M University conducted the Brazos Valley Slopes Archaeological Project in Brazos County (Thoms 1993). The sites are situated in the uplands and valley slopes of the Brazos River. "One of the most important aspects of land use in this region (especially in the uplands) is the abundance of chert in local gravel deposits. These gravels are found on the surface of many of the ridge tops and slopes and served as a major source of raw material for prehistoric lithic tool manufacture. Low density scatters of lithic debris suggest components of a widespread, lithic procurement and manufacturing areas that extend into the

32 | CHAPTER 2

uplands throughout the region" (Dickens 1993a). Lithic analyst William A. Dickens (1993a:113–144) discusses the tool types, reduction strategies, and local gravels in the report by Thoms (1993).

Raw Materials

Agate is a cryptocrystalline form of silica, also known as chalcedony. It is found in various parts of the state, especially in the Trans-Pecos (Cloud and Mallouf 1993) and South Texas. Per Reger, González, and Skowronek (2020:8), most common varieties in the Lower Rio Grande Valley are "moss and plume, with explosions of dark inclusions in an otherwise translucent or semitransparent white matrix." "Other agate varieties have a cloudy appearance but exhibit fine concentric banding when held to bright light." Agates are most abundant in gravels associated with the Frio and Goliad formations and Nuevo Leon on the Mexican side of the Lower Rio Grande Valley. Artifacts made of agate are most often present in the assemblages from Zapata and Starr Counties. A representative set of agate cobbles and artifact types *Palmillas*, *Pandora*, and *Tortugas* from the Frio formation in Zapata County are illustrated by Reger (2020:Figures 10a and 10b).

Alibates chert (a.k.a. Alibates agatized dolomite) is found in the Canadian River Valley north of Amarillo. Outcrops are present on both sides of the valley. The outcrop on the southern side has been designated the Alibates Flint Quarries National Monument (41PT1) and is listed in the NRHP (66000822). The quarry occupies a footprint of about 300 acres containing 250–300 individual quarry pits. Alibates is described as a multi-colored, fine-grained microcrystalline material "occurring as large lenses and nodules, as a result of silicification of the dolomite" (Quigg et al. 2011:194). Johnson (1994:Figure 38a) illustrates a *Perdiz* point made from Alibates chert at the Buckhollow site (41KM16) in Kimble County, Texas. Mercado-Allinger (2004) reported an alibates biface cache in the panhandle known as the Hackberry Cache (41RB95). Campbell (1970: 43) writes, "Alibates agate is an agatized dolomite occurring in the Quartermaster formation of the upper Permian age along the Canadian River north of Amarillo. It is characterized by banded colors, usually white and purple, but also including browns, yellows, and reds." Six *Fresno* points provided by an anonymous source are depicted here. Reger, González, and Skowronek (2020:Figure 13) illustrate a large cobble and three projectile points from South Texas classified as alibates chert. The cobble is in the Museum of South Texas History, and the points, identified as *Marcos*, *Palmillas*, and *Tortugas*, are in private collections in Starr and Zapata Counties.

Basalt is an igneous rock formed by the rapid cooling of low-viscosity lava rich in magnesium and iron exposed at or very near the surface of a rocky planet or moon. More than 90% of all volcanic rock on earth is basalt (Wikipedia). Although no arrow points made from basalt were found at Pueblo Sin Casas (FB6273) in El Paso County, numerous tools and flakes of this material were present that accounted for 2% of the total (Scarbrough and Foster 1993).

Black chert originates in the Tamaulipas Limestone formation in the mountains of Mexico and can be found as gravel beds south of the Rio Grande (Imlay 1931). This material was interpreted by Shiner (1983) as a "black marine chert." The source is near Linares, Mexico, on the eastern edge of the Sierra Madre Oriental in the Mexican state of Tamaulipas, where black chert co-occurring with limestone is frequently mentioned in geological reports. There is consensus that black chert artifacts were made of material from primary deposits in the Sierra Madre Oriental and secondary gravel deposits in streams draining the mountains, but no additional details of this material were provided beyond referencing it as "black." Black chert points are illustrated by Reger, González, and Skowronek (2020:Figure 5). It has been reported that this chert has excellent conchoidal fracture (Russell K. Skowronek, personal communication, September 25, 2023).

"Black banded metamorphic is a dark grey to black rock that often displays fine-scale brownish banding. In projectile points, the bands range in appearance from coarsely banded (1 cm wide) to very finely banded, to highly lustrous uniform black" (Reger et al. 2020:6, Figure 7b). This unusual rock possesses exceptional flaking properties and is virtually indistinguishable from obsidian on visual examination. X-ray diffraction analysis on seven specimens (Reger et al. 2020:Figure 8) precluded the possibility of it being a volcanic glass. Diffraction patterns show no glass component. It is composed of crystalline material, dominantly quartz, and sometimes with feldspar. During the process of grinding to make powder slides for X-ray diffraction analysis, it was observed the hardness and physical properties are unlike those of obsidian and chert. "The primary source is the Sierra Madre Oriental where sandstone, shale, limestone with intercalated chert were contact metamorphosed by volcanic activity and the isolated massif south of Burgos in Tamaulipas" (Imlay 1931). Secondary sources are the gravel beds in the rivers draining these mountains (Reger et al. 2020:Figure 2). Artifacts made from this rock are most frequently found in collections from Mexico, consistent with the proposed source (Reger et al. 2020:6).

Edwards Plateau chert is one of the largest sources in the United States and the largest in Texas (Banks 1990:59). Frederick and Ringstaff (1994) note that "the Edwards Group comprises one of the largest chert resources on the Great Plains." In Texas, Edwards chert is found in a large area that is approximately 100 kilometers north–south and 280 kilometers east–west. It encompasses 41 counties and extends into Mexico (Hester 1980:Figure 2–4). Kirk R. Geno (1984) summarizes the origin and distribution of chert in Edwards limestone in Central Texas. Unfortunately, artifacts manufactured from this source are virtually impossible to trace to a specific location because of the vastness of the area where they occur and the overall similarity of the material throughout these two areas. Artifacts of Edwards chert have been reported in other states such as the Byrd Mountain lithic cache (34GR149) in southwestern Oklahoma. Van Tries Button (1989) discusses this isolated cache of 21 Edwards chert specimens in the abstract of his report: "I suggest that exchange of the ownership of caches of exotic lithics may have played a role in prehistoric economies. Seeing cache ownership, not the lithics themselves, as the medium of exchange may provide a better explanation than owners' forgetfulness for failure to retrieve such caches." A cache of Edwards chert described as unique was found in Rockwall County (Crook and Hughston 2009a). Larry Nelson's (1968) master's thesis is titled "The Effect of Annealing on the Properties of Edwards Plateau Flint." Silica (SiO_2) in chert creates the desired conchoidal fracture that makes this material workable by flaking. J. S. Pittman (1959) addresses its presence in Edwards limestone.

Paul V. Heinrich (1984) discusses lithic resources in western Louisiana. This is pertinent to the overlap and/or the possible absence of certain raw materials in East Texas. For example, he (Heinrich 1984:186) writes, "The occurrence of limestone as a native and a prehistorically utilized lithic material was investigated. Chemical tests and field investigations found that limestone was neither used nor occurs in western Louisiana as a lithic resource." He provides an extensive discussion of silicified wood, its formation, distribution, and knapping qualities. "Within western Louisiana, six major lithic materials occur in the outcropping tertiary strata. They are silicified wood, Eagle Hill Chert, gravel chert, Fleming Gravel Chert, Fleming Opal, and Catahoula Sedimentary Quartzite." The Fleming and Catahoula formations extend into East Texas.

El Sauz chert first appeared in the literature as a distinctive type when it was named by Robert Mallouf in a report by Larry D. Banks (1990). In 2014, Gonzalez, Hinthorne, Skowronek, Eubanks, and Kumpe published perhaps the definitive article on this chert titled "Characteristics and Genesis of *El Sauz* Chert, an Important Prehistoric Lithic Resource in South Texas." This distinctive material is found in the Oligocene-Miocene Catahoula Formation that occurs along the Gulf of Mexico coastal plain from Mississippi to the Rio Grande in Starr County, Texas. In the Lower Rio Grande Valley, its apparent major source consists of two quarries in Starr County reported on by Kumpe and Kryzwonski (2009). It is fine grained and consists of various bright colors including red and yellow, with gray being the most common. It has a unique chemical signature rich in aluminum that allows it to be traced to its sources (Gonzalez et al. 2014; González et al. 2024). Galloway and Kaiser (1980) discuss the origin, geochemical evolution, and characteristics of uranium deposits in the Catahoula formation of the Texas Coastal Plain. Artifacts formed from this material date from the Early Archaic (3500 to 6000 BC) to the Late Prehistoric (AD 700) and into historic times. Examples of projectile points made from this chert include *Cameron*, *Caracara*, *Hidalgo*, *Langtry*, and *Matamoros* (Gonzales et al. 2014:Figure 1). Kelley and Graves (1980) participated in the El Sauz project in Starr County.

Felsite is a very fine-grained volcanic rock. Hedrick (1993:3) describes it as an "extrusive material with a texture that is so fine that individual

36 | CHAPTER 2

grains are microscopic and cannot be seen with a hand lens." This raw material was commonly used in the manufacture of tools in the area by prehistoric groups from the Middle Archaic through the Late Prehistoric periods. Hedrick (1993:5) writes that "very few [felsite] projectile points have been observed, probably because the material does not lend itself well to fine percussion or pressure flaking."

Georgetown Flint is present along the eastern edge of the Edwards Plateau, specifically Williamson County and possibly southern Bell County. Because of the bluish tint in many specimens, ledge chert found in the Georgetown area is often referred to as "Georgetown Blue." Artifacts made from this material are often identifiable as originating from this source. It is an excellent medium for the manufacture of stone tools. Consequently, it was highly valued in prehistoric times just as it is today with modern flint knappers.

Jarilla chert is named for its occurrence in the Jarilla Mountains in Otero County, New Mexico. It is reported on in detail by Lucas and Krainer (2002) in *Geology of White Sands* published by the New Mexico Geological Society. Artifacts made from this material have been reported at sites on Fort Bliss in El Paso County by Mauldin (1993). At site FB5207, phases known as El Paso and Mesilla were recognized. *Jarilla* chert accounts for 66% of the El Paso assemblage and 50% of the Mesilla assemblage (Mauldin 1993:44–45). Table V-5 in Mauldin's report titled "The DIVAD Archaeological Project" presents the percentage of material by material and artifact type at site FB5027. *Jarilla* chert flakes in the El Paso phase outnumbered those in the Mesilla phase 74 to 53. Shatter was statistically equal with 46 pieces in the El Paso phase and 40 pieces in the Mesilla phase. The El Paso phase yielded 93 tools and cores to 57 for the Mesilla phase.

Pisgah Ridge chert occurs within Tehuacana Limestone in north central Texas, Kaufman, and adjacent counties. It was documented by archaeologists from Southern Methodist University during their survey of the Richland Chambers reservoir, particularly at Bird Point Island and Adams Ranch sites (McGregor 1987a, 1987b). McGregor noted that the usage of that material, which occurs as narrow distinctive outcrops, was contracted over time from the Middle–Late Archaic into the Late Prehistoric time periods. Arrow points of this material are clustered closer to the source areas while Archaic dart points are dispersed a greater distance from the source.

Manning Fused Glass is a unique material of volcanic origin found in Texas that was used for the manufacture of arrow points, dart points, and miscellaneous bifaces. It forms when combustion of the lignite beds in localized areas melted the tuff deposits. The degree of fusion varies, and where it was most intense, actual melting of the microscopic glass sherds has produced small aggregates of brightly colored glassy material. "Fused tuff is, like obsidian, a volcanic glass and has a similar fracture" (Brown 1976:190). This material crops out in a narrow band across the Gulf Coastal Plain of Southeast Texas and has been reported at sites in eight counties (Appendix D).

Manning Fused Glass deposits are situated approximately 190 kilometers inland and pass through (from west to east) Polk, Trinity, Walker, Grimes, Brazos, Burleson, Washington, Lee, Fayette, and Gonzales Counties (Brown 1976:Figure 3). The best-known exposure of fused tuff in the Manning formation is the Chalk Creek quarry in northern Walker County. This quarry is identified by the Bureau of Economic Geology as sample locality 235-T-2 and by TARL as rock sample locality M41-WA1. Artifacts made from this material date from Paleoindian times and into the Late Prehistoric, with Late Prehistoric arrow points being better represented in the archaeological record. Fused glass has been documented at sites in Cherokee, Houston, Limestone, Polk, Rusk, San Jacinto, Trinity, and Walker Counties (Brown 1976:Figure 3). The archaeological site recorded nearest the outcrop at Chalk Creek is 41WA71; Kenneth M. Brown (1976) wrote a well-researched article about this colorful material and its use by prehistoric groups in Texas. Brown (1976:190) illustrates and describes its formation and characteristics. Prior to the publication of his article, we visited the quarry and sites 41WA71 and 41TN11 where fused glass artifacts have been found. A controlled surface collection of a 1 × 1 meter square was conducted at 41WA71, and the amount of fused glass waste material (a.k.a. *debitage*) comprised 60% to 70% of the total assemblage. Two bifaces of fused glass were encountered at 41WA71 by the author, but the finds came too late for them to be included in Brown's article. Brown (1976:Figure

38 | CHAPTER 2

5) illustrates arrow points made of Manning Fused Glass from 41SJ19, a private collection in Madison County, 41HO4, and 41CE19. All but one of these specimens are described as *Alba* or *Catahoula*. The only complete specimen in his article is a probable arrow point from 41TN11. It does not appear to conform to a known type. Brown (1976:Figure 5) also illustrates four arrow point preform failures found on the surface of the George C. Davis site (41CE19) with one coming from the plow zone above Mound B.

Maravillas chert is associated with the Maravillas formation of western Texas and co-occurs with *Caballos* novaculite around Maravillas Gap in Brewster County. It primarily occurs as nodules and lenticular masses. It ranges in color from a dark gray to black. Fine white chalcedony veins or fine pale green banding may be present. It is also referred to as Maravillas Gap chert and Canyon chert (Udden et al. 1916).

Novaculite is best known for occurring in the Arkansas novaculite formation in the Ouachita Mountains of central Arkansas and southeastern Oklahoma. The proximity of the major source of this material to northeastern Texas suggests it may have been used as a trade item from Arkansas and Oklahoma. Not surprisingly, this material has been documented in sites in northeastern Texas. Novaculite arrow points have been documented at sites in Red River County such as Rowland Clark (41RR77) (Perino 1994) and as far south as the George C. Davis site in Cherokee County (Newell and Krieger 1949). Novaculite varies in color (white, light to dark gray, pink, red, tan, and black), but light colors are most common. It is typically translucent. Ridges of *Caballos* novaculite occur in the Lightning Hills of Brewster County (Leo 1975; McBride and Thomson 1970). Owl Creek Black is one of the many varieties of Fort Hood chert that occur mainly along Owl Creek in Bell and Coryell Counties. The best grade is reported to be "jet black" in color. According to John Fish (personal communication, April 4, 2022), this is one of the better varieties of chert for knapping as it has fewer impurities and inclusions. Lintz (personal communication, October 8, 2020) disputes this label because chert of the same color and texture is found elsewhere in the expansive Edwards Plateau region.

Obsidian is arguably the most recognized rock in this category. It is described as volcanic glass that is rich in natural silica that typically consists

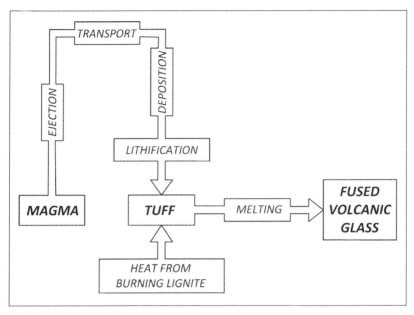

Figure 2.2. Formation of Manning Fused Glass (drafted by K. M. Brown).

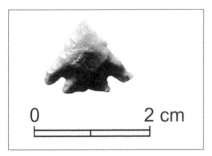

Figure 2.3. Arrow point from 41TN11 (photo courtesy of K. M. Brown).

of rhyolitic that forms when magma erupts from deep under the earth onto or near the earth's surface. Then, it rapidly chills against air, water, or some colder rock. It was a desired medium for tool manufacture because it produces a very sharp edge and is relatively free of impurities that place restrictions on one's ability to knapp chert and other materials. The sharpness of obsidian is reflected in the fact that the renowned flintknapper,

40 | CHAPTER 2

Donald Crabtree, underwent open-heart surgery that was performed with blades he made for that purpose. The tools were so sharp that there was hardly a scar from the incision http://flintknappinghalloffame.blogspot.com/2013/01/don-crabtree-hall-of-fame-flintknapper-3.html. The practice of using stone tools in modern surgery is discussed by B. A. Buck (1982).

Because it is restricted to areas where volcanic activity has taken place, it is not native to Texas. Per Hester (1986:2), "there are no known geologic sources of artifact-quality material of this sort in Texas." Specific areas where there is a linkage between distant sources and artifacts found in Texas include the Mineral Mountain Range in Utah; Obsidian Cliff in Wyoming; Glass and Burns Buttes in Oregon; Timber Butte and Dairy and Wright Creeks (a.k.a. the Malad source) in Idaho (Hester 1986); and the Jemez Mountains and Sierra de los Valles in New Mexico. Hughes and Hester (2009:82) have been quoted as saying that obsidian sources in the Jemez Mountains were the most frequently used obsidian in archaeological sites in Texas, especially after AD 1000.

Michael J. Shott (2021) discusses the analysis of debris and tools from two prehistoric obsidian quarries, the Modena and Tempiute obsidian sources in Nevada. Although the specimens from these quarries have not been linked to sites in Texas, they provide useful information regarding debitage and tools found at quarries that may be applicable to Texas.

Obsidian artifacts have been documented in South Texas, especially at Brownsville Complex sites (Anderson 1932; Hester 1980, 1986); eastern Texas (Perttula and Hester 2016); northeastern Texas (Timothy K. Perttula, personal communication 2020); the Texas Panhandle (Lintz, personal communication 2020); and the Southern Plains (Baugh and Nelson (1987). An example of obsidian reaching the neighboring state of Louisiana is a single flake tool from the Twin Bird Islands site (16CD118) in an article by Pevny (2014).

Thomas R. Hester is one of the pioneers in Texas archaeology who is dedicated to finding the sources of obsidian artifacts in Texas. A breakthrough occurred when a "subcircular worked piece of obsidian" from 41LK51 at Choke Canyon was recovered by archaeologists from the University of Texas at San Antonio (Hall et al. 1986:100). This artifact, along with information about the presence of obsidian in Texas and the possibility of a trade network are discussed in Appendix V of the Choke Canyon report (Hester et al. 1986). Analysis revealed that it belongs to the Escondido Ranch Group, a type defined by a specimen found at Escondido Ranch in Dimmit County. This group is very distinctive because of its high barium (Ba) content, unlike any known source from Mexico or the southwestern United States. Hester (1986:5) believes that the exportation of obsidian over great distances indicates that trade systems transported this material and also may be indicative of new ideas and technologies. Early attempts by archaeologists to trace obsidian artifacts found in Texas to their source were problematic.

Scarbrough and Foster (1993:17) discuss the presence of obsidian in the El Paso area: "Obsidian in the region occurs only as small water-worn pebbles in the gravels of the ancestral Rio Grande that once flowed through the area." Per David L. Carmichael (1986:167), "No obsidian outcrops occur in the El Paso area. Several varieties of obsidian, probably representing several different upstream sources, are found in the gravels. Gravels from the east side of Fillmore Pass, the Black Hills on the southwest side of the Organs and near McCombs Avenue in El Paso, Texas are known to contain concentrations of obsidian pebbles." The current channel of the Rio Grande is more than 20 kilometers to the south of Pueblo Sin Casas (FB6273) where cores, flakes, and projectile points were recovered. Four percent of the 3,017 pieces of lithic material analyzed consisted of obsidian. The obsidian points from FB6273 are depicted in Scarbrough and Foster (1993:Figure II-5). They describe the obsidian from Pueblo Sin Casas as "black opaque" (Scarbrough and Foster 1993:Table II-1).

Foster (1993:17) discusses the chipped stone artifacts from Pueblo Sin Casas (FB6273) in El Paso County. The raw materials used were quartzite (49%), chert (19%), rhyolite (13%), obsidian (4%), and basalt (2%). Fifty-six pieces of "Rancheria chert" were present in the assemblage. This material occurs in the Rancheria formation in the Franklin and Hueco Mountains in western Texas. The formation consists mainly of dense carboniferous silty limestone containing considerable amounts of chert. Foster (1993:19) writes that it is "fairly common and comes in nodular and tabular forms with a cortex of porous, fine-grained limestone. In fact, the chert itself is often porous." Colors range from brown to gray, and it is generally of good

42 | CHAPTER 2

quality (Carmichael 1986:167).

Specimen (TOP-2090) from the Buddy Mangold site (41ME132) in Medina County provided geochemical evidence for a Mexican source of origin. The very informative article by Hughes and Hester (2009:77–84) discusses the process used to determine the source and characteristics of this artifact. The authors concluded that this singular artifact from 41ME132 was manufactured from obsidian of the Mexican Ojozarco chemical type. They estimate the distance from 41ME132 to the source at 675 miles. Considering the extremely rare occurrence of this material in Texas and the lack of associated artifacts of Mexican origin, they write: "It seems unlikely that it was obtained via any formal long-range exchange network or exchange system but may have found its way to the Mangold site through a series of casual or infrequent encounters between peoples living in these areas" (Hughes and Hester 2009:82).

A sample of sites in Texas where obsidian has been found in an archaeological context include 41BL104 (flake) in Bell County (Hester 1986); 41BQ46 (flake) in Bosque County (Hester 1986); 41BX300 (flake) in Bexar County (Hester 1986); 41COL9 (5 arrow points and 2 pieces of worked obsidian) in Collin County (Crook and Hughston 2015c); 41COL34 (one triangular and one side-notched arrow point in Collin County (Crook 2013); 41LL4 (flake) in Llano County (Hester 1986); 41OL6 (flakes) in Oldham County (Kennard 1975); 41OL25 (flakes) in Oldham County (Kennard 1975); 41SW23 (flakes) in Swisher County (Hughes and Willey 1978); 41BI46 (flake) in Briscoe County (Hughes and Willey 1978); 41SS2 (arrow point fragment, 2 unifaces & 5 flakes) in San Saba County; 41SV5 (2 flakes) in Somervell County (Moore 1991b); 41TE98 (stemmed arrow point) in Terrell County (Hester 1986); 41TV133 (flake) in Travis County (Hester 1986); X41 HI 30 (biface) in Hill County; 41WY40 in Willacy County; 41UV2 in Uvalde County; 41ME132 (worked biface tip) in Medina County; and 41JF50 in Jefferson County.

Sites without TARL trinomials are LBL TEX-8-12 (biface fragment and 5 flakes) in Johnson County; LBL TEX-1 (side-notched arrow point) in Medina County (Hester 1986); LBL TEX-23 (flake) in Real County (Hester 1986); and the Branch Site #2 (one triangular arrow point and one end scraper (Crook 1985). Obsidian arrow points identified as known types include *Alba, Catahoula, and Washita* (various sources).

Other sources relevant to the presence of obsidian in Texas include Asaro and Stross (1994); Hester (1988); Hester et al. (1975, 1991, 1992, 1996, 1999); Hughes (1988a, 1988b); and Mitchell, Hester, Asaro, and Stross (1980).

Opalite is a silica-replaced caliche that occurs in portions of the upper Ogallala formation in the Southern and Central Great Plains. Lintz (1998) provides a thorough discussion of its origins, stratigraphic description, and distribution as well as artifacts made of this material. He (Lintz 1998:107) notes that "very little archaeological or geological discussion has focused on the occurrence and prehistoric cultural use of opalite on the Southern High Plains." A major exposure of opalite is in the Palo Duro Creek valley of the upper Texas Panhandle. Lintz (1998:Figure 1) illustrates the distribution of the Ogallala formation and its opalite outcrops in the Texas and Oklahoma panhandles. He summarized the geological literature on the origin of opalite and provides detailed descriptions of the stratigraphy of its exposure at the Palo Duro Creek valley. He (Lintz 1998:Figure 5) illustrates arrow point fragments including side-notched and corner-notched types found in the vicinity of Palo Duro Creek. Typed arrow points of this material in the Palo Duro River basin include one *Washita* point (Anthony 1991); one *Fresno* point (Quigg, et al. 1993); and three unclassified points (Anthony 1991). An opalite arrow point was reported at site 41HF8 in Hansford County (TARL records).

Potter chert is a fine-grained quartzite or silicified sandstone, found in the Potter Member of the Pliocene Ogallala formation. The Potter gravels of the Ogallala formation are exposed along the Canadian River breaks and along the eastern Caprock Escarpment. "The distinctive grainy, gray-brown material is dense and especially suitable for choppers and hammerstones" (Campbell n.d.:43). It also works well for making projectile points and tools. The final report documenting the results of the survey at Mackenzie Reservoir presents the findings at eight sites in Briscoe and Swisher Counties (Hughes and Willey 1978). Artifacts from Potter chert were present at most sites. Lithic artifacts and refuse at Deadman's Shelter (41SW23) were, along with Tecovas Jasper, predominant. At the two occupational levels, strata B and D, Potter chert was ubiquitous. At stratum B, 245 artifacts (39.2%) of Potter chert were found, and the numbers at stratum D were 1,034 (66.0%) of the total. The amount of Potter chert in stratum D was more than any other excavated site in the reservoir (Hughes and Willey 1978:188).

Quartzite is a metamorphic rock that forms when sandstone rich in quartz (parent material) is altered by heat, pressure, and chemical activity. Its texture is described as nonfoliated and medium-grained. The hardness can vary, but it is not prone to scratching or etching. It is found over much of Texas and was used by Indigenous groups to make stone tools, including arrow points. Examples are documented in *An Archeological Survey of Walker County, Texas* (Moore 1976:20, Plate 1).

Rancheria chert makes up 56% pieces of the chipped stone artifacts from Pueblo Sin Casas (FB6273) in El Paso County (Foster 1993:17). This material occurs in the Rancheria formation in the Franklin and Hueco Mountains in western Texas. The formation consists mainly of dense carboniferous silty limestone containing considerable amounts of chert. Foster (1993:19) writes that it is "fairly common and comes in nodular and tabular forms with a cortex of porous, fine-grained limestone. In fact, the chert itself is often porous." Colors range from brown to gray, and it is generally of good quality (Carmichael 1986:167).

Rhyolite occurs in the El Paso area, mainly in the Franklin and Organ Mountains and their alluvial fans. "The local rhyolites are generally dark red, pinkish, purple, or black in color" (Scarbrough and Foster 1993:21). Thunderbird rhyolite has been documented as a common raw material from Jornada Mogollon sites Gobernadora (41EP321) and Ojasen (41EP289) in El Paso County but was mostly used for retouched and unretouched flake tools rather than bifaces and projectile points (see Shafer et al. 1999). Rebeckite rhyolite is found in Big Bend National Park (see Cloud and Mallouf 1996:174).

Scarbrough and Foster (1993:17) discuss the chipped stone artifacts from Pueblo Sin Casas (FB6273) in El Paso County. Thirteen percent were made from rhyolite. Reger, González, and Skowronek (2020:8) include rhyolite under the heading Undifferentiated Volcanic Rocks. They write that it is "also found in the Lower River Grande Valley where specimens of maroon color with visible quartz phenocrysts are scattered throughout the matrix, but yellow rhyolites with a distinctive dull patina are also present." Cobbles and points made from this material are depicted in their figures 9a and 9b (Reger et al. 2020:9). In total, 5% of the studied collections (n = 50) were made of volcanic rocks. Igneous materials from Mexico may contribute to the gravels found in the Rio Grande. The most common forms are red and brown rhyolite (Reger et al. 2020:8).

LeRoy Johnson (2000) discusses the colors and sources of chert at the Bessie Kruze site (41MM13) on the Blackland Prairie of Williamson County. In his dialogue, he mentions a little known chert that he refers to as Round Rock chert. He writes that his conclusions regarding sources were taken from formation outcrops, stream gravels, and high elevation lag deposits. An assemblage of a "dozen or so flakes" represent a "different chert and a different source." "This black or nearly black (very dark gray to very dark grayish brown) chert is colloquially called Round Rock flint, and it, too was carried down Brushy Creek (and nearby streams) to the neighborhood of the Kruze site. In actuality, the material comes ultimately from the eastern margin of the Edwards Formation in Williamson County and northernmost Travis County" (Johnson 2000:116). A similar outcropping of possible identical black occurs on the bluffs of the Colorado River below Tom Miller Dam.

Silicified wood (a.k.a. petrified wood) is found in a large area that incorporates most of East Texas extending to the Arkansas and Oklahoma borders and into Louisiana. A major source of silicified wood in East Texas is the Catahoula Formation. Due to the composition of this material, many artifacts appear to be crudely made when, in actuality, the material being knapped does not allow for precise reduction. Occasionally, exceptional pieces were used, with the result of a well-made point. Silicified wood is also found in the Oligocene-Miocene Catahoula formation that occurs along the Gulf of Mexico coastal plain from Mississippi to the Rio Grande in Starr County, Texas, where it consists of Catahoula volcanic ash 20 meters thick in places. Geologists believe it is the result of a single caldera eruption. Reger, González, and Skowronek (2020:8–9) discuss the presence of silicified wood in South Texas: "The Lower Rio Grande Valley has a wealth of silicified wood with good qualities for knapping. There are distinctly different sources for this material: Frio Formation gravels deposited by the ancestral Rio Grande, and silicified wood found in situ within the

46 | CHAPTER 2

Catahoula Formation. The latter is known for the highly prized silicified palm (Palmoxilum) (Figure 11A and B). According to Galloway (1977) and supported by our own observations, these materials can be distinguished by the amount of weathering and abrasion they have undergone during transport as bed load. Older, more rounded silicified wood fragments associated to the Frio Formation have been heavily reworked during transport as bed load by streams. Younger, more angular and less weathered silicified wood fragments are likely from the Catahoula Formation and can be found on the western side of this formation. Unfortunately, these distinctions are lost in chipped stone artifacts, and at present it is not possible to distinguish them."

Tecovas Jasper is a high-quality material found in the Quitaque area of Briscoe County that is often referred to as Quitaque flint. It is widespread along the eastern Caprock Escarpment of the Llano Estacado (Green and Kelley 1960). It also consists of various colors. Archaeologists often describe these materials as having different visual characteristics. However, there is commonality in the range of their color, texture, banding patterns, and translucency. "Because the ranges of variability in macroscopically visible characteristics of Alibates and Tecovas Jasper are so similar, it is often difficult to accurately sort prehistoric artifacts into typological categories reflecting their presumed geological point of origin" (Quigg et al. 2011:191). This can result in archaeologists inadvertently associating artifacts from these deposits with the incorrect geological source. A very thorough discussion of these two source materials is authored by J. Michael Quigg, Matthew T. Boulanger, and Michael D. Glascock in their article titled "Geochemical Characterization of Tecovas and Alibates Source Samples" (Quigg et al. 2011). Artifacts of Tecovas Jasper were numerous at site 41SW23 in the Mackenzie Reservoir (Hughes and Willey 1978). Two occupation strata were identified, strata B and D. Artifacts of this material in stratum B numbered 326 (52.2%), as opposed to 389 (24.4%) of the total (Hughes and Willey 1978:188).

"Uvalde gravels" is a term that includes a variety of raw materials such as chert, quartz, quartzite, jasper, limestone, and silicified wood. These gravels are present as lag deposits of rivers and major streams that occur in a broad area of the state (Byrd 1971). They are especially common in

South Texas where they are found on hills and high terraces (Turner et al. 2011:10). This is the second largest source of knappable materials in the state as it extends from the Rio Grande to the Oklahoma border (see Turner et al. 2011:Figure 2–4).

McGregor (1995:187–202) provides valuable insight to lithic resources at Joe Pool Lake in the Upper Trinity River region. The presumed absence of chert in this area is contradicted by Mentzer and Slaughter (1971:217–218) who report that "chert nodules, although relatively small in size, occur in the upland gravel deposits." Daniel R. Prikryl (1987:91) writes that "some of the local chert material is virtually indistinguishable from Edwards Plateau cherts." He examined the material of 1,274 diagnostic projectile points and concluded that they were made from chert or quartzite and present in all time periods from Paleo-Indian to the Late Prehistoric. At sites 41DL148 and 41DL149 in the Joe Pool Reservoir (Dallas County), sixty-five *Alba* and *Alba*-like points were recovered, and all were made from local chert as opposed to three from quartzite and none from silicified wood (McGregor 1995:Table 3). To put this in a different perspective, 94.7% of the debitage from site 41DL199 in the reservoir area was chert as opposed to 0.4% of quartzite, 0.6% of silicified wood, and 0.7% classified as other (McGregor 1995:Table 1).

CHAPTER 3

Projectile Point Typologies

WHEN THE Texas Archeological and Paleontological Society was founded in 1929, projectile point typology was not well established for Texas. Davis (1995:13) writes that "the naming and describing of points and tools is a relatively new event, not only in Texas but throughout North America." The first point to be named was *Folsom* by J. D. Figgins in 1927 for the location of the find near the town of Folsom, New Mexico (Cook 1927; Figgins 1927; Wormington 1957). This practice was followed by the naming of *Scottsbluff* in 1932 and *Clovis* in 1933, also for nearby towns. Cyrus Ray was the first president of the Texas Archeological Society and a major contributor to the initial issues of the *Bulletin*. In an article published in volume 2, Ray (1930:58) refers to three specimens as simply "flint points."

In 1935, the Central Texas Archeological Society was founded in Waco, Texas. In volume 1, Frank H. Watt's article "Stone Implements of Central Texas Area," described points by their shape using the terms triangular, oval, and diamond. Watt (1935:17) presented this information in a "Classification Chart of Projectile Points." Specific characteristics of body, edges, notches, and base were included, but no names were assigned.

Frank Bryan was a geologist and avocational archaeologist. In volume 2 of the *Bulletin of the Central Texas Archeological Society* (published in 1936), his article "Preliminary Report on the Archeology of Western Limestone County" discussed the benefits of naming points. "In conclusion, it is believed that enough work has now been done in this section of Central Texas to justify giving names of certain types of artifacts found here. Until a specific artifact is tied down and given a name, it has a tendency to float

50 | CHAPTER 3

around as an indefinite something. It is the rule, where original research reveals something of scientific interest, to name the object after the locality or something connected with the location where they were discovered or first carefully studied." Plate XV contained outlines of the various points and tools found in the area. The arrow point labeled "m" on Plate XV was named *Navasot Beveled Point* because of its abundance near the Navasota River, and specimen "q" was assigned the name *Dead-Man Triangle Point*. Davis (1995:14) believes Frank Bryan should be regarded as the "Father of Texas Point Typology."

Alex D. Krieger (1944:271–288) published an article in *American Antiquity* titled "The Typological Concept." This was the first attempt at systematic typing of projectile points in Texas. Point names were binomials and typically descriptive, such as *Alba Barbed, Bonham Barbed*, and *Scallorn Stemmed*. This practice was continued in publications by Krieger (1946); Kelley (1947b); Newell and Krieger (1949:51–52, Figure 56); Stephenson (1952:Figure 95, Row E); Miller and Jelks (1952:178, Plate 25); Jelks (1953:Plate 19, F–H); and Ford (1952:115, Figure 45). Joe Ben Wheat (1953:197) commented on the value of point typology in his report on the Addicks Basin survey in Harris County: "The binomial nomenclature of projectile points, in use by the Council of Texas Archeologists, and recently adopted by the Southwestern Archeological Conference, Point of Pines, Arizona has been used in this report. This system, long used in pottery designation, combines the type-site name and a word or phrase descriptive of the most characteristic or consistent feature of the projectile point."

In 1954, no articles had been submitted to the *Bulletin of the Texas Archeological Society* (paleontological had been removed from the title). At the time, Dee Ann Suhm was a graduate student in anthropology at the University of Texas at Austin. She had been working on a very ambitious project of sorting through the thousands of points in the TARL collections to refine typology for Texas projectile points. The result was the publication of volume 25 of the *Bulletin of the Texas Archeological Society*. It combined the previous independent work of Krieger and Jelks and is recognized as the first definitive source for Texas point typology and the first for much of the country. This volume included ceramics and the first in-depth discussion of culture complexes and traits in the state. It was extremely successful, and archaeologists in other states relied on it to identify some of their types. A major change was the simplification of point types such as *Alba Barbed* to *Alba*. Each figure depicting artifacts has a scale of 10 centimeters at the bottom of the page. Additionally, the range of length and width of each type is included in the text. The points are illustrated by photos and are housed in TARL's type collection. Projectile point typology guides for states like Alabama and Mississippi relied heavily on types originally defined in volume 25, and to this day, rightly or wrongly, insist on applying Texas-derived type names to many of their point types. Because of the immense popularity of the 1954 *Bulletin*, a revised edition titled *Handbook of Texas Archeology: Type Descriptions* was compiled by Suhm and Jelks and published in 1962, but it did not include the overview of the various archaeological regions in the state. This version was also available in a spiral-bound form that would allow for future pages to be added, but this never took place.

It was not until 1985 that another typology book for Texas appeared. Sue Ellen Turner and Thomas R. Hester published *A Field Guide to Stone Artifacts of Texas Indians*. The focus of this book was the inclusion of points that the authors considered to be valid types. Kathy Roemer was the illustrator who drafted pen and ink drawings. Additionally, the authors included a physical description of each type and supplemental information such as distribution, age, known sites where the type was found, and references that discuss and/or illustrate the type. They discussed the process used to make projectile points and their context and chronology. This book also included various tools in addition to projectile points. No dimensions for the various types are given, and the illustrations are without a scale. It was very successful, and new editions were published in 1993 and 1999 (also without scales). Kathy Roemer was the illustrator in each of these volumes.

Edward B. Jelks (1993:9–15) published "Observations on the Distribution of Certain Arrow Point Types in Texas and Adjacent States." In this article, he examined "the relatively rapid spread of material culture traits from one group to another across wide geographical areas." His examples of this phenomenon are "several widely recognized projectile point types commonly found in Texas and adjacent regions." He states that "two major genera of arrow point forms are clearly discernible in the archaeological record in the United States and adjacent parts of Canada and Mexico: a generally earlier genus of stemmed forms and a generally later genus of

52 | CHAPTER 3

triangular forms." There are numerous defined types and varieties within each genus. He organized his arrow point sequence by date and stem forms. The sequence begins with expanding stem and rectanguloid stem forms that range in age from AD 700 to AD 1200. Expanding stem points consist of *Alba*, *Edwards*, and *Scallorn*. Circa AD 1100 to AD 1300, the expanding stem tradition was largely replaced by the contracting stem forms *Bassett*, *Livermore*, and *Perdiz*. Regarding the triangular forms, Jelks (1993:12) states: "There is considerable diversity among the types and varieties of triangular arrow points found in Texas. Some are side-notched, others have only basal notches, and several types are unnotched. As a genus, they are relatively late." The major unnotched triangular types found in Texas include *Cameron*, *Fresno*, *Guerrero*, *McGloin*, *Maud*, *Talco*, and *Starr*. Jelks writes that triangular points appeared circa AD 1100 to AD 1200 and persisted into historic times. The notched triangular arrow points found in Texas "appear to represent extensions of the Plains triangular series to the north and west." They occur most frequently in northern and western Texas and include *Garza*, *Harrell*, *Washita*, and *Toyah*. He (Jelks 1993:14) concludes that "over the middle latitudes of North America, from northern Mexico to southern Canada, the sequence of early expanding or rectanguloid stemmed forms to later triangular forms may be observed in most regions; but contracting stem arrow points are generally absent outside of Texas and adjacent areas." Specific comments for these types are presented in the formal discussion of types in chapter 7.

Two publications appeared in 1995. Elton R. Prewitt is the former owner of Prewitt & Associates Inc. His area of interest focused on Central Texas, and his passion was projectile point typology. His major contribution to this subject appeared in volume 66 of the *Bulletin of the Texas Archeological Society* in 1995. His article was titled "Distributions of Typed Projectile Points in Texas." He plotted a range of numbers for 151 arrow point and dart point types by county. Prewitt's findings are based on a review of 716 sources and 60,519 specimens. Although this was a monumental effort, he wrote that there are gaps in 67 of the 254 counties because they lacked published data. These counties were not mentioned. There were fewer than three or more published reports for 110 counties when this article was published. Although extensive, the 716 sources do not represent 100 percent of the data available at the time. This article, however, is the only research on this topic that discusses the status of recognized types statewide in this format. Patterson (1995) commented on Prewitt's study from the perspective of Southeast Texas. His main criticism was Prewitt's coverage of Southeast Texas was not "thorough."

Dan R. Davis Jr. (1995) published his version of Texas artifact typology titled *Prehistoric Artifacts of the Texas Indians: An Identification and Reference Guide* that referenced arrow points and dart points. It is out of print and commands a high price when available.

In 2011, Turner and Hester revised their typology book and changed the name to *Stone Artifacts of Texas Indians*. The same format was used but more information was added, and the artifacts were illustrated by Richard L. McReynolds. The dimensions of the various types are not stated, and the figures lack scales. This volume does not include point types *Agee, Cliffton, Colbert, Form 2, Granbury, Homan, Ray*, and *Rockwall*. Per Hester (personal communication on June 6, 2022), the third edition was the last to be published.

The vastness of the Trans-Pecos Region of Texas has typically been overlooked in terms of previously unrecorded types. The first attempt to remedy this problem was by Robert J. Mallouf and his staff, who proposed new types and revised some previous point classifications. These new types were discussed and illustrated in *La Tierra* (Mallouf 2012) and the publication *Archaeological Explorations of the Eastern Trans-Pecos and Big Bend: Collected Papers*, edited by Dasch and Mallouf (2013). New types such as *Alazán, Diablo*, and *Means* are discussed. There have been publications on artifact typology in other states, and some of these were used during this project. These publications are relevant because they mention types reportedly found in Texas as well as types that bear a strong similarity to some Texas specimens.

The title of this book, *Arrow Points of Texas and Its Borderlands* is a reference to those types found on both sides of arbitrary state boundaries that border Texas. The following discussions involve studies by archaeologists in adjacent states.

Robert E. Bell was a professor of anthropology at the University of Oklahoma in Norman. In 1952, he produced a brief mimeographed article titled

54 | CHAPTER 3

"Indian Arrowheads" in the Department of Anthropology's *Archaeological Newsletter*. This article included general comments plus brief descriptions and outlines of thirteen named points. It was so popular that Robert E. Bell and Roland S. Hall (1953) produced "Selected Projectile Point Types of the United States," which appeared in volume 1 of the *Bulletin of the Oklahoma Anthropological Society*. Hall prepared the drawings, and 44 projectile points were described. Five specimens described as arrow points also found in Texas were mentioned. They are *Alba Barbed, Bonham Barbed, Hayes Barbed, Perdiz Pointed Stem,* and *Scallorn Stemmed*. Richard P. Wheeler (1954) authored a second article with the same name in volume 2 of the bulletin of the newly formed Oklahoma Anthropological Society. He presented data for eleven types that were not included in the previous bulletin. No arrow points were included.

Bell recognized the need for a new and more inclusive document on the types of projectile points found in Oklahoma. His goal was to provide more information for each type in conjunction with illustrations of several examples drawn to actual size. Unfortunately, there is no scale with any of these drawings. He wrote that the project was not "coming together as quickly as anticipated." Therefore, it was decided at the annual meeting of the Oklahoma Anthropological Society in 1957 to publish only the information for the types that had been completed at the time with the other types to appear in later bulletins. Eventually, four bulletins were published that contained information about points reportedly found in Oklahoma and adjacent states. Some examples, such as *Sallisaw* (Perino 1968:82, Plate 41) are mainly Oklahoma types often found at Caddo sites, but this type may also be present at Caddo sites in parts of Texas.

The first entry in the new series was titled Special Bulletin No. 1. It was published in 1958 by the Society and titled *Guide to the Identification of Certain American Indian Projectile Points*. Robert E. Bell was the author. Fifty points were described, and they were illustrated by Bell, Max Hibshman, and Mary Frances Fenton. In his introduction, Bell emphasized that his work serves only as a guide to aid in the identification of point types. He stated that these descriptions and drawings do not replace the experience obtained by seeing the actual specimens. Seven specimens described as arrow points found in Oklahoma and Texas were mentioned.

Projectile Point Typologies | 55

They are *Alba*, *Bassett*, *Harrell*, *Hayes*, *Maud*, *Talco*, and *Washita*. This bulletin and the three that follow provide dimensions of the various types, but the figures lack scales.

In 1960, Bell authored Special Bulletin No. 2. It was a continuation of the work published in 1958 as Special Bulletin No. 1. This bulletin also described 50 projectile points. Bell stated that at the time of this publication there were perhaps as many as 200 named points in the United States. The specimens discussed represented those for which adequate information was available. Most of the artifacts were obtained from the collections housed at the University of Oklahoma in Norman. The primary artists were Max Hibshman and Mary Fenton. A few were penned by Ben Williams and the author when necessary. Eleven specimens described as arrow points found in Texas and Oklahoma were mentioned. They are *Bonham*, *Catahoula*, *Cliffton*, *Fresno*, *Friley*, *Huffaker*, *Livermore*, *Perdiz*, *Scallorn*, *Toyah*, and *Young*.

Special Bulletin No. 3 was compiled by Gregory H. Perino and published by the Society in 1968. It also described and illustrated 50 points. Dr. Bell was experiencing an increase in academic responsibilities, and Perino was selected as the new editor of this series. The artists included Don Dickson, Robert Edler, Mett Shippee, and Perino. Six named specimens described as arrow points found in Texas and Oklahoma were mentioned. They are *Agee*, *Benton type A*, *Benton type B*, *Edwards*, *Garza*, and *Howard*. The *Benton* points are examples of metal points made and used during the historic period.

Gregory H. Perino was the editor and author of Special Bulletin No. 4, which was published by the Society in 1971. This volume also described 50 points. In the introduction, Perino wrote that at the time of this publication there were more than 300 typed points, and more were being named every year. Only one specimen, *Rockwall*, is mentioned as having been found in Texas. He continued to illustrate and describe projectile points in three volumes that he published privately in 1985, 1991, and 2002 as *Selected Preforms, Points, and Knives of the North American Indians*.

In 2007, the Oklahoma Anthropological Society published Special Bulletin No. 26 titled "Southern Plains Lithics: The Small Points." This volume describes and illustrates arrow points found in Arkansas, Colorado,

56 | CHAPTER 3

Kansas, Louisiana, Missouri, Nebraska, New Mexico, Oklahoma, and Texas (Duncan et al. 2007). The project began in 1993 when Dr. Gene Hellstern formed a committee to research known point types from the Southern Plains region of North America. This was a joint effort with archaeologists from TARL, Gilcrease Museum, Panhandle-Plains Historical Museum, Museum of the Red River, Arkansas Archeological Survey, and the Sam Noble Oklahoma Museum of Natural History. Although the efforts by Robert E. Bell and Gregory H. Perino continue to be used as valid sources for projectile point typology in Oklahoma, the authors of this volume concentrated on redefining the geographic distribution of the various types. They also included radiocarbon dates, when possible, and additional references. Illustrations were provided by Robert E. Bell, Pam Headrick, Bobby Nickey, Frieda Vereecken-Odell, Gregory H. Perino, Frank Weir, and Don Wykoff. Texas points are numerous and include *Agee, Alba, Bassett, Bonham, Cuney, Deadman's, Edwards, Fresno, Friley, Garza, Harrell, Hayes, Howard, Maud, Morris, Perdiz, Rockwall, Scallorn, Starr, Talco, Toyah,* and *Turney.* Average dimensions are stated, but the figures lack scales.

Clarence H. Webb (2000:1) addressed the typology issue in *Stone Points and Tools of Northwestern Louisiana*: "The reader should know that lithic types are not sacrosanct. They are developed by a person or a group of people who study samples from a site, a cultural group, of a given area, who attach a name or names to perceived objects to develop a tool for study and comparison. Some point types (like *Evans* or *Friley*) have distinct attributes that make identification easy; others offer more difficulties and overlaps, or variations are numerous." Points described by Webb (2000:14–16) as occurring on both sides of the artificial boundaries of Texas and Louisiana are *Alba, Bassett, Bayou Goula, Bonham, Catahoula, Colbert, Friley, Hayes, Homan, Maud, Perdiz,* and *Scallorn.*

Samuel O. McGahey was an archaeologist with the Mississippi Department of Archives and History who had a strong interest in projectile point typology. In 2000, this agency published *Mississippi Projectile Point Guide* as the culmination of his research. Although one state removed from Texas, this guide is relevant because it discusses *Scallorn* as a type found in Mississippi.

Noel D. Justice compiled *Stone Age Spear and Arrow Points of the Midcontinental and Eastern United States,* which was published by Indiana University Press in 1987. Although most of the examples are from other states, this book is relevant to Texas because some specimens have been reported in parts of the state. The only Texas examples mentioned are *Alba, Scallorn,* and *Morris.* Types from the neighboring states of Arkansas and Louisiana are also included. Examples of some types are depicted in excellent color photographs, and the detailed descriptions are illustrated by drawings enhanced by a scale for each specimen. His approach is unlike other typology books in that he describes types as part of clusters, wide areas of distribution of each type. For example, *Alba* is a Texas type found in East Texas with specimens reported in lesser numbers in Arkansas, Louisiana, and Oklahoma. Justice (1987:235–237) reports that the *Alba* Cluster includes sites as far away as Indiana, Illinois, and Missouri.

The perusal of typology books and publications to identify arrow point types found in Texas was the primary source for the decision about which points should be included in this volume. The sources listed in chapter 6 of this book were written and compiled by archaeologists whose reputations are considered well-reasoned and valid.

Conversely, there exists numerous books, websites, and Facebook groups compiled by nonprofessionals that also describe arrow point types. It's obvious that the creators of these books and other materials relied on the efforts of professional archaeologists, but some types are questionable and reflect the opinion of collectors. A most thorough source on the internet is "Projectile Point Identification Guide," touted by its creators as "the largest most comprehensive on-line identification guide." All 50 states are included, and the types included are identified as valid or typed by collectors. It is a very useful source for a first or second sorting of types and a good platform for visual variability in point types. It was not created by professional archaeologists; therefore, some comments should be viewed with caution.

Arrow points with established names such as *Catahoula* and *Scallorn* are easily distinguishable by their shape. Variations among all types occur, and this can make typing difficult. The area where certain types

58 | CHAPTER 3

are known to occur is never perfectly clear. Reasons for certain points to be found away from what is considered their core area include trade and travel for hunting and/or warfare. A different explanation is implied by Campbell (1979:22), who cites other sources that state the Manos Prietas Indians of northeastern Coahuila exchanged bows and arrows with other groups to "symbolize peaceful relations." Also, the territory of the various groups changed as they moved about the state and into the missions. A reminder of the limited choices available when shaping a projectile point was made clear to me when I visited the National Museum of Finland and saw projectile points virtually indistinguishable, except for the type of stone, from types in Southeast Texas.

CHAPTER 4

Archaeological Planning Regions

THE BORDERS of Texas encompass more square miles than any state except Alaska. As a result, there is a huge variation of terrain and vegetation within its boundaries. Elevations range from sea level in the coastal areas along the Gulf of Mexico to 8,715 feet at the top of Guadalupe Peak in Culberson County. Plant communities have been identified as alpine, desert, forest, swamp, and coastal. This variation in environmental settings was a major factor in the diversity of lifeways among the prehistoric inhabitants of Texas and the early settlers. To better understand how people adapted to the different conditions across the state, the Texas Historical Commission (THC) began a program of identifying the regions of Texas according to the archaeological data from these regions that were known at the time. Other archaeologists may have differing opinions about the names of these regions and the counties therein. In this book, I'm adhering to those established by the THC.

Preservation planning in Texas began in earnest in 1968 when the THC divided Texas into four major "planning regions," with each one composed of archaeological subregions based on unique environmental and archaeological characteristics. This division resulted in the creation of the Eastern Planning Region, Central and Southern Planning Region, Plains Planning Region, and the Trans-Pecos Planning Region. The counties in each region are listed in Appendix E.

These regions were to be discussed in planning documents that could be used to "provide recommendations to federal agencies, to direct the effort to list sites in the National Register of Historic Places, and to preserve significant sites through other mechanisms" (Kenmotsu and Perttula

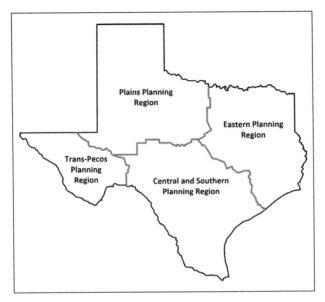

Figure 4.1. Planning regions in Texas (drafted by Lili Lyddon).

1993:4–5). The planning documents are based on geographic areas that in most cases correspond to regional archaeological syntheses prepared for the Southwestern Division, US Army Corps of Engineers. The maps depicted in this chapter are provided courtesy of the Texas Historical Commission. Each major region is subdivided into smaller specific regions.

Two formal planning documents have been completed. They present data for the Eastern Planning Region (Kenmotsu and Perttula 1993) and the Central and Southern Planning Region (Mercado-Allinger et al. 1996). These documents are very thorough and should be considered required reading for any major archaeological project prior to entering the field. As with all such compilations, new data is created immediately after publication, but the heart of the research remains and will always be a valuable resource. According to Patricia A. Mercado-Allinger (personal communication, 2018), the Plains Planning Region and the Trans-Pecos Planning Region are not likely to be published. There are discrepancies between some of the counties presented in the planning document for the Central and Southern Planning Region and those that were selected for the

Archeological Bibliography for the Central Region of Texas (Simons and Moore 1997). Those counties in the bibliographies are used here because the changes were made after additional research, and they are linked to the bibliographies for research purposes.

As an extension of the planning documents, the Office of the State Archeologist, Texas Historical Commission, compiled bibliographies of the Southern Coastal Corridor Region (Bailey 1988), Northern Panhandle Region (Simons 1988), Southeastern Region (Moore and Simons 1989), Northeastern Region (Martin 1990), and Central Texas Region (Simons and Moore (1997) as special reports. Each bibliography contains far more information than just citations of archaeological publications. Added value consists of an Index of Key Words, Site Numbers, Counties, Ethnohistorical and Historical Sources, and Environmental Bibliographies.

Eastern Planning Region

This planning document for the Eastern Region contains three separate subregions—Prairie-Savanna, Northeast Texas, and Southeast Texas. The planners realized that these regions were based on data available at the time they were created, and that they may not coincide exactly with cultural and geographical units as identified by other researchers (see Perttula 2004:Table 1.1).

Prairie-Savanna

This subregion consists of 26 counties that are bordered on the north by Oklahoma, on the south by the Southeast Texas subregion and the Central and Southern Planning Region, on the east by the Northeast Texas subregion, and on the west by the Plains Planning Region. Per Daniel Prikryl (1993:191), "The prehistoric archeology of the Prairie-Savanna has not received as much attention as many other regions of Texas." He writes that this is "unfortunate because many sites have been damaged or destroyed in past years, and threats continue." Prikryl (1993:191–204) presents an overview of the history and future of this region in chapter 3.1, "Introduction to Section III: Regional Preservation Plan for Archeological Resources, Prairie-Savanna Archeological Region" (Kenmotsu and Perttula

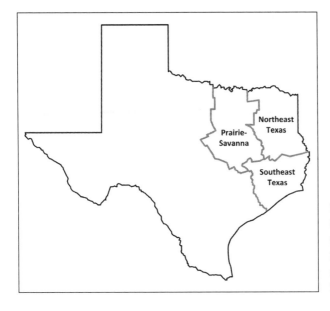

Figure 4.2. Subregions in the Eastern Planning Region (drafted by Lili Lyddon).

1993). No bibliography for this region has been compiled by the THC.

Southeast Texas

This subregion consists of 19 counties in the southeastern corner of the state. It is defined on the north by the Northeast Texas and Prairie-Savanna subregions, on the east by the Texas-Louisiana border, on the west by the Central and Southern Planning Region, and on the south by Mexico. This area is approximately the same as defined by Patterson in his database for the southeastern coastal margin (1989a) and bibliography of the upper Texas coast (1989b). Perttula presents an overview of the history and future of this region in chapter 4.1, "Introduction to Section IV: Regional Preservation Plan for Archeological Resources, Southeast Texas Archeological Region" (Kenmotsu and Perttula 1993:207–213). In 1965, all Southeast Texas could be regarded as unknown archaeologically (Shafer, personal communication). This statement was based, in part, on his work in the San Jacinto River Basin in Montgomery County (Shafer 1968). Moore and Simons (1989) compiled *Archeological Bibliography for the Southeastern Region of Texas.*

Northeast Texas

This subregion consists of 31 counties in the northeastern corner of the state. It is defined on the north by the Red River, on the south by the Southeast Texas subregion, on the east by Louisiana, and on the west by the Prairie-Savanna subregion. There is no separate chapter that discusses the Northeast Texas subregion in this planning document. William A. Martin (1990) compiled *Archeological Bibliography for the Northeastern Region of Texas.*

Central and Southern Planning Region

This planning document contains five separate subregions—Central Texas, Central Coastal Plains, Lower Pecos, Southern Coastal Corridor, and Rio Grande Plains. The goals of this planning document are the same as those for the previously published Eastern Planning Region by Kenmotsu and Perttula (1993). The present document was intended to represent the efforts of the THC to plan and conduct preservation efforts in the central and southern portions of Texas. In the introduction, Mercado-Allinger, Kenmotsu, and Perttula (1996:3–27) discuss the history of preservation in the state and the salient points of the Commission's efforts to protect archaeological resources and how they are to be implemented in such sections as "Chronology of Preservation Planning in Texas," "Implementation Procedures," and "The Physical Setting" of the region. Sites listed in the National Register of Historic Places are named, and the geographical regions by county are provided. As stated, one of the persistent problems facing preservationists is the constant destruction of archaeological sites by man and nature. Chapter 1.2 reviews the damage caused by these events and names the regions that have been the most affected. Mercado-Allinger, Kenmotsu, and Perttula (1996:44) write that the data presented in this document make "it possible to anticipate potential impacts to significant archeological resources and to make informed management decisions about them." Unlike the planning document for the Eastern Planning Region by Kenmotsu and Perttula (1993), this one

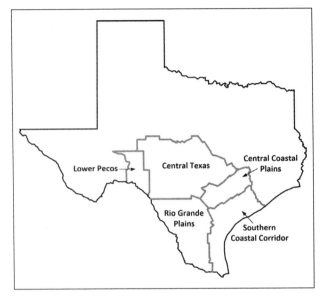

Figure 4.3. Subregions in the Central and Southern Planning Region (drafted by Lili Lyddon).

lacks discussions of each subregion. Instead, all discussions tend to focus on the entire region.

Central Coastal Plains

This subregion consists of ten counties. It is defined on the north by the Central Texas and Prairie-Savanna subregions, on the south by the Southern Coastal Corridor subregion, on the east by the Eastern Planning Region, and on the west by the Rio Grande Plains subregion. No bibliography for this region has been compiled by the THC.

Central Texas

This subregion consists of 34 counties in the center of the state as defined by Simons and Moore (1997) in the *Archeological Bibliography for the Central Region of Texas*. It is bordered on the north by the unnamed portion of the Plains Planning Region, on the south by the Rio Grande Plains and the Central Coastal Plains archaeological subregions, on the east by the

Prairie-Savanna subregion, and on the west by the Lower Pecos subregion. Crockett County is one of the two counties that make up the Lower Pecos subregion, but it also appears in the bibliography by Simons and Moore (1997) as part of the Central Texas subregion. A larger contradiction is the presence of an entire row of counties referred to in the planning document for the central and southern regions as part of the Central Texas subregion, but they were omitted in the bibliography by Simons and Moore (1997). These counties are (from west to east) Sterling, Coke, Runnels, Coleman, Brown, Comanche, and Hamilton. In this publication, these counties are part of the Plains Planning Region that was not named. The assumption is the bibliography is more correct since it was published after the planning document.

Lower Pecos

This subregion consists of two counties. It is defined on the north by the Plains Planning Region, on the south by the border with Mexico, on the east by the Central Texas and Southern Planning Region, and on the west by the Trans-Pecos Planning Region. No bibliography for this region has been compiled by the THC.

Southern Coastal Corridor

This subregion consists of 15 counties along the central and lower coast of Texas. It is defined on the north by the Central Coastal Plains subregion, on the south by the border with Mexico and the Gulf of Mexico, on the east by the Southeast Texas Subregion, and on the west by the Rio Grande Plains subregion. Gail Bailey (1987) compiled *Archeological Bibliography for the Southern Coastal Corridor Region of Texas.*

Rio Grande Plains

This region consists of 19 counties. It is defined on the north by the Central Texas subregion, on the south by the border with Mexico, on the east by the Southern Coastal Corridor and Central Coastal Plains subregions, and on the south and west by the border with Mexico. This region has not been published as part of the Planning Document series, and there are no current plans to do so (Patricia A. Mercado-Allinger, personal

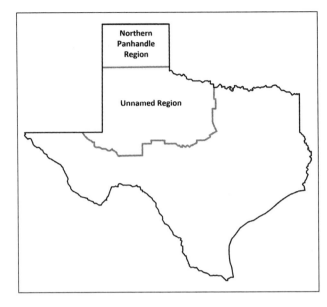

Figure 4.4. Northern Panhandle and unnamed regions (drafted by Lili Lyddon).

communication 2018). No bibliography for this region has been compiled by the THC.

Plains Planning Region

This planning document contains one defined subregion—Northern Panhandle and a large group of counties not included in the planning region at this time, referred to here as an "Unnamed Region." The area covered encompasses portions of the Canadian River Basin and adjacent sections of the High Plains. Per Patricia Mercado-Allinger (personal communication 2020), the Unnamed Region to the south is not likely to be published in this series.

Northern Panhandle

This subregion consists of 20 counties in the northernmost part of Texas. It is defined on the north and east by the border with Oklahoma, on the south by the Trans-Pecos, Central, and Southern subregions, and on the west by the border with New Mexico. Helen Simons (1988) compiled *Archeological Bibliography for the Northern Panhandle Region of Texas.*

Unnamed Region

The 69 counties that comprise this subregion are bounded by the Northern Panhandle subregion on the north, the Central and Southern Planning Region on the south, the Eastern Planning Region on the east, and the Trans-Pecos Region.

Trans-Pecos Planning Region

This region consists of nine counties in far western Texas. The boundaries of this region are New Mexico to the north, Mexico to the south and west, and the Plains and Central and Southern Planning Regions to the east.

CHAPTER 5

Relevant Literature

PDATES ON the status of the various archaeological regions in Texas appear periodically in the literature. Obviously, the counties defined in these regions don't match exactly with those established by the THC for planning purposes. These reports are not about projectile point typology, but many discuss types of points associated with each region. Cyrus N. Ray was president of the newly organized Texas Archeological and Paleontological Society, which published its initial Bulletin in 1929. His article titled "A Differentiation of the Prehistoric Cultures of the Abilene Section" discussed the Sand Dune Culture and the Culture of the Bifurcated Base (Ray 1929:7–22). Although he refers to this region solely as "near Abilene, Texas," this article exemplifies an early attempt at discussing a broad area. In many ways, Texas archaeology was in its infancy as evidenced by the following statement from T. N. Campbell in his discussion of the Johnson site of the Aransas focus (1947:40): "Thus far, no excavated site on the Texas coast has been reported with full descriptive details." "Only one archaeologist, E. B. Sayles, has attempted to synthesize the rather heterogeneous data on the archaeology of the coastal strip, but this synthesis involved very little data derived from excavation." Sayles (n.d.) notes are on file at TARL.

The first statewide overview was the highly acclaimed *Bulletin of the Texas Archeological Society* (volume 25), which was published in 1954 and authored by Dee Ann Suhm and Alex D. Krieger with a contribution by Edward B. Jelks. The areas discussed are Trans-Pecos, Panhandle-Plains, North-Central Texas, Central Texas, Coastal Texas, Southwest Texas, and East Texas. This extremely popular volume was out of print in 1956, and

70 | CHAPTER 5

there were numerous requests for a reprint. In the foreword, Edward B. Jelks, E. Mott Davis, and Henry F. Sturgis discuss the sequence of events that transpired following the issuance of the 1954 Bulletin: "It was originally planned that the *Handbook* would be reissued in essentially its original form, and that, in addition, a series of papers on special problems in the different parts of Texas would be published. Also, a volume on field techniques was to be prepared. Most of these plans went awry because of pressure on the editors' time and slowness on the part of the authors submitting manuscripts, and therefore a different order of events is now contemplated." The first part of the *Handbook* that dealt with areas and complexes was not reissued. It was replaced by reviews of *Texas Archeology* with chapters on Northeast Texas Archeology by Clarence H. Webb, Central Texas Archeology by Dee Ann Suhm, Trans-Pecos Texas Archeology by Donald J. Lehmer, and the Central and Southern Sections of the Texas Coast by T. N. Campbell. Additionally, W. W. Newcomb Jr. discussed Indian tribes of Texas, while T. N. Campbell authored "Texas Archeology: A Guide to the Literature." The long-awaited response was published in volume 29 of the *Bulletin of the Texas Archeological Society* (published in 1960 for 1958). It was titled "A Review of Texas Archeology" and was edited by T. N. Campbell, with assistance from assistant editors E. Mott Davis and Edward B. Jelks. The contents consisted of "Indian Tribes of Texas" (W. W. Newcomb); "A Review of Northeast Texas Archeology" (Clarence B. Webb); "A Review of Southeast Texas Archeology" (Dee Ann Suhm); "A Review of Trans-Pecos Archeology" (Donald J. Lehmer); "Archeology of the Central and Southern Sections of the Texas Coast" (T. N. Campbell); and "A Guide to the Literature" (compiled and edited by T. N. Campbell).

In the foreword by Edward B. Jelks, E. Mott Davis, and Henry F. Sturgis, the authors state the following: "This, then, is the long-awaited 1958 issue of the *Bulletin*, and the beginning of the revision of *An Introductory Handbook of Texas Archeology*. It is our hope and belief that the members of the Society will find the papers of general interest, and that those members engaged in active research will find them of particular value."

The popular discussion of projectile points and ceramics was finally issued in 1962 as a special publication by the Society and the Texas Memorial Museum and titled *Handbook of Texas Archeology: Type Descriptions* (Suhm and Jelks 1962). It was sold out and has become another sought-after publication.

LeRoy Johnson's (1967) study titled *Toward a Statistical Overview of the Archaic Cultures of Central and Southwestern Texas* appeared as Bulletin 12 of the Texas Memorial Museum. His approach was to compare total lithic collections from nine Texas sites by a "simple form of cluster analysis with ordered matrix." Most the focus of his research is the Texas Archaic. However, arrow points *Bonham*, *Livermore*, *Perdiz*, and *Scallorn* were included in this study. His Figure 2 depicts outlines of points he refers to as period markers.

Thomas R. Hester is one of the more prolific publishers of information regarding Texas archaeology. In 1980, he published *Digging into South Texas Prehistory: A Guide for Amateur Archaeologists*. Chapters relevant to typology are "Historic Indians of South Texas," "Prehistoric Sites in South Texas," "Major Artifact Types of South Texas," and "11,000 Years of South Texas Prehistory." He also played a major role in the creation of the journal *La Tierra* published by the Southeast Texas Archaeological Association beginning with the first issue in 1971. A substantial amount of information for this book was taken from this journal.

Lawrence E. Aten published his critically acclaimed study titled *Indians of the Upper Texas Coast* in 1983; it was an outgrowth of his PhD dissertation (Aten 1979). His research focused on a wide swath along the Texas coast from the Louisiana border to the Guadalupe River northeast of Goliad, Texas. In the preface he writes that this book is "pertinent to scholars interested in the Archaeology of Texas, of the Southeastern United States, and of coastal zones in General."

Daniel E. Fox is a noted Texas historical archaeologist. His very well researched book *Traces of Texas History: Archeological Evidence of the Past 450 Years* was published in 1983. Of importance here is the fact that he discusses the archaeological investigations at missions in Texas. This information provides insight into the lives of the Indians who inhabited the missions and made arrow points of stone, metal, and glass.

The utility of computers to document records became realized in the late 1970s, and their role today is mandatory if the vast cultural resources

72 | CHAPTER 5

of Texas are to be made available for research. The first systematic computerization of the prehistoric record in Texas appeared in 1984 in *Prehistoric Archeological Sites in Texas: A Statistical Overview* (Biesaart et al. 1985). It quickly became a popular research tool, but it went out of print shortly after it was issued.

The Department of Antiquities Protection, Texas Historical Commission, published several major documents dividing the state into planning regions, but only two were published, *Overviews of the Eastern Planning Region* (Kenmotsu and Perttula 1993) and *Central and Southern Planning Region* (Mercado-Allinger et al. 1996). These are discussed in chapter 4.

This agency also published volume 1 of *Advances in Texas Archeology: Contributions from Cultural Resource Management* in 1995 (James E. Bruseth and Timothy K. Perttula editors). Albeit not a source that focuses on artifact typology, it is a valuable companion source as it is more than simple reportage. Most pertinent to this work is inclusive statements about associated artifacts to include types and age. Even though each chapter contains useful information for much of the state, the one titled "Lithic Resource Availability in the Upper Trinity Region: The Evidence from Joe Pool Lake" by Daniel E. McGregor is the most relevant to this study.

The Texas Archeological Society published Bulletin 66 in 1995; it focused on the current knowledge of the prehistory and early history of the state in two parts.

Part 1 contains Elton R. Prewitt's article "Distributions of Typed Points in Texas." Part 2 reviews "The Archeology of Southeast Texas" by Leland Patterson, "Prehistoric Occupation of the Central and Lower Texas Coast: A Regional Overview" by Robert A. Ricklis, "The Archeology of the Post Oak Savannah of East Central Texas" by Ross C. Fields, "The Archeology of the Piney Woods and Post Oak Savannah of Northeast Texas" by Timothy K. Perttula, "Forty Years of Archeology in Central Texas" by Michael B. Collins, "The Prehistory of South Texas" by Thomas R. Hester, and "The Lower Pecos Region of Texas and Northern Mexico" by Solveig A. Turpin.

The same year [1995], avocational archaeologist Dan R. Davis Jr.'s book *Prehistoric Artifacts of the Texas Indians: An Identification and Reference Guide* was published by the Pecos Publishing Company in Fort Sumner,

New Mexico. His work was a compilation of data from other sources. The points are illustrated by photographs accompanied by scales. No dimensions are given.

Timothy K. Perttula (2004) edited *The Prehistory of Texas*. Some of the chapters in this volume were updated as more comprehensive and expanded versions of papers that were originally published in Bulletin 66 by the Texas Archeological Society in 1995. Part 1 is titled "Texas Prehistory." The remainder of the book is devoted to the current knowledge of the archaeology of Central Texas by Michael B. Collins, South Texas by Thomas R. Hester, the Central and Lower Texas Coast and Southeast Texas by Robert A. Ricklis, the Jornada Mogollon and Eastern Trans-Pecos Regions of West Texas by Myles R. Miller and Nancy A. Kenmotsu, hunters and farmers of the High Plains and Canyonlands by Solveig A. Turpin, Southern High Plains by Eileen Johnson and Vance T. Holliday, Palo Duro Complex by Douglas K. Boyd, Post Oak Savanna of East-Central Texas by Ross C. Fields, and Caddoan Archeology of the Northeastern Texas Pineywoods by Timothy K. Perttula. This is an expressly appropriate source, as diagnostic arrow point types for these regions are considered.

In 2015, Texas A&M University Press published *Pioneering Archaeology in the Texas Coastal Bend: The Pape-Tunnell Collection* by John W. Tunnell Jr. and Jace W. Tunnell. It is a most valuable resource that documents the field work and collections by two avocational archaeologists, John W. Tunnell and Harold Pape on the Texas coast in Aransas, Kleberg, Nueces, Refugio, and San Patrice Counties in the 1920s and 1930s. Not only did they amass a huge collection of prehistoric artifacts, but they also kept detailed records of their finds. The artifacts, notes, and maps were stored in boxes where they had been forgotten until the 1990s when they were discovered by members of the family. John W. Tunnell Jr. and Jace W. Tunnel collaborated to organize the collection and notes that were eventually published in 2015. The contribution that can be made by avocational archaeologists is evident in this book. At the time of their explorations, the archaeology of Texas was in its infancy, and few sites were being investigated by professional archaeologists. Consequently, the Pape-Tunnell collection represents a huge amount of archaeological data that would be literally impossible to replicate today. One of their most prolific areas,

74 | CHAPTER 5

Webb Island in San Pedro Bay, no longer exists. Other sites have been lost to erosion and development. Many of their sites are Late Prehistoric, and photos of arrow points from the coastal area of Texas are abundant. Much of this collection was donated to TARL, where it is housed as the Pape-Tunnel Collection. Thomas R. Hester praised the Tunnells for the efforts they spent documenting their collection.

Other efforts to analyze private collections include the following: Mary Jo Galindo (1988) analyzed the Riley Point Collection from Mier, Tamaulipas. Her results can be found in an unpublished manuscript on file at TARL.

Kindall and Patterson (1986) examined Andy Kyle's collection from sites in East Texas that includes *Alba, Bonham, Catahoula, Friley, Perdiz,* and *Scallorn* arrow points.

E. Mott Davis was a regular attendee at the annual field school sponsored by the Texas Archeological Society. "He is respected by his professional peers and revered by a vast legion of volunteer and professional archeologists in Texas" (Tunnell et al. 1998). The Texas Archeological Research Laboratory (1998) published a collection of his writings titled *Chapters in the History of Texas Archeology: Selected Papers by E. Mott Davis.*

CHAPTER 6

Arrow Points

Agee

ORIGINAL RECORDER: W. Raymond Wood (1963) defined this arrow point based on examples found at the Crenshaw site in Miller County, Arkansas. He named it for W. P. Agee Jr. who identified it in 1906.

OTHER NAMES: None reported.

SIMILAR TYPES: *Alba*, *Catahoula*, *Homan*, and *Rockwall* (Duncan et al. 2007:3).

AGE: Davis (1995) offers an approximate time frame for the use of this point as AD 700 to AD 1300. Lemley (1936) believes this type is representative of a pre-Caddo culture.

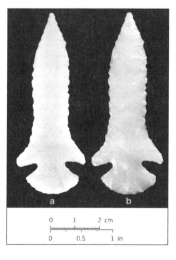

Figure 6.1. Agee point (photo courtesy of Sam C. Johnson, Caddo Trading Company).

76 | CHAPTER 6

DESCRIPTION: Duncan et al. (2007:3) cites Wood (1963), White and others (1963), and Perino (1968:4) in his physical description of *Agee*. "This type has a convex base with fairly deep U- and V-shaped corner notches. The blade shape is referred to as excurvate/incurvate. Notches on the blade are a prominent feature and occur at an angle of 45 degrees. Some specimens have two sets of notches. The barbs are pointed or flat-ended, depending on the orientation of the notches. These points were manufactured by carefully controlled pressure flaking. The edges were trimmed by minute flaking, and some points are serrated. At the Crenshaw site, the length varied from 3.5 cm to 5.5 cm. The width varied from 1.5 cm to 2.0 cm, and the maximum thickness was 0.25 cm." This type is not discussed by Suhm and Jelks (1962) or Turner, Hester, and McReynolds (2011).

CULTURAL AFFILIATION: Wood (1963) associates *Agee* with the Coles Creek culture (primarily as grave goods) and with the Caddo. James Brown (1996) believes it is associated with the Early Caddoan period in Oklahoma.

KNOWN SITES: Sam C. Johnson (telephone conversation, April 29, 2022) says that the main source (e.g., type site) for *Agee* points is Crenshaw Mounds (3-MI-0006) in Miller County, Arkansas. The examples illustrated are courtesy of Johnson. Specimen "a" is made from novaculite. The material used to create specimen "b" has not been identified. Other sites with *Agee* points are Bowman (3 LR 00046) in Little River County, Arkansas and the Kidd site in Pike County. Examples have been documented at 3-CN-000117 in Calhoun County, Arkansas, and 34LF40 (Spiro Mounds) in eastern Oklahoma.

SOURCES FOR ILLUSTRATIONS AND DESCRIPTIONS: Brown (1976); Davis (1995); Duncan and others (2007); Perino (1968, 1985, 1991); Turner and Hester (1985); and Wood (1963).

COMMENTS: Davis (1995) states that *Agee* may have been a ceremonial point because it has been found in caches associated with burials. He also believes that *Agee* and *Homan* points may be part of a continuum since they are very similar in general appearance.

Perino (1991) refers to his illustrations of *Agee* points as variants used for special occasions. The excellent workmanship, length of some specimens,

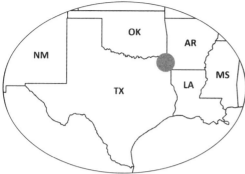

Figure 6.2. Distribution of Agee points (drafted by Lili G. Lyddon).

extreme thinness of this type, and association with burials suggests to this author that their function may have been other than as an actual projectile.

Duncan and others (2007:5–7) illustrate 32 *Agee* points from this site. They (Duncan et al. 2007:4) write that the distinctions between *Agee* and other types "appear to relate to barb length, flaking, size, and width." They (Duncan et al. 2007:3) report the dimensions of *Agee* points at the Crenshaw site as follows:

Length: 3.5 cm to 5.5 cm
Maximum width: 1.5 cm to 2.0 cm
Maximum thickness: 0.25 cm

James A. Brown (1976) refers to Specimen "E" in Perino's (1991) figure as a sociotechnic point of the Spiro Phase and earlier. He describes the rest of the specimens as sociotechnic points of the late Coles Creek culture that were intended as nonutilitarian ceremonial objects.

Agee is included in *A Field Guide to Stone Artifacts* (Turner and Hester 1985:162) but omitted from *Stone Artifacts of Texas Indians* (Turner et al. 2011).

DISTRIBUTION: Gregory Perino (1968:4) writes that it is primarily found in southwest Arkansas, but specimens have been reported in northwestern Louisiana, northeastern Texas, and southeastern Oklahoma.

Figure 6.3. Ahumada point (replica by Matt Soultz).

Ahumada

ORIGINAL RECORDER: Milton F. Krone (1976) named it for the nearby town of Villa Ahumada in Chihuahua, Mexico.

OTHER NAMES: None reported.

SIMILAR TYPES: *Livermore, Maljamar, Pendejo,* and *Van Horn.*

AGE: AD 750 to AD 900 (Krone 1976).

DESCRIPTION: Krone (1976:42) describes this type as a "medium-sized arrow point with a narrow triangular blade, short protruding barbs, and a bulbous stem." The blades are always serrated. He does not provide dimensions.

CULTURAL AFFILIATION: Unknown.

KNOWN SITES: In Mexico, this type has been reported at Villa Ahumada, Rio Santa Maria, and Soto Ranch.

SOURCES FOR ILLUSTRATIONS AND DESCRIPTIONS: Krone (1976).

COMMENTS: Krone (1976:42) found this point on hunter-gatherer complex sites scattered throughout areas where water was available and centered in

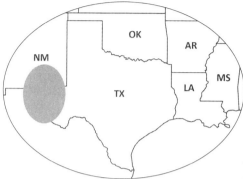

Figure 6.4. Distribution of Ahumada points (drafted by Lili G. Lyddon).

northern Chihuahua, Mexico. He describes these sites as "ranging from small single-fire hearths to large scatters of lithic debris that continue for miles along arroyos and rivers." These sites contain little or no pottery. According to him, Alan L. Phelps (1966) offered the best relative estimate of the age of this type based on cruciform artifacts he found at sites like those where *Ahumada* points occur. His dates for the Cruciform type are based on pottery analysis, with the *Ahumada* point being associated with the prepottery phase of the culture.

The *Maljamar* point is also similar in form to *Ahumada*, but it is mainly found at sites in southern New Mexico and the adjacent panhandle of Texas to both the south and east.

Andy Cloud (personal communication, 2018) observed that the term *Ahumada* is not used by most archaeologists in the El Paso area. Cloud refers to the *Van Horn* arrow point as the correct name for this type, but I have not yet found any reference to this type or any citation regarding dimensions.

Ahumada is not included in *Stone Artifacts of Texas Indians* (Turner et al. 2011).

DISTRIBUTION: The geographical center of this type is near the town of *Villa Ahumada* in Mexico (Krone 1976), but it has also been encountered in Culberson and Hudspeth Counties in the Trans-Pecos region of Texas (Prewitt 1995). Robert J. Mallouf (personal communication, 2018) says this type is frequently found in the Eastern Trans-Pecos and Big Bend regions.

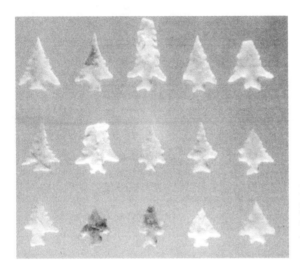

Figure 6.5. Alazán points (photo courtesy of the Center for the Studies of the Big Bend).

Alazán

ORIGINAL RECORDER: This arrow point was first recognized by John A. "Jack" Hedrick of the El Paso Archaeological Society during surveys of the Van Horn Plateau area in the 1970s and 1980s. Hedrick (1975) published the initial descriptions of this point in *The Artifact*, but it was never given an official name. He later discussed it in a publication describing five arrow point types from the Plateau Complex (Hedrick 1986). Robert J. Mallouf formally named this point for specimens found in the Alazán Hills of southeastern Presidio County, Texas. He published additional information related to *Alazán* in 1985, 2009, 2012, and 2013.

OTHER NAMES: None reported.

SIMILAR TYPES: *Cuney, Livermore,* and *Scallorn.*

AGE: Hedrick (1986) does not attempt to place this arrow point style chronologically, other than noting its repeated occurrence in surface contexts with Late Prehistoric types *Perdiz, Scallorn,* and *Toyah*. A specimen that is very similar to this type found at 41PS915 was dated at AD 1130 to AD 1380 (Seebach 2007). The presence of *Alazán* arrow points with *Livermore, Toyah,* and other types in the John Z. and Exa Means Cache in the

Y-6 Hills near Lobo Valley (Culberson County) implies a possible age range of from AD 800 to AD 1350 (Mallouf 1985a; 2012:16). Recent radiocarbon assays of cultural features at sites in the Big Bend region appear to narrow the chronological range for *Alazán* arrow points (through association with *Toyah* points) to circa AD 1150 to AD 1350 or somewhat later (Corrick 2000; Cloud et al. 1994; Cloud and Piehl 2008).

DESCRIPTION: Mallouf (2012:14) describes this type as possessing triangular blades. "The lateral edges are usually straight but may be slightly concave to slightly convex or sometimes slightly recurved. The blades range in size from wide to narrow, and the lateral edges are frequently serrated. Refurbishing of blades was a common practice. Sometimes, the distal tips were beveled, giving them a needle-like appearance. The barbs may project out at right angles to the long axis of the point or slope downward. Occasionally, they flare outward. Stem necks vary from narrow to wide and are typically short and small relative to the overall size of the point. They may be parallel sided to moderately expanding with a concave or 'fish tail' base. Finally, they are lenticular to plano-convex in cross-section."

Mallouf (2012:15) provided the following measurements for *Alazán* points:

Range of maximum length: 17.7 cm to 31.7 cm
Mean length: 22.3 cm
Range of maximum width: 8.1 cm to 21.5 cm
Mean width: 15.3 cm
Range of maximum neck width: 4.5 cm to 8.3 cm
Mean neck width: 5.9 cm
Range of maximum thickness: 2.1 cm to 4.3 cm
Mean thickness: 2.9 cm

CULTURAL AFFILIATION: The association of *Alazán* arrow points with *Livermore* and *Toyah* from the John Z. and Exa Means Cache is suggestive, but not conclusive, of affinities with the Livermore Phase of the eastern Trans-Pecos Region. As noted, *Alazán* points have been recovered from most, if not all, areas of the eastern Trans-Pecos and from a wide variety of contexts. However, additional research is necessary to confidently assign cultural affinities to this point type (Mallouf 1985a; 2012:13).

82 | CHAPTER 6

KNOWN SITES: John Z. and Exa Means Projectile Point Cache (41JD212); Roark Cave (41BS3); Tres Metates Rockshelter (41PS915); Upper Farmersville (41COL34), 41BS466, 41BS522, 41CU658, 41COL34; and private collections. Turner, Hester, and McReynolds (2011) report that this type has been found at sites in the salt flats and Rosillos Mountains.

SOURCES FOR ILLUSTRATIONS AND DESCRIPTIONS: Hedrick (1975, 1986); Ingand colleagues (1996); Katz and Lukowski (1981); Mallouf (1985a, 2009, 2012, 2013); Mallouf and Wulfkuhle (1989); Marmaduke (1978); Ricklis and Collins (1994:45); Roney (1985); Crook (2008–2009); Turner, Hester, and McReynolds (2011); and Turpin (1998).

COMMENTS: Data recovery since the middle of the 1980s supports Hedrick's original contention that this point style is distinctive and in need of further research (Mallouf 2012).

Robert J. Mallouf's (2009, 2012, 2013) classification of projectile points in the Eastern Trans-Pecos and Big Bend region of Texas is the most recent and comprehensive discussion of this type. Mallouf (2012:16) notes that "Leslie (1978) does not include this arrow point style in his typology of the Mescalero Escarpment area of New Mexico."

Hedrick (1986:15) refers to the geographical distribution of this type as the Plateau Complex in southern Culberson County. Mallouf (2012:16) describes sites in this area as occurring in "hard-packed sand and dune sand areas parallel to intermittent water courses of Plateau and Sacaton Draws in the northern part of the complex and China and Michigan Draws in the southern part of the complex." These draws flow to the north and northwest and empty into the southern end of Wild Horse Basin.

Brockmoller (1987) identified and classified projectile points from the Plateau Complex in *The Artifact* (25(1):1–48.

DISTRIBUTION: Based on archaeological surveys and private collections, this type is frequently found in the eastern and Big Bend areas of the Trans-Pecos region. Mallouf (2012:15) provides the following statements: It is, "known to occur in the Terlingua Creek, Bear Creek, Mountains, Big Canyon, Chisos Mountains, Maravillas Creek, and Persimmon Gap areas of the Big Bend Proper." He also writes that they "appear to have an increasing frequency to the north, being known from the Davis Mountains,

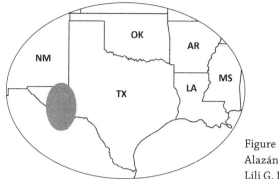

Figure 6.6. Distribution of Alazán points (drafted by Lili G. Lyddon).

Y-6 Hills, Lobo Valley, and Plateau areas." Specimens have also been reported from sites in the Guadalupe Mountains, Delaware Mountains, and Salt Basin areas.

Alba

ORIGINAL RECORDER: Alex D. Krieger (1946) named this point for the town of Alba in Wood County where the first specimens were found. The initial description was based on examples found at the M. D. Harrell site (41YN1) in Young County.

OTHER NAMES: *Alba Barbed* (Krieger 1946; Newell and Krieger 1949). Suhm and Krieger (1954:494) shortened the name to *Alba* and described it in more detail. The *Alba* point illustrated here was found at 41SJ13 in San Jacinto County by the author.

SIMILAR TYPES: *Bonham* (Shafer 2006); *Colbert*, *Hayes*, and *Homan* (Duncan et al. 2007).

AGE: Crook and Hughston (2015b:34–35) were able to get radiometric data from a femur at the Lower Rockwall site (41RW1). The results were reported as AD 1240 ± 30 BP, with a 1-sigma calibration date range of AD 715 to AD 775, and a 2-sigma calibration of AD 680 to AD 880. Suhm and Krieger (1954) estimate the age of this point at about AD 1000 to AD 1200 or later. Turner, Hester, and McReynolds (2011) date it to sometime between

Figure 6.7. Alba point from 41SJ13 (photo courtesy of Brian Wootan).

AD 800 and AD 1200. *Alba* points were common in Coles Creek, Plaquemine, and early Caddoan cultures around AD 500 to AD 700 (Webb 2000). Crook (2017) dates this type to the Wylie Phase, circa AD 700 or AD 800 to AD 1250.

DESCRIPTION: Suhm and Krieger (1954:494) describe *Alba* as a "triangular point with lateral edges that are usually concave or recurved but seldom straight. Sometimes the edges are finely serrated. The shoulders are wide, 'outflaring' and usually barbed. The edges of the stems are usually parallel, but occasionally they are contracted or slightly expanded." Stems can be straight or bulbous. Some specimens were made from flakes. Suhm and Krieger (1954:494) provide the following measurements for *Alba* points:

Length: 1.8 to 3.5 cm
Maximum width: uniform at about 1.5 cm
Average stem length: 0.7 cm or one-fourth to one-fifth of the total point.

Webb (2000:14) presents the following average measurements from a sample of 82 specimens in Louisiana:

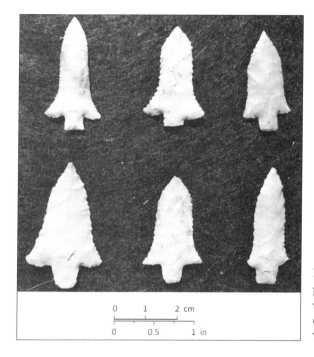

Figure 6.8. Alba points depicting various stem shapes (photo courtesy of Thomas Oakes).

Length: 32 mm
Width: 18.35 mm
Weight: 1.06 grams
Stem: about ¼ of total length

CULTURAL AFFILIATION: Webb (1959:162) cites Webb and Dobb (1939) and Newell and Krieger (1949) when stating, "This is the typical resident small point of Alto and Gahagan foci of the Gibson Aspect." Ford (1951) found *Alba* points in Louisiana at sites described as Haley-era and Spiro-era. He also cites *Alba* as a less common type in Coles Creek–era and Plaquemine-era sites in central Louisiana. Crook (2017:53) places it in the Wylie Phase.

KNOWN SITES: M. D. Harrell (41YN1); George C. Davis 41CE19); Pecan Springs (41EL11); A. C. Mackin (41LR39); the Reese site (41WA55); J. B.

86 | CHAPTER 6

White (41MM341); Bentsen-Clark (41RR41); the Kyle site (41HI1); Lower Rockwall (41RW1); Trammell Crow Pond (41WD185); Tankersley Creek (41TT108), 41CX5, 41DL148, 41DL149, 41DL406, 41SJ13, 41HR279, and sites in the Cedar Creek reservoir (Story 1965).

In Louisiana, *Alba* points have been reported at Belcher Mound (16CD13) in Caddo Parish. In Oklahoma, examples have been reported at Spiro mounds (34LF40) and Craig Mound (34LF46).

SOURCES FOR ILLUSTRATIONS AND DESCRIPTIONS: Aten (1983); Banks and Winters (1975); Bell (1958); Davis (1995); Duncan and others (2007); Fields (1988, 2004); Gadus and others (2006); Jelks (1962, 1993); Krieger (1946); Moore (1976); Newell and Krieger (1949); Perino (1985); Shafer (1973); Sorrow (1966); Suhm and Jelks (1962); Suhm and Krieger (1954); Turner and Hester (1985, 1993, 1999); Turner, Hester, and McReynolds (2011); Webb (1959, 2000); Young (1981b); Perttula and others (1986); Story (1981); and Crook (2008–2009, 2011).

COMMENTS: *Alba* was the predominant (a.k.a. resident) type at the George C. Davis site with 174 specimens documented. Newell and Krieger (1949:161) write that their research demonstrates that "*Alba Barbed*" points (and, by inference, the bow and arrow) were in use before the mound was erected. They continue: "In fact, the occurrence of these small points in features 30, 31, and 45 (Table 16) shows the type present beneath the initial four "small mounds." "This also means they were adopted before 'dart points,' and sandy pottery were abandoned."

Shafer (1973:194) describes and illustrates a "very compact cluster" of 150 *Alba* points at the George C. Davis site that are very similar morphologically and were likely stored in a basket-like container of wood or cane." These specimens were made of nonlocal chert. Their similar appearance suggests that they may have been made by the same knapper. This hypothesis was proposed for clusters of arrow points in a burial context at the Dan Holdeman site (Perino 1997:5600).

Harry J. Shafer (2006) proposed a *Bonham-Alba* classification that encompasses specimens dating around AD 100 from central Texas into eastern Texas. In her publication titled "Lithic and Mineral Artifacts," Baskin (1981:264) divides *Alba* points from the George C. Davis site into the following categories: Contracting Stem Edge Group, Form 1 (concave base);

Contracting Stem Edge Group, Form 2 (convex base); Contracting Stem Edge Group, Form 4 (platform base); and Parallel Stem Edge Group, Form 1 (convex base). Examples of these forms are illustrated in her Figure 32.

Joe Ben Wheat (1953:Plate 53) illustrates points that he describes as *Alba*. Some specimens are clearly *Catahoula*, a type that was not recognized until 1956.

Per Banks and Winters (1975), *Alba* points made from novaculite were found at the Bentsen-Clark site (41RR41). One example from 41WD185 was made from Ogallala chert (Perttula et al. 1986:544).

Wilson W. Crook III (2017) discusses types of damage to *Alba* points and other Late Prehistoric types from a sample of 750 specimens.

Arrow points classified as *Alba* were present at the Dan Holdeman site (41RR11) in Red River County. Excavators unearthed three groups of *Alba* points at Burial 51 (Perino 1995:56). The first group consisted of arrow points made of Ogallala quartzite and Edwards chert. The points in Group 2 were brown and red siltstone, while the remainder were identified as Edwards chert. Forty-five examples had been placed next to the head in Burial 45.

Webb (2000:14) states that ¾ of *Alba* points found in Louisiana are "made of local pebble cherts or quartzites in tan, gray, brown, black, and red colors. Most of the others are made of novaculite and quartzite from the Ouachita or Kiamichi Mountains. Occasionally, specimens are made of gray chert."

At the Gilkey Hill site (41DL406), the *Alba* type is the most common. A total of 189 specimens was recovered with 77 classified as *Alba*. Eighteen were made of chert, and 59 were fashioned from quartzite (Crook 2011:Table 1).

One *Alba* point made from Manning Fused Glass was recovered from the George C. Davis site (Baskin 1981; Brown 1976).

Alba-like points made of obsidian have been reported in Collin County at the Upper Farmersville site (41COL34), the Branch site (41COL9), and the Branch #2 site (Crook 2013:Table 1). X-ray fluorescence analysis revealed the probable source of the *Alba* points from 41COL9 is Browns Bench (Idaho-Nevada-Utah) and Massacre Lake/Guano Valley in Oregon (Crook 2016:27). He (Crook 2016) presents a thorough discussion of the methods used to determine the source of obsidian for these points and other relevant data regarding obsidian.

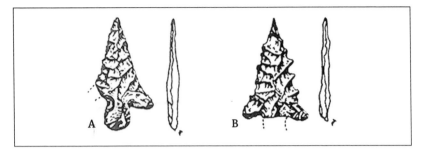

Figure 6.9. Arrow points from 41NV670 (image courtesy of the author).

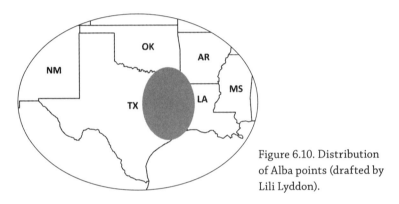

Figure 6.10. Distribution of Alba points (drafted by Lili Lyddon).

Two arrow points were found near the skeletal remains of *Bison bison* in Navarro County (41NV670). One has a bulbar stem and closely resembles the *Alba* type. The other is missing the stem and was not typed (Moore et al. 1997:Figure 9).

DISTRIBUTION: East Texas and adjacent parts of Louisiana (Suhm and Krieger 1954). According to Davis (1995:192), this type is primarily found in eastern and northeastern Texas. Specimens have been found in other areas of the state, but in fewer numbers such as a lone specimen from the Kyle site (41HI1), a rockshelter in Hill County. Examples from Arkansas, Mississippi, and Oklahoma have also been reported (Duncan et al. 2007:9). Webb (2000:14) writes that this type has been found "as far north as the Cahokia site (11-MS-2) in East St. Louis, Illinois probably as trade items."

Turner, Hester, and McReynolds (2011:177) cite its distribution as eastern and central Texas, the coastal plain, and Louisiana. Aten (1983) reports *Alba* points in the area he refers to as the Upper Texas Coast.

Figure 6.11. Anagua points (replicas by Matt Soultz).

Anagua

ORIGINAL RECORDER: Unknown

OTHER NAMES: None reported

SIMILAR TYPES: *Scallorn*

AGE: *Anagua* is a Late Prehistoric type that Turner, Hester, and McReynolds (2011) say is possibly contemporaneous with *Scallorn*.

DESCRIPTION: Turner, Hester, and McReynolds (2011:178) describe this type as a slender, triangular, corner-notched point. "The edges are straight or lateral and sometimes slightly convex, culminating in prominent barbs. The lateral edges are well-flaked, serrated, and/or notched. The bases are deeply concave, and the cross-section is lenticular."

CULTURAL AFFILIATION: Unknown.

KNOWN SITES: In Victoria County, *Anagua* points have been reported at 41VT3, 41VT9, 41VT12, 41VT34, 41VT69, 41VT81, and 41VT98. In Refugio County, they have been found at 41RF10 and 41RF11.

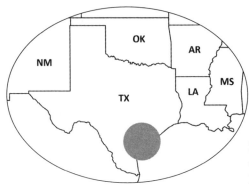

Figure 6.12. Distribution of Anagua points (drafted by Lili Lyddon).

SOURCES FOR ILLUSTRATIONS AND DESCRIPTIONS: Turner, Hester, and McReynolds (2011).

COMMENTS: Examples of this type are housed at the Museum of the Coastal Bend at Victoria College in Victoria, Texas. They are part of the Birmingham, Bluhm, Branch, and Vogt collections. *Anagua* points are often found in association with ceramics, *Scallorn* and *Perdiz* points.

DISTRIBUTION: Turner, Hester, and McReynolds (2011:178) write that this type is common to the lower Guadalupe River drainage system within the Southern Coastal Corridor Archeological Region.

Bassett

ORIGINAL RECORDER: This type was named and described by Clarence H. Webb (1948) for examples found near the community of Bassett, Texas, in Bowie County. He originally referred to it as *Bassett Pointed Stem*. Suhm and Krieger (1954:494) shortened the name to *Bassett* and described it in more detail.

OTHER NAMES: None reported.

SIMILAR TYPES: None reported. However, glass points bearing similarities to this type have been reported.

AGE: AD 1200 to AD 1600 (Suhm and Krieger 1954:494). Turner, Hester, and McReynolds (2011:179) estimate its age at AD 1400 to AD 1700. Webb (2000) places it at AD 1200 to AD 1500.

Figure 6.13. Basset points (photo courtesy of TARL).

DESCRIPTION: Suhm and Krieger (1954:494) describe the *Basset* point as very small with a triangular blade. "The edges can be straight or sometimes slightly concave or convex. The stem is tiny and protrudes from the center of a concave base. This is a well-made point that often exhibits exceedingly fine edge serrations." Webb (2000:15) writes that Louisiana specimens "were made from flakes of local materials, like tan, brown, gray, and black cherts, petrified wood, or occasionally novaculite." Some were made on flakes.

Suhm and Krieger (1954:494) provided the following measurements:

Length: 1.7 cm to 4.2 cm with a few more than 3.5 cm
Width: 1.2 cm to 1.8 cm
Stem length: 0.1 cm to 0.5 cm, but rarely more than 0.3 cm

CULTURAL AFFILIATION: According to Suhm and Krieger (1954:494), *Bassett* points are a "common type in the Belcher and Texarkana foci, and they occur less frequently in the Titus Focus and during the Fulton Aspect of the Neo-American stage." Webb (2000) provides evidence that they are common in Louisiana and often associated with Caddoan pottery from the middle period of the Bossier and Belcher foci.

KNOWN SITES: Sites in Texas where *Bassett* points have been recorded include Carpenter (41CP5), A. C. Mackin (41LR39), Jones Hill (41PK8), Williams (41CP10), Womack (41LR1), Resch (41HS16), and 41BP206. Four specimens have also been reported from Belcher Mound (16CD13) in Louisiana.

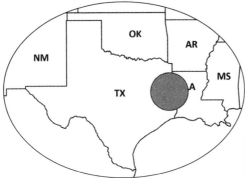

Figure 6.14. Distribution of Bassett points (drafted by Lili Lyddon).

SOURCES FOR ILLUSTRATIONS AND DESCRIPTIONS: Bell (1958); Davis (1995); Duncan and others (2007); Harris and others (1965); McClurkan (1968); Perino (1985); Suhm and Jelks (1962); Suhm and Krieger (1954); Taylor (1989); Turner and Hester (1985, 1993, 1999); Turner, Hester, and McReynolds (2011); Turner and Smith (2002); Thurmond (1985); and Webb (1948, 1959, 2000).

COMMENTS: Suhm and Krieger (1954:494) state that these points are "very fine and thinly chipped" and "exceedingly fine edge serration is common." Harris and others (1965) interpreted the two *Basset* points found at the Womack site (41LR1) as representing trade from the east. McClurkan (1968:11, Table 6) states that "all but one of the four *Bassett* points found at the Jones Hill site are stemmed types with no discernable pattern to their distribution," which he cautions might have been due to a small sample of 41 specimens.

Mallouf (1976:228) writes that the one *Bassett* point from the A. C. Makin site retains the "characteristic exaggerated percussion bulb of bipolar knapping technique on one face." The blow originated from the proximal end of the specimen.

In Louisiana, *Basset* points are found around lakes, in valleys, and upland streams (Webb 2000). Webb states they were usually made of local materials such as chert, silicified wood, and occasionally novaculite.

Duncan et al. (2007:19) identify the type site as Belcher Mound (16CD13) in Caddo Parish, Louisiana.

Thurmond (1985:189–191) places the *Bassett* point in the Late Caddoan Period, Titus Phase (AD 1600–AD 1700). It is accompanied by arrow points *Maud*, *Reed*, and *Talco*.

DISTRIBUTION: Northeastern Texas and parts of Arkansas and Louisiana (Suhm and Krieger 1954:494; Turner, Hester, and McReynolds 2011:179).

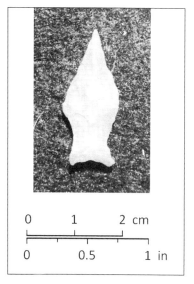

Figure 6.15. Bayou Goula point (photo courtesy of Thomas Oakes).

Bayou Goula

ORIGINAL RECORDER: This type was named and described by George I. Quimby and Clarence H. Webb (1948) for examples found at the type site, Bayou Goula, in Iberville Parish, Louisiana.

OTHER NAMES: *Bayou Goula Fishtail, Bayougoula*

SIMILAR TYPES: *Collins* (Mississippi type). Some compare it to *Friley*.

AGE: AD 950–AD 1000

DESCRIPTION: McGahey (2000:204) describes this point in the following: "Bayougoula Fishtailed points are small to medium-sized arrow points with side notches, concave bases, and leaf or ovate blades. Occasional specimens are serrated along the blade edges, and reworked specimens lose the

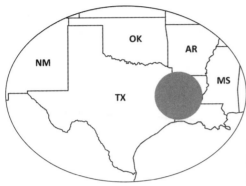

Figure 6.16. Distribution of Bayou Goula points (drafted by Lili Lyddon).

ovate shape as resharpening occurs. The outline then becomes an elongated diamond shape. Many distal ends, like those of the *Collins* type, are sharp and needle-like. Many specimens reveal evidence of heat treating, and an occasional specimen may be completely reddened by the process." "The raw material is almost invariably the nearest available tan gravel chert."

CULTURAL AFFILIATION: Late prehistoric, possibly Mississippian

KNOWN SITES: Bayou Goula (16-IV-11)

SOURCES FOR ILLUSTRATIONS AND DESCRIPTIONS: Quimby (1957), Williams and Brain (1983:222), Perino (1985:29), and McGahey (2000:204–205).

COMMENTS: The following measurements were provided during a telephone conversation with John Fish on October 10, 2023.

> Average length: 32 mm
> Range of length: 23 mm to 45 mm
> Average width: 14 mm
> Range of width: 11 mm to 20 mm
> Average thickness: 4 mm
> Range of thickness: 3 mm to 6 mm

DISTRIBUTION: Perino (1985:29) writes that this type is found in southern Louisiana and Mississippi and northward to Illinois and Wisconsin. There are scattered reports of it extending into East Texas.

Figure 6.17. Bonham points (photo courtesy of John Fish).

Bonham

ORIGINAL RECORDER: This point was named by Alex D. Krieger (1946) for examples found at the Sanders site (41LR2) in Lamar County. He referred to this type as *Bonham Barbed*, but the name was shortened to *Bonham* by Suhm and Krieger (1954:496).

OTHER NAMES: *Bonham Barbed*

SIMILAR TYPES: Suhm and Krieger (1954:496) note its similarity to *Alba* and *Hayes*.

AGE: Suhm and Krieger (1954:496) estimate its age at AD 800 to AD 1200. Davis (1995:180) dates it to circa AD 800 to AD 1600. In Louisiana, Webb (2000) dates them to circa AD 900 to AD 1200.

DESCRIPTION: Suhm and Krieger (1954:496) describe *Bonham* as "having a slender triangular blade that is occasionally serrated. The edges are usually straight but sometimes are recurved or slightly convex. The shoulders can

96 | CHAPTER 6

be squared or have small barbs. Stems are very narrow and have parallel edges. Bases are straight to slightly convex." Turner, Hester, and McReynolds (2011:180) write that most specimens are fully bifacial and have lenticular cross sections. They provided the following measurements for *Bonham* points:

Length: 2 to 4 cm to 4.5 cm
Width: 1 cm to 1.5 cm
Stem length: 0.5 cm to 0.7 cm

CULTURAL AFFILIATION: According to Krieger (1946) and Suhm and Krieger (1954:496), this is a common type of the Sander Focus, and it also occurs in the later stages of the Spiro Focus. Turner, Hester, and McReynolds (2011:180) describe it as a Late Prehistoric type that extends into historic times.

KNOWN SITES: Kyle (41HI1); A. C. Mackin (41LR39); Sanders (41LR2); Hoxie Bridge (41WM103); Love-Fox (41WM230); George C. Davis (41CE19); Baylor (41ML35); Roark Cave (41BS3); Limerick (41RA8, 41SE17, 41VT38); and sites in the Cedar Creek Reservoir (Henderson and Kaufman Counties) (Story 1965).

SOURCES FOR ILLUSTRATIONS AND DESCRIPTIONS: Bell (1960); Bell and Hall (1953); Davis (1995); Duncan et al. (2007); Kelley (1963); Krieger (1946); Perino (1985); Ricklis (2010); Shafer (2006); Suhm and Jelks (1962); Suhm and Krieger (1954); Turner and Hester (1985, 1993, 1999); Turner, Hester, and McReynolds (2011); Hedrick (1989); and Webb (2000).

COMMENTS: According to Davis (1995:196), "*Bonham* and *Alba* points are quite similar in general outline and appearance, but the primary difference is that the parallel stem on the *Bonham* point is narrower than those on the *Alba* type."

Harry J. Shafer (2006) proposed a *Bonham-Alba* classification that encompasses specimens dating around AD 100 from central Texas into eastern Texas.

Mallouf (1976) describes the four *Bonham* points from the A. C. Makin site as being made from dark red jasper, dark purple novaculite, and Bigfork chert (black and green varieties).

Arrow Points | 97

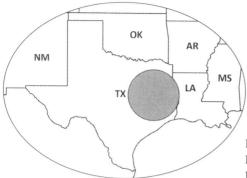

Figure 6.18. Distribution of Bonham points (drafted by Lili Lyddon).

Smitty Schmeidlin (1997) reports a single *Bonham* point at 41VT38, the presumed third location of *Mission Espíritu Santo de Zuñiga* (41VT11).

Authentic *Bohnam* points are housed at TARL but were not available for photographing.

DISTRIBUTION: Suhm and Krieger (1954:496) write "*Bonham* points are found in the northern part of East Texas, especially in the Red River valley, eastern Oklahoma, and North-Central Texas. A few specimens have been reported from the northern part of Central Texas and possibly as far west as the Pecos River."

Turner, Hester, and McReynolds (2011:180) write that it is found at sites in north central and northeastern Texas. Webb (2000) reports that they are found in Oklahoma but less frequently than in northeastern Texas.

Bulbar Stemmed

ORIGINAL RECORDER: James E. Corbin (1963) first observed this type during his work at sites in the Coastal Bend of Texas, initially, referring to it as an "unknown arrow point." In his 1974 article titled "A Model for Cultural Succession for the Coastal Bend Area of Texas," he does not describe this point but refers to it as *"Bulbar"* in his figures 9 and 10. This type was not formally described until Turner and Hester (1985:166) did so in their *Field Guide to Stone Artifacts of Texas Indians.*

CHAPTER 6

Figure 6.19. Bulbar Stemmed point from 41WH8 (photo courtesy of TARL).

OTHER NAMES: *Bulbar*

SIMILAR TYPES: Turner, Hester, and McReynolds (2011:181) state: "These points are sometimes similar to *Perdiz* and may represent a regional variant in the Corpus Christi region and northern Padre Island." However, according to Corbin (1974), they are a type separate from *Perdiz*. *Bulbar Stemmed* points are also similar in form to *Alba*.

AGE: Late Prehistoric point that was still in use during historic times (Turner, Hester, and McReynolds 2011:181). Davis (1995:198) assigns it a time frame of circa AD 700 to AD 1700.

DESCRIPTION: The stem shape reportedly varies in length and width, according to Turner, Hester, and McReynolds (2011:181). The defining characteristic is a pronounced rounded or bulbous stem (Corbin 1974), unlike its *Alba* counterpart that has parallel stem edges and straight bases. No average dimensions were found for this type.

CULTURAL AFFILIATION: Unknown.

KNOWN SITES: McGloin Bluff (41SP11), Shanklin (41WH8), Mitchell Ridge (41GV66), Guadalupe Bay (41CL2), and 41WH19.

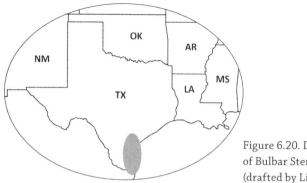

Figure 6.20. Distribution of Bulbar Stemmed points (drafted by Lili Lyddon).

SOURCES FOR ILLUSTRATIONS AND DESCRIPTIONS: Corbin (1963, 1974); Hester (1980); Davis (1995); Gunter (1985); Perino (1985); Ricklis (1994); Turner and Hester (1985, 1993, 1999); Turner, Hester, and McReynolds (2011); and Weinstein (2002).

COMMENTS: This type is reported as being in a historic context at site 41WH19 in Wharton County. If it was present in historic times, it is possible that the Karankawa who lived in the area may have used it.

Richard A. Weinstein (2002) has identified three varieties based on the shape of the stem that he refers to as *Bulbar Stemmed,* var. *bulbar, calhoun,* and *rupley lake.* They are described in Volume 2 (Appendix K) of his report on the Guadalupe Bay site.

DISTRIBUTION: Southern Coastal Corridor and Southeastern Texas.

Cameron

ORIGINAL RECORDER: R. S. MacNeish (1958) named this point for examples from Cameron County in the Lower Rio Grande Valley where it is most commonly found. Originally, it was referred to as *Cameron Triangular.* Robert J. Mallouf and Anthony Zavaleta (1979) shortened the name to *Cameron* based on their work at the Unland site.

OTHER NAMES: *Cameron Triangular.*

Figure 6.21. Cameron points from South Texas (photo courtesy of TARL).

SIMILAR TYPES: *Cameron* is similar to *Fresno*, but smaller and thicker (Turner, Hester, and McReynolds 2011:182). Davis (1995:200) states that *Cameron* points are no more than 17 mm long, and the *Fresno* point is no less than 20 mm long.

AGE: This point was made and used sometime between AD 1200 and AD 1750. Its placement in the Historic Period is based on the fact that some *Cameron* points were made from glass (Turner, Hester, and McReynolds 2011:182).

DESCRIPTION: Turner, Hester, and McReynolds (2011:182) write: "this is a tiny equilateral point with straight to slightly convex edges." Some specimens are unifacial. Dimensions are not given.

CULTURAL AFFILIATION: Unknown.

KNOWN SITES: Unland (41CF111), 41KL13, 41KL14, 41KL26, 41KL27, 41KL30, 41KL35 through 41KL38, 41VT8, and McGill Ranch (no TARL number).

SOURCES FOR ILLUSTRATIONS AND DESCRIPTIONS: Davis (1995); Gunter (1985); Hester (1969, 1980); Mallouf, Baskin, and Killen (1977); Perino (1991); Saunders (1985); Turner and Hester (1985, 1993, 1999); Jelks (1993); Fox and Tomka (2006); and Turner, Hester, and McReynolds (2011).

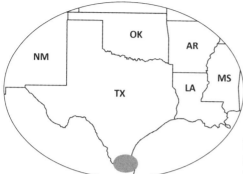

Figure 6.22. Distribution of Cameron points (drafted by Lili Lyddon).

COMMENTS: Hester (1969) reported on investigations in Kenedy and Kleberg Counties, and he described 36 arrow points that he classified as *Cameron*. He was unable to identify consistent morphological patterns in the entire sample of triangular points. Therefore, he arbitrarily classified those specimens that were less than 20 mm in length as *Cameron*, while points greater than 20 mm were classified as *Fresno*.

Hester (1969) believes that it is possible that both arbitrary groups are the same type.

Perino (1991) theorized that *Cameron* may have developed from the earlier *Catán* arrow point. He also states that in historic times *Cameron* was sometimes made of glass. Most often, they were reduced from cobbles of Edwards Plateau chert found in riverine systems flowing into the Gulf (Perino 1991).

Like Hester (1969), Davis (1995:200) believes that the *Cameron* point may be part of a continuum that includes the *Matamoros* dart point and the *Fresno* arrow point.

Robert J. Mallouf, Barbara J. Baskin, and K. L. Killen (1977) collaborated to write a predictive assessment of cultural resources in Hidalgo and Willacy Counties. This report is relevant to the *Cameron* type and the area in which it is found.

DISTRIBUTION: Turner, Hester, and McReynolds (2011) place its location as the Rio Grande Delta, Baffin Bay, and the Corpus Christi area.

Figure 6.23. Caracara point (replica by Matt Soultz; photo courtesy of Brian Wootan).

Caracara

ORIGINAL RECORDER: R. K. Saunders (Saunders and Hester 1993:22–31) described this point, but no report or other reference is mentioned.

OTHER NAMES: None reported.

SIMILAR TYPES: This type was previously referred to as *Harrell* and *Scallorn* by artifact collectors.

AGE: Turner, Hester, and McReynolds (2011) estimate the age of the *Caracara* point at AD 700 to AD 1100.

DESCRIPTION: This is a small very thin point that exhibits side-notching. According to Turner, Hester, and McReynolds (2011:183), "the lateral edges are "convex to nearly straight and are often serrated. The rounded or basal 'ears' usually extend slightly beyond the width of the shoulders. The bases are typically straight, but they also may be slightly concave or convex." Although examples illustrated by Boyd and Perttula (2000) are accompanied by scales, no average dimensions are given.

CULTURAL AFFILIATION: Unknown.

KNOWN SITES: Sites in Texas are Beacon Harbor Lodge (41ZP7), Old Zapata Burial (41ZP85), and Rough Enough Rockshelter (41VV1987). Sites in Mexico are the Arroyo Salinillas Cremation Burial and Southern Island Burials 2 and 3.

SOURCES FOR ILLUSTRATIONS AND DESCRIPTIONS: Boyd (1997); Boyd and Wilson (1999); Boyd and Perttula (2000); Perino (1991); Saunders and Hester (1993); Turner and Hester (1993, 1999); Hester (1995); Turner, Hester, and McReynolds (2011); Stillwell (2011); and Wilson and Hester (1996).

COMMENTS: According to James B. Boyd and Timothy K. Perttula (2000), *Caracara* points have been found at burials in the Falcon Lake area, and some were embedded in human bones as evidence of violence or warfare.

At the Old Zapata Burial site, 13 *Carcara* points, broken and complete, were found with a disturbed burial by Cynthia Scott of Zapata that had been exposed and vandalized when the lake levels were low. The complete specimens were sold to a private collector and were not available for study. Fortunately, the five broken ones were loaned to Boyd and Perttula for examination. This is the most thorough discussion of *Caracara* points I have found.

James Boyd discovered and salvaged a burial of two adults and an infant from 41ZP7. His efforts are discussed in detail along with osteological analysis by Wilson and Hester (1996). Grave goods with the primary individual consisted of *Caracara* arrow points, bone beads, and perforated human teeth that possibly functioned as a necklace.

Saunders and Hester (1993:22–31) discuss side-notched arrow points from the Falcon Lake region of Texas and Mexico. Their discussion of *Caracara* includes two figures of examples of this type.

DISTRIBUTION: This type is from southern Texas. Examples have been found in Duval, Hidalgo, Starr, Webb, and Zapata Counties and on the adjacent Mexican side of the border. Boyd and Perttula (2000:6) believe the core region for this type is in and around Falcon Reservoir.

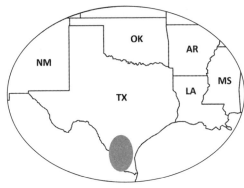

Figure 6.24. Distribution of Caracara points (drafted by Lili Lyddon).

Catahoula

ORIGINAL RECORDER: This type was first named in 1956 by Clarence H. Webb and Hiram F. Gregory (Baker and Webb 1976:226) based on specimens found at the Sanson site (16RA1) near Catahoula Lake in central Louisiana. The point was not described in detail until 1960 when it appeared in *Special Bulletin Number 2* of the Oklahoma Anthropological Society (Bell 1960).

OTHER NAMES: Referred to by Wheat (1953) as *Alba Barbed*.

SIMILAR TYPES: *Catahoula* points are like the *Agee* type. Both have short stems, but *Agee* points expand more strongly toward the base, which is markedly convex (Davis 1995:202). The examples illustrated here are from site 41WA55 in Walker County.

AGE: The age of this point is uncertain, but it was probably associated with Plaquemine materials in Louisiana (Bell 1960). Based on research by Baker and Webb (1976), it was most common from AD 800 to AD 1100 with the possibility that it began as a type in AD 500 to AD 600 and lasted until AD 1200 to AD 1300. Turner, Hester, and McReynolds (2011:185) estimate its age between AD 700 and AD 1100. Crook and Hughston (2015b:34–35) were able to get radiometric data from a femur at the Lower Rockwall site (41RW1). The results were reported as 1240 ± 30 BP. The 1-sigma calibration is AD 715 to AD 775, and the 2-sigma calibration is AD 680 to AD 880. In a later article, Crook (2017) dates this type

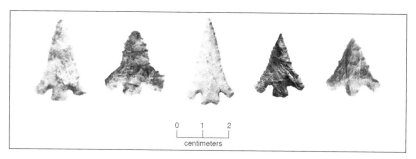

Figure 6.25. Catahoula points from 41WA55 (photo courtesy of Tanner Singleton).

DESCRIPTION: Baker and Webb (1976:225–251) describe this point as having a wide base with a fan-shaped stem and distinctive square barbs. "The blade edges are commonly recurved, often markedly concave, so that the blade appears short in reference to the broad shoulders. The stem is short, wide, expanding and normally convex at the base. The notches are likely to be rather narrow and delimit a large and broad barb which is the most distinctive feature of this type. Some specimens are almost as wide as they are long" (Baker and Webb 1976). Webb (2000:15) provides the following average measurements for Louisiana specimens:

Length: 28.4 mm
Width: 21.6 mm
Thickness: 4 mm
Weight: 1.9 grams

CULTURAL AFFILIATION: Some sites in Louisiana that yielded *Catahoula* points date to the Alto Focus. Webb (2000) maintains that this type is only occasionally found in Caddo village middens or burials. Crook (2017) dates this type to the Wylie Phase, circa AD 700 or AD 800 to AD 1250.

KNOWN SITES: 41HR273, 41HR269, 41HR301, 41HR616, 41HR696, Resch (41HS16), Jones Hill (41PK8), 41PK69, Gilbert (41RA13), Upper Rockwall (41RW2), Upper Farmersville (41COL34), Glen Hill (41RW4), Tankersley Creek (41TT108), 41TN11, Reese (41WA55), 41DL406, and sites in the San Jacinto River Basin and Addicks Reservoir. In Louisiana, they have been recorded at 16BO2, 16BI1, 16CD8, 16CD12, 16CT11, 16CT89, 16CT128, 16DS4, 16DS5, 16GR2, 16GR7, 16NA5, 16NA7, 16NA10, 16RA1, and 16RR1.

106 | CHAPTER 6

SOURCES FOR ILLUSTRATIONS AND DESCRIPTIONS: Baker and Webb (1976); Bell (1960); Davis (1995); Fields (1988, 2004); Moore (1976); Patterson (1976); Perino (1985); Skinner, Harris, and Anderson (1969); Sollberger (1967); Turner and Hester (1985, 1993, 1999); Turner, Hester, and McReynolds (2011); Crook (2008–2009, 2011); Young (1981b); Ross (1966); and Webb (2000). Story (1965) described *Catahoula*-like points at sites in the Cedar Creek Reservoir, Henderson and Kaufman Counties.

COMMENTS: Following Bell (1960), the next major reference to this type was in volume 3 of the *Bulletin of the Louisiana Archaeological Society* by Baker and Webb (1976). At that time, the authors had examined nearly 150 *Catahoula* points from more than 40 sites in central and northern Louisiana. In addition, they studied 63 preforms from sites where *Catahoula* points were predominant. Most of the specimens appear to have been collected from campsites, but they have also been found at mound sites with ceremonial burials.

Six *Catahoula* points were found at the Gahagan site (16RR1) by Webb and Dodd (1939), and an equal number was recovered from Mounds Plantation (16CD12) (Webb and McKinney 1975). Both sites contained Caddoan burials dating to the Alto Focus.

Most of the examples (93%) studied by Baker and Webb (1976) were made from local chert available in pebble form in the area where the *Catahoula* points were found. Others were made from fossiliferous chert, flint, and quartzite.

The presence of *Catahoula* points at mound sites suggests they may have had some ceremonial significance, and some archaeologists postulate that they may have been used in trade. However, the presence of performs at some sites may be evidence that they were also produced at the sites where they were found.

At the Gilkey Hill site (41DL406), the *Catahoula* type is the second most common. A total of 189 arrow points were recovered with 39 specimens classified as *Catahoula*. Two were made of chert, and 37 were fashioned from quartzite (Crook 2011:Table 1).

An article by Baker and Webb (1976) provided a well-researched discussion of the history and distribution of this type in Louisiana and other states, and published measurements of 143 specimens and the relationship of *Catahoula* to other types. Their article is the most thorough on this type that I have encountered.

Leland W. Patterson (1987) describes a new artifact type named *Catahoula Perforator*. This artifact is a *Catahoula* point that has been reworked to create a drill or perforator. The examples he describes were found on the surface of site 41HR182 in Harris County.

Patterson refers to them as a separate type because similar specimens have been found at sites on the Upper Texas Coast. According to Patterson (1976), Wheat (1953) and Greengo (1964) incorrectly described *Catahoula* points as *Alba*.

Other sources include Wilson W. Crook III (2017), who discusses types of damage to *Catahoula* points and other Late Prehistoric types from a sample of 750 points. Skinner, Harris, and Anderson (1969:Figure 26) illustrate the steps involved in making a *Catahoula* point, and Joe Ben Wheat (1953:Plate 53) illustrates points that he describes as *Alba*, although some specimens are clearly *Catahoula*.

Catahoula-like points made of obsidian have been reported in Collin County at 41COL34 (Crook 2013:37) and 41COL9 (Crook 2013:39). X-ray Fluorescence analysis revealed the probable source of the points from 41COL9 is Owyhee, Toy Pass (Idaho) and Browns Bench (Idaho-Nevada-Utah) (Crook 2016:27). Crook (2016) presents a thorough discussion of the methods used to determine the source of obsidian for these points and other relevant data regarding obsidian.

Twenty-two *Catahoula* points were recovered from site 41SJ160. The length ranged from 1.7 cm to 2.5 cm. Shoulder width ranged from 1.6 cm to 2.3 cm. The weight varied from 0.8 g to 1.0 g (Keller and Weir 1979:39).

DISTRIBUTION: Leland W. Patterson (1976:219) presented a study of the *Catahoula* type. His research found that it has an "east–west spatial distribution from Alabama to Nevada, and a north–south distribution from Missouri to the Gulf Coast." I doubt the validity of this statement. In Texas, it is most common in the Northeast and Southeast Texas subregions. Elsewhere, it has been reported from sites in Louisiana, southwestern Arkansas, and southeastern Oklahoma.

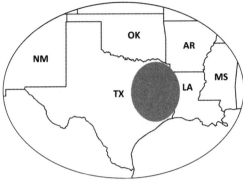

Figure 6.26. Distribution of Catahoula points (drafted by Lili Lyddon).

Figure 6.27. Chadbourne point from 41TA58 (photo courtesy of TARL).

Chadbourne

ORIGINAL RECORDER: Darrell G. Creel named the *Chadbourne* point based on its occurrence in the area around Fort Chadbourne in Coke County, Texas. Illustrated example housed at TARL and not to scale.

OTHER NAMES: None reported.

SIMILAR TYPES: None reported.

AGE: circa AD 900 to AD 1300 (Turner, Hester, and McReynolds 2011) and possibly earlier.

DESCRIPTION: Turner, Hester, and McReynolds (2011:186) describe this type as elongate and triangular. The lateral edges are straight to convex. It has small shoulders and a wide and slightly expanding stem that often ends in a concave base. No dimensions are given.

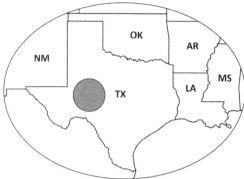

Figure 6.28. Distribution of Chadbourne points (drafted by Lili Lyddon).

CULTURAL AFFILIATION: Darrell Creel attributed this type to the Blow Out Mountain Complex, whose type site is 41TA30 (TARL files).

KNOWN SITES: 41CK87, 41TA58, and 41TA66. Joe Ben Wheat (1947) encountered *Chadbourne* points at the W. A. Myatt site (no TARL number).

SOURCES FOR ILLUSTRATIONS AND DESCRIPTIONS: Turner and Hester (1993, 1999); Wheat (1947); and Turner, Hester, and McReynolds (2011).

COMMENTS: *Chadbourne* points are often found with *Scallorn* and *Moran* points (Turner, Hester, and McReynolds 2011:186). Examples of this type are housed in the Sayles Collection at TARL (Sayles 1935).

Creel (1990) proposed that *Chadbourne* is a *Darl* variant that was made small for use with the bow and arrow. Before Creel identified this type as *Chadbourne*, he discussed its characteristics in his report on the excavations at 41TG91.

DISTRIBUTION: According to Turner, Hester, and McReynolds (2011:186), *Chadbourne* is found in west-central Texas and sites in the drainages of the Colorado and Concho Rivers and the Clear Fork of the Brazos. It has been found in the Central Texas archeological subregion and the unnamed subregion of the Texas Panhandle.

Figure 6.29. Clifton points (photo courtesy of TARL).

Clifton

ORIGINAL RECORDER: The *Clifton* point was named *Contracting Stem* by Alex D. Krieger (1946:496) for examples found in northern Texas near the town of Clifton in Bosque County. Krieger misspelled the name of the town, but Suhm and Krieger (1954) decided to use his spelling rather than correct it.

J. Charles Kelley (1947b) referred to this point as *Clinton Contracting Stem* (obviously a typographical error). The name was shortened by Suhm and Krieger (1954) during the writing of *An Introductory Handbook of Texas Archeology*.

Walter W. Taylor (1966) referred to it as the *Ojo* point based on examples found in northeastern Mexico; however, I have found no evidence of a proposal to make *Ojo* a valid type in Texas.

OTHER NAMES: *Clinton Contracting Stem* and *Ojo*.

SIMILAR TYPES: *Bassett*

AGE: According to Suhm and Krieger (1954:496), *Clifton* dates from circa AD 1200 to AD 1500. Prewitt (1981) places it in the Neo-Archaic.

DESCRIPTION: Suhm and Krieger (1954:496) describe *Clifton* as having a "roughly triangular blade, crudely chipped, often modified on only one face, or one face more than the other. Shoulders may project at right-angle but often are difficult to distinguish from the short, pointed stem. Blade edges may be fairly straight but often convex, concave, or asymmetrical." They provide the following dimensions:

Length: 2 cm to 4 cm
Width: 1.5 cm to 2 cm
Stems vary from barely visible to about 0.5 cm in length.

CULTURAL AFFILIATION: Henrietta Focus (Suhm and Krieger 1954); Toyah Phase (Prewitt 1981). Cloud and Mallouf (1996:173) state that "*Cliffton* (along with Perdiz) is the second most common arrow point found in Big Bend National Park." They are believed to be typically associated with Cielo Complex encampments.

KNOWN SITES: Kyle (41HI1), Oblate (41CM1), Roark Cave (41BS3), Peerless Bottoms (41HP175), 41HR279, 41HR301, 41SE17, 41AU37, 41JW8, and sites in the Cedar Creek Reservoir (Henderson and Kaufman Counties) (Story 1965).

SOURCES FOR ILLUSTRATIONS AND DESCRIPTIONS: Beasley (1978); Bell (1960); Davis (1995); Duffield (1963); Fields (1988, 2004); Kelley (1963); Krieger (1946); McClurkan (1968); Mitchell and Van der Veer (1983); Suhm and Krieger (1954); Tunnell (1962); Jelks (1993); Hester (1980); Hall (1981); (Cloud and Mallouf 1996:173); and Turner and Hester (1985, 1993, 1999).

COMMENTS: According to Turner, Hester, and McReynolds (2011:206), "Preforms or poorly made *Perdiz* points have sometimes been called '*Cliffton*.' A detailed study of *Perdiz* points from the Buckhollow site points to technological data that invalidate *Cliffton* as a type."

Prewitt (1981) presents a detailed discussion of the Toyah Phase in his article titled "Cultural Chronology in Central Texas."

Cliffton is included in *A Field Guide to Stone Artifacts* (Turner and Hester 1985:169) but omitted from *Stone Artifacts of Texas Indians* (Turner, Hester, and McReynolds 2011).

DISTRIBUTION: From the Red River to the central Gulf Coast (Turner and Hester 1999). Archeological regions include Central Texas, Rio Grande Plains, Trans-Pecos, Upper Texas Coast, and the Prairie-Savanna.

112 | **CHAPTER 6**

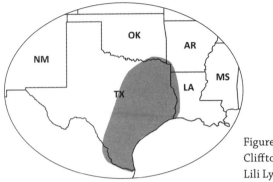

Figure 6.30. Distribution of Cliffton points (drafted by Lili Lyddon).

Figure 6.31. Colbert points (photo courtesy of Thomas Oakes).

Colbert

ORIGINAL RECORDER: This point was named and described by Clarence H. Webb (1963) based on examples found at the Colbert site in Bienville Parish, Louisiana where this type was frequently encountered.

OTHER NAMES: None reported.

SIMILAR TYPES: According to Webb, *Colbert* resembles *Alba, Hayes, Homan,* and *Scallorn.*

AGE: Turner and Hester (1985:170) estimate the age of this type at AD 950 to AD 1585. Webb (2000) dates this type at Louisiana sites to circa AD 900 to AD 1100.

DESCRIPTION: This type is not described by Suhm and Krieger (1954) or Turner, Hester, and McReynolds (2011). Davis (1995:206) refers to it as "A small point with a triangular outline. The lateral edges are concave to recurved and may exhibit minute serrations. The strong shoulders are barbed and have a flared appearance. The short stem expands toward the base. The base is usually straight or mildly convex but is occasionally concave." Webb (1963:180) writes that they typically measure 1.2 cm to 3.2 cm in length and 9 mm to 2 cm in width.

CULTURAL AFFILIATION: Webb (1948, 1963, 2000) found this type at an Alto Focus site, and he says there is an association with late Coles Creek cultures.

KNOWN SITES: Trichel (41SJ16), 41PK21, and sites at Cooper Lake. Examples from Louisiana have been found at Colbert (16 BI 2), Smithport Landing (16 DS 4), and Mound Plantation (16 CD 12). In Arkansas, it has been found at Crenshaw Mounds (3 MI 0006).

SOURCES FOR ILLUSTRATIONS AND DESCRIPTIONS: Davis (1995); Fields (2004); Turner and Hester (1985, 1993, 1999); Baskin (1981); McClurkan (1968); and Webb (1948, 1963, 2000).

COMMENTS: According to Webb, the Colbert site was the first to be identified as having an Alto Focus component. He mentions the *Colbert* point in his 1963 article but does not discuss the Colbert site. Webb writes that 21 arrow points found at Smithport Landing were characterized by expanding stems produced by corner notching and blades like those on the *Alba* type. Webb also states that this point has been the subject of considerable discussion because of its frequency in Louisiana and Arkansas. Some reports present it as *Alba* or *Scallorn*, but Webb (1963:180) believed that *Colbert* has "meaningful and distinct differences" from those types. He (Webb 2000:16) states that this type is found on pottery sites in the uplands and on lateral lakes in Louisiana (e.g., Caddo, Cross, and Clear Lakes).

According to Davis (1995:206), the main distinction is that *Colbert*

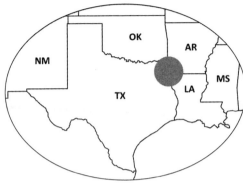

Figure 6.32. Distribution of Colbert points (drafted by Lili Lyddon).

points have shoulders and barbs that are flared, which is uncharacteristic of the *Alba* point.

Six *Colbert* points were reported from site 41SJ160. The lengths ranged from 2.5 cm to 2.6 cm. Shoulder widths ranged from 1.4 cm to 1.7 cm. The weight for each specimen weighed was 0.8 g (Keller and Weir 1979:39).

Colbert is included in *A Field Guide to Stone Artifacts* (Turner and Hester 1985:170) but omitted from *Stone Artifacts of Texas Indians* (Turner et al. 2011).

DISTRIBUTION: Northeast and Southeast Texas Archeological regions, Arkansas, and Louisiana.

Cuney

ORIGINAL RECORDER: The *Cuney* point was named by Dee Ann Suhm and Alex D. Krieger (1954:498) for examples found at the Jim Allen site (41CE12) in Cherokee County. It was named for the nearby town of Cuney.

OTHER NAMES: None reported.

SIMILAR TYPES: According to Perino (1991), *Cuney* points are similar to *Sabinal* and *Rockwall*, except the stems on *Rockwall* are broader and more expanded. Davis (1995:208) recognizes a similarity between *Cuney* and *Alba*.

Figure 6.33. Cuney points (photo courtesy of John Fish).

AGE: Suhm and Krieger (1954) estimate its age at AD 1600 to AD 1800. Turner, Hester, and McReynolds (2011) refer to it as a Late Prehistoric type that persisted into historic times, but they do not give a date.

DESCRIPTION: Suhm and Krieger (1954:498) describe *Cuney* as having a triangular blade with straight or concave edges. The barbs extend downward or flare outward. Stems are parallel-edged or slightly expanded. The base is concave and varies from a "shallow curve to a deep U-shaped notch" (Suhm and Krieger 1954:498). Some were made on flakes.

CULTURAL AFFILIATION: Suhm and Krieger (1954:498) believe this type was associated with the Allen Focus (Fulton Aspect) during the Historic Stage. They suggest that it might have been a type made by Caddoan tribes of the Hasinai branch. Turner, Hester, and McReynolds (2011) say that it is associated with the Allen Phase in the Caddo area.

SOURCES FOR ILLUSTRATIONS AND DESCRIPTIONS: Perino (1991); Saner and others (2019); Suhm and Jelks (1962); Suhm and Krieger (1954); Turner and Hester (1985, 1993, 1999); and Turner, Hester, and McReynolds (2011).

COMMENTS: Davis (1995:208) states that the primary difference between *Cuney* and *Alba* is that the stem on the *Cuney* type expands more strongly toward the base, while the base of the *Alba* type is straight or mildly convex.

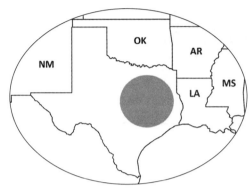

Figure 6.34. Distribution of Cuney points (drafted by Lili Lyddon).

Suhm and Krieger (1954:498) give the following dimensions for *Cuney* points:

Total Length: 2 to 4.5 cm
Maximum width: about 1 to 2 cm
Stem: 0.4 to 0.7 cm wide and length about the same. Stems about one-half to one-sixth of total length

KNOWN SITES: Jim Allen (41CE12) (a.k.a. J. P. Allen site), Pecan Springs (41EL11), Scorpion Cave (41ME7), Smith Rockshelter (41TV42), Shanklin (41WH8), Hagler (41PP325), 41DM31, 41DM33, 41KR600, 41ZV155, and sites at Lake Monticello and sites in the Cedar Creek Reservoir (Henderson and Kaufman Counties) (Story 1965). Two *Cuney* points were reported at the Strawberry Hill site (41SJ160). (Keller and Weir 1979:39) provide the following measurements for a single specimen found at 41SJ160: Length 2.5 cm. Shoulder width 1.6 cm. Weight 0.8 g.

DISTRIBUTION: When this type was first introduced, its distribution was principally in Cherokee, Anderson, and Henderson Counties with lesser numbers reported as far north as the Red River and westward into Central Texas. It has also been found at sites in the Southern Coastal Corridor, Rio Grande Plains, and Prairie-Savanna subregions.

Arrow Points | 117

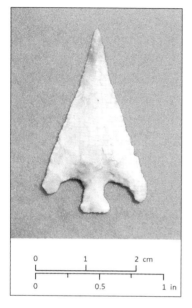

Figure 6.35. Deadman's point (photo courtesy of John Fish).

Deadman's

ORIGINAL RECORDER: The *Deadman's* point was named and described by Patrick S. Willey and Jack T. Hughes (1978) based on examples found at Deadman's Shelter (41SW23) in Swisher County in the Texas Panhandle. It was the predominant point at this site and was described as a distinctive base-notched arrow point with long slender barbs and stem.

OTHER NAMES: None reported.

SIMILAR TYPES: *Bulbar Stemmed*, *Moran*, and *Scallorn* (Duncan et al. 2007).

AGE: This may be the earliest known arrow point in Texas with an estimated age of AD 400 to AD 800 (Davis 1995). Turner, Hester, and McReynolds (2011) refer to it as simply Late Prehistoric.

DESCRIPTION: This type does not appear in Suhm and Krieger (1954). Per Turner, Hester, and McReynolds (2011:188), this is a "short, wide triangular point that has convex lateral edges that are sometimes serrated. The long,

118 | CHAPTER 6

slender stem is straight to expanding with a rounded basal edge. Deep basal notches are rarely one-third the length of the point." Dimensions are not given.

CULTURAL AFFILIATION: Douglas K. Boyd (1995) includes this type in the Late Prehistoric Palo Duro Complex of the Caprock Canyonlands in the Texas Panhandle.

KNOWN SITES: Deadman's Shelter (41SW23) is the type site. This point has been reported from sites at Palo Duro Canyon in Armstrong and Randall Counties, McKenzie Reservoir in Briscoe and Swisher Counties, and Lake Alan Henry in Garza County. Sites in Garza County include 41GR256, 41GR325, and 41GR438. Other sites include 41HL66 in Hall County and 41LU29 and 41LU34 in Lubbock County (Brown 1985). Site 41OC93 in Ochiltree County yielded a *Deadman's* point made from Alibates chert.

SOURCES FOR ILLUSTRATIONS AND DESCRIPTIONS: Boyd (1995, 2004); Boyd and others (1989); Brown (1985); Davis (1995); Perino (1985); Turner and Hester (1985, 1993, 1999), Turner, Hester, and McReynolds (2011); and Willey and Hughes (1978).

COMMENTS: According to Davis (1995:210), this point is unique, and there are no types similar enough to cause confusion in the identification of a specimen as *Deadman's*.

Dimensions from the type site are reported as follows (Hughes and Willey 1978:187).

Total length: 11 mm to 42 mm (average 21.9 mm)
Total width: 9 mm to 19 mm (average 13.9 mm)
Total thickness: 2 mm to 4 mm (average 3 mm)
Stem length: 3 mm to 9 mm (average 7.25 mm)
Maximum stem width: 3 mm to 8.5 mm (average 6 mm)
Maximum stem length: 2 mm to 6 mm (average 4.25 mm)

Deadman's Shelter was formerly referred to as the Deadman's Terrace site with the same trinomial—41SW23. Hughes and Willey (1978:149) write that "Breakage is frequent, especially from the stem to the body (Figure 55 w-a'), and lateral edges from the body (Figure 55 b-j')."

Arrow Points | 119

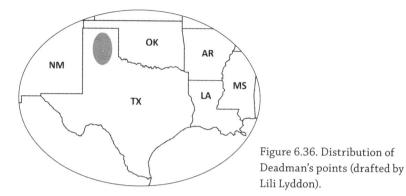

Figure 6.36. Distribution of Deadman's points (drafted by Lili Lyddon).

DISTRIBUTION: This type is primarily found in the Texas Panhandle and Llano Estacado regions. According to Robert J. Mallouf (personal communication, 2016), it is sometimes found in the Eastern and Big Bend areas of the Trans-Pecos. He describes its frequency as rare.

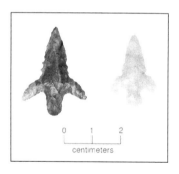

Figure 6.37. Diablo points (photo courtesy of TARL).

Diablo

ORIGINAL RECORDER: Robert J. Mallouf (2013) described this type based on examples found in the Sierra Diablo Mountains in the Trans-Pecos region of Texas.

OTHER NAMES: None reported.

SIMILAR TYPES: *Guadalupe, Livermore,* and *Neff.*

AGE: Mallouf (2013:198) writes that the "direct association of *Diablo* points with *Livermore, Toyah*, and other arrow point styles in the John Z. and Exa Means Cache (41JD212) is strongly suggestive of an age range of circa AD 800 to AD 1350." Cloud (2004:96, Figure 46) reported an arrow point that conforms well to the *Diablo* type at the Arroyo de la Presa site on the Rio Grande near Presidio. It was recovered from a stratum radiocarbon dated AD 690 to AD 890 (beta 155178). Leslie (1978) suggested an age range of AD 1000 to AD 1200 for similar points in southeastern New Mexico. Justice (2002:231) believes a reasonable span of use was circa AD 100 to AD 800 with a possible extension to AD 1200. Donald Lehmer (1948:30, Plate VII-f) mentioned an intrusive *Livermore* point at the Mesilla Phase site of Los Tules in the El Paso Area, which Mallouf (2012:8) called an excellent example of a *Diablo* point. Radiocarbon assays for *Toyah* points in the Texas Big Bend range from AD 1150 to AD 1350 (Mallouf 2012:8; Corrick 2000; Cloud 2001). Mallouf believes that this time frame may also provide an approximate terminal span for *Diablo* points.

DESCRIPTION: This type does not appear in Suhm and Krieger (1954). Mallouf's (2013:195–198) description of *Diablo* "is based on an examination of 18 complete or nearly complete specimens from the Means Cache, multiple examples in private collections, and comparative data from examples in the archaeological literature of the region." Mallouf (2013:195–198) writes that, "*Diablo* arrow points are typified by narrow, short to moderately long triangular blades having straight to slightly convex lateral edges. In some examples, blade edges are recurved. Moderate to strong serration of lateral edges that extend all the way to the distal blade tip is common, and occasional notching of the blade just above the barbs serves to exaggerate the blade/barb juncture. Remnants of the original flake removal scar are sometimes present on one blade face." "The barbs are often wide relative to the overall point length and are typically strong to exaggerated, often exhibiting a severe arching curve that results in a hook-like configuration that is enhanced by deep corner notching. In some examples, barbs simply project at right angles to the long axis of the point. Stems are variable and may be slightly bulbous, parallel-sided, or expanding. In both expanding and bulbous stem examples, stem elements usually constitute only 20 to 30 percent of overall specimen length." In cross-section, this type is usually lenticular, but some examples may be plano-convex.

CULTURAL AFFILIATION: Mallouf (2013) believes *Diablo* may belong to the Late Prehistoric Livermore Phase because of the presence of *Diablo* points in the Livermore Cache assemblage that is dominated by *Livermore* points. He also states that this designation is problematical because *Diablo* points are not an element of Livermore Phase components at Tall Rockshelter in the Davis Mountains.

KNOWN SITES: Arroyo de la Presa (41PS800), Tall Rockshelter (41JD10), John Z. Livermore Cache (41JD66), and Exa Means Projectile Point Cache (41JD212).

SOURCES FOR ILLUSTRATIONS AND DESCRIPTIONS: Riches (1976); Boisvert (1985); Cloud (2004); Justice (2002); Katz and Katz (1974); Leslie (1978); Mallouf (2009, 2012, 2013); Roney (1995:53, Figure 6,e-l); Turner, Hester, and McReynolds (2011); Wheaton (2009); and Wiseman (1971).

COMMENTS: According to Mallouf (2013), this point style has recently been lumped within a Livermore Cluster construct and included in a typological subset termed the *Guadalupe* point by Justice (2002). Mallouf (2013:194) describes this point as "being comprised of a confusing array of projectile styles that includes both dart and arrow points. Unfortunately, this commendable attempt by Justice to resolve several long-standing regional typological issues serves only to complicate matters further."

Boisvert (1985) illustrates four *Livermore* points that bear some resemblance to *Diablo*. The major contribution of his article is the very thorough discussion of lithics found in the Guadalupe region where the *Diablo* type has been reported.

Robert J. Mallouf's (2013) classification of projectile points in the Eastern Trans-Pecos and Big Bend of Texas is the most recent and comprehensive discussion of this type available.

Wiseman (1971) reported on an arrow point from the Neff site in New Mexico that is like *Diablo*.

Mallouf (2012:4) writes that "Similarities with the *Diablo* point with the *Neff* point style as defined by Wiseman (1971) are noted, and there can be

122 | CHAPTER 6

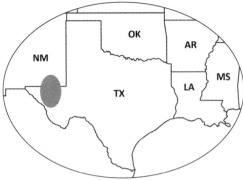

Figure 6.38. Distribution of Diablo points (drafted by Lili Lyddon).

little doubt that the two types are interrelated. However, *Neff* points are narrowly characterized as having expanding stems and L-shaped tangs (barbs?), while *Diablo* points are morphologically more diverse, the latter including parallel-sided and bulbous, as well as expanded stems—all apparently representative of a single technological tradition. In addition, while *Diablo* points, like *Neff* points, usually exhibit hook-like barbs, they may also have barbs that are essentially perpendicular to the long axis of the specimen—in a fashion more similar to *Livermore* points."

Wiseman (1971:24) notes that examples of *Neff* points from the Neff site are "not truly representative of type specimens examined in private collections but does go on to describe the range of variability that distinguishes the type."

Mallouf (2013:196) provides the following dimensions:

Length: 25.5 to 40.6 cm
Width: 14.0 cm to 21.3 cm
Thickness: 3.3 cm to 4.8 cm

Neff points may best be described as a provisional type.

DISTRIBUTION: Its known distribution in Texas includes the Davis Mountains, northern Lobo Valley, Salt Basin, Sierra Diablo, Delaware Mountains, and Guadalupe Mountains. *Diablo* points are much less common south of the Davis Mountains in the Big Bend area of Texas. Other specimens have been found in the Chinati Mountains and Midland County. In southeastern New Mexico, the distribution includes the Guadalupe Mountains north to the Capitan Mountains and east to the Mescalero Escarpment. According to Robert J. Mallouf (personal communication, 2018), this type has been found at sites in the Eastern and Big Bend areas of the Trans-Pecos.

Figure 6.39. Edwards point (photo courtesy of John Fish).

Edwards

ORIGINAL RECORDER: J. B. Sollberger (1967) was the first to recognize this type and describe it. The name was derived from the Edwards Plateau where these specimens were initially found. Much of his early studies were in Kerr County where he found and described *Edwards* points at the Lamb's Creek site and rockshelters such as Goat's Bluff and August's Bluff, which have not been assigned trinomials.

OTHER NAMES: None reported.

SIMILAR TYPES: *Edwards* points are similar to the *Scallorn type* as both have prominent barbs and stems that expand strongly at the base. The

124 | **CHAPTER 6**

major difference is that the stem of an *Edwards* point is deeply divided into two long barb-like projections with a concave base, while *Scallorn* bases expand.

AGE: It may be the earliest arrow point in the state based on a radiocarbon date that indicates it first appeared circa AD 900 to AD 1000 (Beasley 1978). Other researchers believe it may have persisted as a specific type until AD 1050. Radiocarbon dates from the Ernest Rainey site date it to the tenth and eleventh centuries (AD 900 to AD 1000) (Turner et al. 2011:190). DESCRIPTION: This type does not appear in Suhm and Jelks (1954). Davis (1995:210) describes it as a "small to large triangular point with lateral edges that may be straight or slightly concave or convex. The lateral edges may be slightly serrated. The point has strong shoulders that are usually well-barbed. The stem is short and expands greatly into two long barb-like projections with a concave base." Turner, Hester, and McReynolds (2011:190) write that these barb-like projections may curve upward or downward. *Edwards* is described as one of the largest arrow points found in Texas, but dimensions are not provided by Davis (1995) or Turner, Hester, and McReynolds (2011).

CULTURAL AFFILIATION: This type dates to the early part of the Late Prehistoric. Duncan and others (2007) say that it may have been associated with the initial adoption of the bow in parts of Texas.

KNOWN SITES: Panther Springs Creek (41BX228); sites at Camp Bullis (41BX36, 41BX377, 41BX379, 41BX383, 41BX385, and 41BX811); Crystal Rivers (41BX195, 41BN113, 41GL19); Lambs Creek (41KR356); La Jita (41UV21); Mingo (41BN101); Ernest Rainey (41BN33, 41DM59), and Goat's Bluff and August's Bluff in Kerr County (No TARL numbers for these two sites).

SOURCES FOR ILLUSTRATIONS AND DESCRIPTIONS: Beasley (1978); Davis (1995); Duncan and others (2007); Hester (1970b, 1978, 2004); Moore (1988a); Perino (1968); Sollberger (1967, 1978); Hester (1980); Turner and Hester (1985, 1993, 1999); Jelks (1993); Hester and Whatley (1992); and Turner, Hester, and McReynolds (2011).

Arrow Points | 125

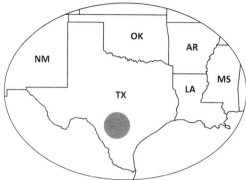

Figure 6.40. Distribution of Edwards points (drafted by Lili Lyddon).

COMMENTS: Sollberger (1967) believes that *Edwards* points were modeled after a variety of Central Texas dart points such as *Ensor, Fairland, Frio,* and *Martindale*. Because of its size and early dates, some archaeologists think it may have been the earliest arrow point style adopted in Texas when the bow and arrow technology was a reduction in the size of projectile points. *Edwards*-like points have been found in apparent association with *Frio, Montell,* and *Pedernales* dart points and *Scallorn* arrow points. No type site was identified. *Edwards* points have been found associated with burials, and some specimens were embedded in the victim's bones.

DISTRIBUTION: Trans-Pecos, Central Texas, and Rio Grande Plains Archeological Regions. *Edwards* points are a rare occurrence in the Trans-Pecos Region (Mallouf, personal communication, 2018).

Form 2

ORIGINAL RECORDER: The article by Kumpe and McReynolds (2017–2018) states that *Form 2* appeared in a report by Frank Weir (1956), but they do not mention who named it.

OTHER NAMES: *Boomerang*

SIMILAR TYPES: *Revilla* and *Starr*

CHAPTER 6

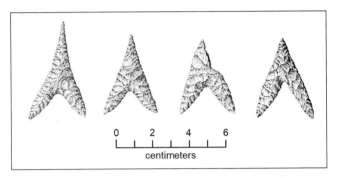

Figure 6.41. Form 2 points (drawing courtesy of Richard McReynolds).

DESCRIPTION: Kumpe and McReynolds (2017–2018:43–45) describe this type as "very thin, skillfully made arrow points," using quality chert. "*Form 2* arrow points are generally triangular in outline with remarkably deep (8 to 16 mm deep) concave bases. The basal notch has convex sides and a rounded apex, which is unlike *Starr*. Beginning at the base, lateral edges of larger complete specimens are convex until above the apex of the basal notch, where they straighten towards the tip. The lateral edges of these larger specimens that have been minimally refurbished are concave overall. Smaller specimens, which have been heavily reworked, may have slightly convex, slightly concave, or even straight lateral edges." They provide the following dimensions:

Length: 27.2 cm to 55.0 cm
Width: 16.9 cm to 29.4 cm
Thickness: 2.5 cm to 4.2 cm
Weight: 0.8 g to 2.3 g

AGE: Late Prehistoric

CULTURAL AFFILIATION: Unknown

KNOWN SITES: 41ZP83, 41ZP154

SOURCES FOR ILLUSTRATIONS AND DESCRIPTIONS: Kumpe, McReynolds, and Chandler (2000); Kumpe and McReynolds (2017–2018); Saunders (1985); and Weir (1956).

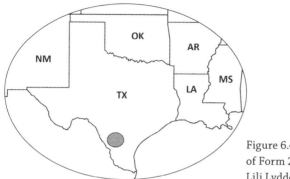

Figure 6.42. Distribution of Form 2 points (drafted by Lili Lyddon).

COMMENTS: Kumpe and McReynolds (2017–2018:43) describe this type as very thin and skillfully made of quality chert. The distinguishing characteristic is the concave base that can be as deep as 16 mm. *Form 2* bears some resemblance to the *Starr* point, but the authors note its convex sides and rounded apex of the basal notch.

Form 2 is not included in *Stone Artifacts of Texas Indians* (Turner, Hester, and McReynolds 2011).

Fresno

ORIGINAL RECORDER: Alex D. Krieger (1946) was the first to describe the *Fresno* point, but he did not name it. He first observed this type at the Harrell site in Young County. J. Charles Kelley (1947b) referred to examples found at the Lehman Rock Shelter in Gillespie County as *Fresno Triangular Blade*, but he did not describe them. Joe Ben Wheat (1953) called similar specimens *Kobs Triangular Points* based on examples from the Kobs site at Addicks Reservoir in Harris County. Dee Ann Suhm and Alex D. Krieger (1954:498) shortened the name to *Fresno* during the writing of *An Introductory Handbook of Texas Archeology*.

OTHER NAMES: *Fresno Triangular Blade*, *Kobs Triangular Point*, and *El Muerto*.

128 | CHAPTER 6

Figure 6.43. Fresno points from Dimmit County (photo courtesy of TARL).

SIMILAR TYPES: *Cameron, Guerrero,* and *Kobs* (Wheat 1953). Suhm and Krieger (1954) say *Fresno* grades into the *Turney* type, which belongs to the historic Allen Focus of East Texas. Specimens also grade into *Talco* of the Titus Focus and the *Starr* type. Forrester (1987b) believes some *Fresno* points may be preforms for side-notched triangular types found at Henrietta Focus sites.

AGE: Suhm and Krieger (1954:498) estimate the age of this type as AD 800 or AD 900 to AD 1600 or later. They say that it was found at historic-age sites Spanish Fort and Womack on the Red River. These sites have also produced Late Prehistoric artifacts. Turner, Hester, and McReynolds (2011:191) simply refer to *Fresno* as Late Prehistoric, AD 1250 to AD 1600. Crook (personal communication, 2019) believes it dates to circa AD 800 to about AD 1250.

DESCRIPTION: Suhm and Krieger (1954:498) describe these points as simple triangles with straight to slightly convex edges, and bases that are usually straight but may be concave or slightly convex. The lateral edges are sometimes finely serrated. The length is 2.0 cm to 3.5 cm, and the width is 1.0 cm to 2.0 cm.

CULTURAL AFFILIATION: According to Suhm and Krieger (1954:498), this type is associated with the Bravo Valley and Central Texas aspects; Brownsville, Galveston Bay, Henrietta, Mier, Rockport, and Wyle foci; and probably other foci in the Historic Stage. Crook (2017:51) reports that *Fresno* points are associated with the Farmersville Phase.

KNOWN SITES: Arrowhead Peak Ruin (41HC19), Harrell (41YN1), Unland (41CF111), Landslide (41BL85), Wunderlich (41CM3), Spanish Fort sites (41MU12, 41MU24, and 41MU28), Womack (41LR1), Lubbock Lake (41LU1), Dillard (41CO174), Pearson (41RA5), Gilbert (41RA13), Peerless Bottoms (41HP175), *Presidio Nuestra Señora de Loreto de la Bahia de Espíritu Santo* (41VT8), Tortuga Flat (41ZV155), Polvo (41PS21), Baker Cave (41VV213), Upper Farmersville (41COL34), 41DL406, 41HG4, 41HG5, 41HG9, 41SE17, 41NU33, 41GR396, 41GR432, 41K742, and 41KL13.

SOURCES FOR ILLUSTRATIONS AND DESCRIPTIONS: Allen et al. (1967); Beasley (1978); Bell (1960); Boyd and others (1989); Crook (2008–2009); Hester (1980); Davis (1995); Duncan et al. (2007); Fields (2004); Fox and Tomka (2006); Johnson, Suhm, and Tunnell (1962); Kelley (1947b); Krieger (1946); Mallouf, Baskin, and Killen (1977); Mokry (1977); Perino (1985); Saunders and Saunders (1978); Suhm and Krieger (1954); Turner and Hester (1985, 1993, 1999); Turner, Hester, and McReynolds (2011); Weir (1956); Tunnell and Tunnell (2015); Jelks (1993); Shackelford (1955); Crook (2011); Hedrick (1989); Word and Douglas (1970); and Wheat (1953).

COMMENTS: This is a simple triangular shaped point, and the edges are rarely serrated. Suhm and Kreiger (1954) stated that the type described by Joe Ben Wheat (1953) as *Kobs* should probably be included with this type.

John T. and Elaine L. Saunders (1978:2–18) discuss a private collection belonging to J. R. Saunders of San Antonio. Mr. Saunders had collected 1,822 pieces of worked stone from his 3,120-acre ranch. The purpose of their analysis was to "devise a method or system by which collections of amateurs can be used in conjunction with professional archaeology." At the time of their study, they found "a paucity of published archaeological data from the Webb County area of Southern Texas." They identified 17 points in the collection as *Fresno*. They also conducted two small area surveys along the east and west banks of Isabella Creek. One *Fresno* point was found along each bank in areas that were thickly vegetated.

130 | **CHAPTER 6**

Duncan and others (2007) present a lengthy discussion of this type and similar types found in other states. Forrester (1987b) believes *Fresno* points may be preforms for side-notched triangular types found at Henrietta Focus sites. Several side-notched points were found a 41RA13 in association with 173 *Fresno* points.

Wilson W. Crook III (2017) discusses types of damage to *Fresno* points and other Late Prehistoric types from a sample of 750 points. Tomka (2016) illustrates his version of how the *Fresno* point was hafted as compared to the *Guerrero* type. These points were found with Late Prehistoric burials at 41ZV155.

At the Gilbert site (Allen et al. 1967), *Fresno* was the dominant type with 173 specimens. All but two were made of chert or another fine cryptocrystalline quartz material. The two exceptions were made of quartzite.

Jelks (1993:12) writes the following: "Some Fresno points in Texas were undoubtedly preforms and not completed points, making accurate definition of the type's distribution difficult." Jelks recalls finding *Fresno* points in the same field contexts with *Scallorn*. "Later, when experimental knappers tried their hands at making Scallorn points, it became obvious that many, if not all of the so-called Fresno points represented a stage in the production of Scallorn points, lacking only the final step of corner-notching. For that reason, the legitimacy of identifying Fresno as a discrete type is highly questionable." "Further refinement of the type and its relationship to more distinctive types is needed for a better understanding of the cultural-temporal affinities of the type."

At the Gilkey Hill site (41DL406), *Fresno* is represented by nine specimens. Three were made of chert, and six were fashioned from quartzite (Crook 2011:Table 1).

Six complete *Fresno* points and eight fragments were recovered from the Greenbelt site (41DY17). The edges vary from straight, slightly convex, to slightly concave. Bases are straight to concave. Widths range from 0.8 cm to 1.8 cm. Lengths range from 1.6 cm to at least 3.5 cm. All were made of Alibates agate (Campbell 1970:44–45).

Four artifacts described as *Fresno* were recovered at Presidio Nuestra Señora de Loreto de la Bahia del Espíritu Santo (41VT8). Two are complete, and two are fragments. Their provenience and metric data are found in

Arrow Points | 131

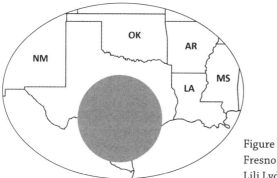

Figure 6.44. Distribution of Fresno points (drafted by Lili Lyddon).

Fox and Tomka (2006:Table 15). "Technologically, two lack the fine edge-pressure retouch found on finished Scallorn points, and therefore, may be late stage Scallorn preforms. Another reason to support this interpretation is that they consistently occur with Scallorn" (Fox and Tomka 2006:102, Figure 35).

DISTRIBUTION: Suhm and Krieger (1954) state that *Fresno* points are found throughout Texas with the fewest examples found in counties next to the Louisiana border. According to Turner, Hester, and McReynolds (2011:191), this type has been widely reported throughout Texas. It occurs most frequently in the central, eastern, and southern parts. Robert J. Mallouf (personal communication, 2018) states that this type is frequently found in the Eastern Trans-Pecos and Big Bend regions.

Friley

ORIGINAL RECORDER: According to Robert E. Bell (1960), *Friley* was named by Clarence H. Webb (1963) for examples found at the Friley site in Louisiana. No trinomial has been assigned to this site.

OTHER NAMES: Webb (2000:16) states that "these points were originally referred to as Gem points because of their frequency on Jim's (Gem?) Island."

SIMILAR TYPES: Davis (1995) says that *Friley* is like the *Steiner* type, except *Friley* has strong broad recurved and barbed shoulders.

132 | CHAPTER 6

Figure 6.45. Friley points (photo courtesy of Thomas Oakes).

AGE: When Bell's (1960) work was published, the age and cultural associations of *Friley* points were not clearly known. Since it was found with pottery, it was presumed to be a Late Prehistoric type. According to Turner, Hester, and McReynolds (2011:192), *Friley* is one of the earliest arrow points to have been used in Texas with an estimated time span of AD 700 to AD 1100.

DESCRIPTION: Davis (1995:216) described *Friley* as a small point with a triangular outline and lateral edges that are usually straight to recurved, and commonly serrated. "The strong shoulders expand with barbs that recurve toward the tip of the point. The stem may be parallel or slightly expanding toward the base. The bases are usually straight but are occasionally slightly concave or convex" (Davis 1995:216). Dimensions are not stated.

CULTURAL AFFILIATION: The *Friley* points found at the Smithport Landing site in De Soto Parish, Louisiana, were assigned to the Alto Focus by

Webb (1963). The specimen from 41MX65 was part of a "poorly known Titus Phase cemetery in Ellison Creek Reservoir" (King and Turner 1993:25).

KNOWN SITES: Friley is the type site in Louisiana, but it has not been assigned a unique trinomial. In Texas, *Friley* points have been found at Roitsch (formerly Sam Kaufman—41RR16), Jones Hill (41PK8), Wolfshead (41SA117), 41PK21, West Island (41MX65), Williams site (41CP10), and various sites in the Cedar Creek Reservoir in Henderson and Kaufman Counties (Story 1965). Gadus, Blake, and Fields (1997) report specimens in the Cooper Lake area of Delta County. Keller and Weir (1979) illustrate an example of this type from the Strawberry Hill site (41SJ160). Story (1965) reports this type from sites in the Cedar Creek Reservoir (Henderson and Kaufman Counties). In Louisiana, it has been found at Smithport Landing (16DS4).

SOURCES FOR ILLUSTRATIONS AND DESCRIPTIONS: Bell (1960); Davis (1995); Duffield (1963); Duncan and others (2007); Fields (2004); Keller and Weir (1979); King and Turner (1993:31); Perino (1985); Turner and Hester (1985, 1993, 1999); Turner, Hester, and McReynolds (2011); Webb (1963, 2000); and Turner and Smith (2002).

COMMENTS: Duffield (1963) divided this type into two subgroups based on recurved or laterally projecting shoulder treatments. He stated that the significance of the variations cannot be accurately determined until specimens at other sites are analyzed.

Bell's discussion of *Friley* is in the fifth printing of his guidebook that was published in 1969.

Friley points are often made of silicified wood of near-opalized quality (Turner, Hester, and McReynolds 2011:192).

Two *Friley* points were recovered from site 41SJ160 (Keller and Weir 1979:39). The length ranged from 1.8 cm and 1.9 cm, but the shoulder width was not measured. They weighed 0.4 g and 0.5 g.

DISTRIBUTION: Bell (1960) says that *Friley* is apparently most common in Natchitoches Parish, Louisiana. It has also been reported from sites in the Northeast and Southeast Texas Archeological regions.

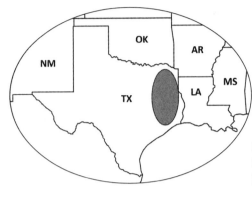

Figure 6.46. Distribution of Friley points (drafted by Lili Lyddon).

Figure 6.47 Gar scale point (photo courtesy of TARL).

Gar Scales

ORIGINAL RECORDER: The first mention of this artifact in Texas is in *An Introductory Handbook of Texas Archeology* by Dee Ann Suhm and Alex D. Krieger (1954:510).

OTHER NAMES: None reported.

SIMILAR TYPES: None reported.

AGE: Davis (1995:218) estimates the age of these presumed points at AD 700 to AD 1600. The latest edition of a typology book (Turner et al. 2011) does not discuss gar scales as possible points.

DESCRIPTION: Davis (1995:218) describes gar scale points as small thin points with a triangular outline and lateral edges that may be straight, concave, or convex. "The shoulders may appear strong to non-existent. The stem usually contracts toward the base giving this point a bi-pointed appearance." Dimensions are not stated.

CULTURAL AFFILIATION: Unknown.

DISTRIBUTION: Gar scales have been found in numerous sites on the Texas coast and some inland sites, especially those on the lower reaches of rivers entering the Gulf of Mexico.

KNOWN SITES: 41HR133 (shell midden on Peggy Lake); Kendrick's Hill site (41JK35); and Possum Bluff (41JK24). Site 41JK35 contained 13 scales with asphaltum, but it covered the faces of the scales as well as the stems.

SOURCES FOR ILLUSTRATIONS AND DESCRIPTIONS: Aten (1983); Costa and Fox (2016); Davis (1995); Jelks (1962); Olsen (1968); Moore (1985); Patterson (1994a, 2001); Perino (1985); Suhm and Krieger (1954:Plate 134); and Tunnell and Tunnell (2015).

COMMENTS: Gar scales are found on alligator garfish (*Atractosteus spatula*). They are hard, boney interlocking scales known as ganoid scales. Their purpose is to provide a protective armor. The shape of these scales is ideal for hafting without serious modification. The natural stem of some specimens has been altered, and cut marks are sometimes present (Suhm and Krieger 1954:510).

Davis (1995) and Costa and Fox (2016) believe that they could have also been used as flaking tools for making arrow points. Because of their diminutive size, they are believed to have only functioned as arrow points.

Costa and Fox (2016) examined gar scales in terms of their durability for use as projectile points. They concluded that they were just as effective as flint if the serrated edges were removed by grinding. Test firing with a calibrated crossbow demonstrated that some points fractured with one shot, while others survived two or more. Four points were shot at pork ribs and passed easily through the skin and rib tissue. Even hits on bone resulted in good penetration. Costa and Fox (2016:28–29) write that "the results of these experiments support the hypothesis that alligator gar scales can be easily modified and utilized as tips for projectile weaponry."

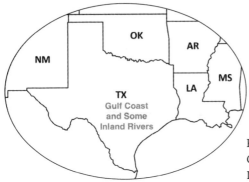

Figure 6.48. Distribution of Gar Scale points (drafted by Lili Lyddon).

Agogino and Shelley (1988) discuss the possibilities of gar scales having been used as projectile points in the southern United States and northern Mexico.

Carl Welch hafted alligator gar scales to wooden shafts to make complete arrows with feathers, and such. He used scales from Missouri. Welch (personal communication, 2022) states that the scales are razor sharp, especially those with a serrated edge. While describing his experiment, he writes that he used a Dermal tool to shorten the long extension of the bottom of the scale to remove some of its slight curvature and to create notches for hafting. An argument for their utility to function as a projectile point is due to their toughness. They are made of enamel like human teeth, the hardest bone associated with living creatures. He also argues that another fact that supports their use as projectiles is they have been found in archaeological sites away from their native habitat.

Wen Yang and colleagues (2013) discuss structure and fracture resistance of alligator gar scales.

The latest edition of a typology book (Turner, Hester, and McReynolds 2011) does not discuss gar scales as possible points as it is restricted to stone tools.

DISTRIBUTION: At sites on the Texas Coastal Plain and the lower reaches of rivers entering the Gulf of Mexico.

Figure 6.49. Garza point (photo courtesy of John Fish).

Garza

ORIGINAL RECORDER: *Garza* was named and described by Frank A. Runkles (1964) for examples found at the Garza site near the town of Post in Garza County. Runkles proposed this type for 13 triangular points that exhibited a centrally placed basal notch.

OTHER NAMES: *Soto*

SIMILAR TYPES: Walter W. Taylor (1966) referred to a similar type found in Mexico as the *Cienegas* point. Davis (1995:232) stated that *Lott* also bears a strong resemblance. *Garza* points lack shoulders, while *Lott* specimens exhibit weak to strong shoulders and occasionally small barbs. Davis (1995:232) said that a "weak shouldered *Lott* point and a *Garza* point are somewhat similar in appearance." Perino (1968) believes *Garza* points are like some *Toyah* points and would become *Toyah* if notched on the sides. He adds that they also resemble the *Harrell* type, and the two are often found together.

AGE: Runkles (1964) believes *Garza* is the same age as *Lott* and *Perdiz*. It is Earl Green's (1962) opinion that the *Garza* point from the Lubbock Lake

138 | CHAPTER 6

site dates to sometime prior to AD 1500. Turner, Hester, and McReynolds (2011:193) estimate the age of this point at AD 1540 to AD 1665. Boyd (2001) refers to sites with *Garza* points as protohistoric.

DESCRIPTION: Davis (1995:220) describes *Garza* as a "small stemless point with triangular blades and lateral edges that may be straight or convex and serrated or smooth. The base is straight to slightly concave with a centrally notched base that is either V-shaped or U-shaped. Basal corners may be slightly rounded but are more often pointed in appearance." Dimensions are not given.

CULTURAL AFFILIATION: Duncan and others (2007:51), citing others, said, "These points are considered part of the cultural inventory of the protohistoric Garza Complex, which is considered a westward extension of the Wheeler Phase on the southern plains, and affiliated with the Tejas" (Plains Caddoan or Wichita).

KNOWN SITES: Garza (41GR40), Lubbock Lake (41LU1), Blue Mountain Rockshelter (41WK4), Cielo Bravo (41PS52), Lott (41GR56), and the Pete Creek site (Parsons 1967).

SOURCES FOR ILLUSTRATIONS AND DESCRIPTIONS: Holden (1938); Parsons (1967); Boyd (2001); Davis (1995); Duncan and others (2007); Perino (1968, 1985); Runkles (1964); Turner and Hester (1985, 1993, 1999); Hedrick (1989); Johnson and others (1977); and Turner, Hester, and McReynolds (2011).

COMMENTS: Most *Garza* points from 41GR40 were made from local flint and chert. One specimen was manufactured from obsidian. Eighty-two percent of the triangular points found at the Garza site were fragmentary, and this suggested to Runkles (1964) that they might represent an intermediate step in the production of *Garza* or *Harrell* points. Evidence from the Garza site indicates that it is associated primarily (or even exclusively) with the triple-notched *Harrell* point and not with the side-notched *Harrell* point.

Mallouf (personal communication, 2018) informed me of a triple-notched arrow point at 41PS194 that he believes to be a *Harrell*.

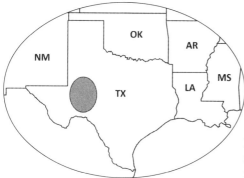

Figure 6.50. Distribution of Garza points (drafted by Lili Lyddon).

The *Soto* point, believed to be similar to *Garza*, was reported by Captain Alan L. Phelps (1964:8) of the US Army; he discovered it in northern Chihuahua, Mexico. The name was derived from a nearby ranch. Phelps (1964:8) said, "*Soto* points range in size from 1.3 cm to 3.5 cm in length and .5 cm to 1.5 cm in width at the base. The base is always notched, sometimes deeply, sometimes shallow, and can be straight or concave. The favored material is agate, but flint and obsidian points are found."

Eileen Johnson and others (1977) discuss the *Garza* occupation in their article "Garza Occupation at the Lubbock Lake Site." Two Garza points were found in activity area FA8-4. One specimen is described as a unifacially flaked basal section with a bifacially flaked notch. The other is represented by two sections in close proximity to each other that could be the result of a break during manufacture.

Boyd (2001:Figure 5) maps the distribution of *Garza* and *Lott* points in the Texas Panhandle-Plains.

DISTRIBUTION: At the time the *Garza* point was proposed, its known extent was bounded on the north by Lamb and Bailey Counties, on the east by southern Floyd to Taylor Counties, on the southwest by Crane County, and on the west by El Paso County (Runkles 1964). A few specimens were reported from widely scattered areas in eastern New Mexico (Doña Ana and Otero Counties) and west to the Pecos River.

Robert J. Mallouf (personal communication, 2018) says that this type is found in the eastern part of the Trans-Pecos and Big Bend region, but it is not a common type in the area.

Duncan and colleagues (2007:51) write that "Garza Complex villages are concentrated along the White River in Blanco Canyon around Lubbock, Texas." Boyd (2001:Figure 5) presents a map of the distribution of *Garza* and *Lott* points in the Texas Panhandle-Plains.

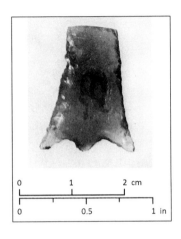

Figure 6.51. Glass point from 41SA25 (Photo courtesy of Texas A&M University Press).

Glass

ORIGINAL RECORDER: Not applicable

OTHER NAMES: Glass points are named for the material they were made from. I am not aware of a taxonomical classification for glass points like their stone counterparts.

SIMILAR TYPES: Some glass points resemble known types of stone points such as *Bassett*, *Cameron*, *Cliffton*, and *Guerrero*.

AGE: Suhm and Krieger (1954:119) write that glass arrow points and scrapers are associated with the Historic Stage. *Guerrero* points made of glass were used in the eighteenth century by mission Indians (Turner et al. 2011:194). The glass arrow point described by Perttula and Marceaux (2018) dates from circa AD 1680 to AD 1720.

DESCRIPTION: See the descriptions for *Bassett*, *Cameron*, *Cliffton*, and *Guerrero*.

CULTURAL AFFILIATION: Glass points were used during historic times. Suhm and Krieger (1954:119–120) state that "surface finds of glass arrow points have been reported at sites associated with the Brownsville Focus." They assert that "since none of these have been excavated, it is uncertain whether this is fortuitous, or the Brownsville Focus lasted into European times." Prewitt and others (1987:24–25) argue that the presence of glass arrow points and other European made objects may associate these sites with the Rockport Focus and beyond.

KNOWN SITES: Swan Lake (41AS16), Live Oak Point (41AS2), Spradley (41NA206), *Mission Dolores de los Ais* (41SA25), Gilbert (41RA13), and Candelario Olivo (a.k.a. Glass Arrow site) in Aransas County (no trinomial).

SOURCES FOR ILLUSTRATIONS AND DESCRIPTIONS: Campbell (1958, 1960); Harris and Tunnell (1966); Prewitt and others (1987); Tunnell and Tunnell (2015); Corbin and others (1990); Perttula and Marceaux (2018). Two glass arrow points are on display at the Bullock Texas State History Museum in Austin as part of a loan by TARL.

COMMENTS: Two green glass arrow points were found on Webb Island in the Laguna Madre, 25 miles south of Puerto Bay by George Martin and Henry Fulton Sadly. Fulton's find was lost after leaving the site (Tunnell and Tunnell 2015:198).

Six green glass arrow points were found at the Swan Lake site (41AS16) in Aransas County (Prewitt et al. 1987:24).

Campbell (1958:163) mentioned previous work in the Rio Grande Delta Region by A. E. Anderson (1932) in the following quote: "Anderson attributed all of his artifacts to a single culture. He mentioned a few projectile points made of glass, but no attempt was made to link the archeological remains with any specific Indian group." Anderson (1930:31) also stated that "Green bottle glass projectile points, similar to those of flint, are found but are scarce."

Campbell (1958) believes glass arrow points at the Live Oak Point site (41AS2) may be linked to the historic Karankawa.

Perttula and Marceaux (2018:22) describe and illustrate a glass point from 41NA206 Nacogdoches County. "It is made of bluish-green glass that is flat and only 2.5 mm in thickness. It was recovered from Unit N54-W59,

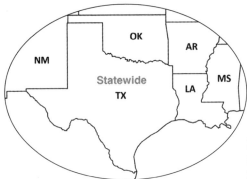

Figure 6.52. Distribution of Glass points (drafted by Lili Lyddon).

level 2 (10–20 cm below the surface). The point is broken, and only the tip and serrated blade remain. It is 17.5 mm in width."

Harris and Tunnell (1967:111) describe seven pieces of clear flat glass that have been bifacially retouched into points or knives. One sherd of clear flat glass and two green bottle fragments have unifacial flaking along one edge which may be intentional retouch or wear from use as scrapers. One example is illustrated in their Figure 48.

Claude McCrocklin (1993:8–13) discusses chipped glass found at historic Indian sites. Even though his article is not about arrow points, he provides insight into methods and materials used that may be applicable to the manufacture of glass arrow points. He writes that "bottle glass, especially wine bottles, was the object of choice. All parts of the bottle; neck, sides, and bottom were used. Flaking removed large chips as well as pressure flakes. Only the sides of bottles were bifacially chipped," and he states that these resemble prehistoric scrapers or knives.

A glass point (not depicted) was found on a deflated surface in Aransas County. It was associated with other points, pottery, and scrapers, a small knife blade, and sherds of green glass believed to be part of a wine bottle used in colonial times (Tunnell and Tunnell 2015:198, Figure 7.12). The authors speculated that, if complete, it would have measured "nearly two inches in length by three-quarters inch in width. The thickness corresponds to that of the wall of the bottle fragments found here."

DISTRIBUTION: Statewide.

Figure 6.53. Granbury point from 41HI1 (photo courtesy of TARL).

Granbury

ORIGINAL RECORDER: *Granbury* points were first recognized at the Kyle site in Hill County by Edward B. Jelks (1962). He named it for Lake Granbury where some of the first specimens were found. This new type was proposed based on 38 specimens described as a series of triangular to subtriangular artifacts classified as arrow points.

OTHER NAMES: None reported.

SIMILAR TYPES: Jelks (1962:35) states that the var. *bono* is similar to the *Fresno* type, but "as a group they are distinct from that type, being generally thicker, heavier, and cruder than *Fresno*." Other varieties noted by Jelks are Granbury var. *joshua* and *parker*, but they "lack sharp angles at the basal corners, which makes them readily distinguishable from the *Fresno* type."

AGE: According to (Prewitt 1981), the *Granbury* point dates to circa AD 700 to AD 1300 due to its association with the Austin Phase.

DESCRIPTION: Jelks (1962:35) describes *Granbury* in the following: "This provisional type includes a series of triangular to subtriangular artifacts

144 | CHAPTER 6

that are classed as arrow points." The blade is triangular "with straight to slightly concave base; lateral edges straight to mildly concave." His discussion of this type includes physical characteristics of the three proposed varieties.

> *bono*—Length 2 cm to 4 cm; maximum width at base: 1.4 cm to
> 2.1 cm; maximum thickness: 3 mm to 6 mm.
> *joshua*—Length 2.6 cm to 5 cm; maximum width at base: 1.5 cm to
> 2.3 cm; maximum thickness: 3 mm to 7 mm.
> *parker*—Length 3.4 cm to 4 cm; maximum width at base: 1.7 cm to
> 2.5 cm; maximum thickness: 4 mm to 7 mm.

CULTURAL AFFILIATION: *Granbury* is a diagnostic type of the Austin Focus (a.k.a. Austin Phase) of the Central Texas Aspect (Jelks 1962; Prewitt 1981). No specimens from the Kyle site were found in the Toyah Focus zone.

KNOWN SITES: Kyle (41HI1), Footbridge (41CM2), Oblate (41CM1), Pecan Springs (41EL11), and 41SE17.

SOURCES FOR ILLUSTRATIONS AND DESCRIPTIONS: Johnson and others (1962); Sorrow (1966); Forrester (1987b); Perino (1991); and Prewitt (1981).

COMMENTS: Prewitt (1981) presents a detailed discussion of the Austin Phase/Focus in his article titled "Cultural Chronology in Central Texas." This type was recognized after the TAS bulletin by Suhm and Krieger (1954) and the typology book by Suhm and Jelks (1962) were published. Forrester (1987b) mentions *Granbury* points, var. *parker* (n = 21) *joshua* (n = 8), and *bono* (n = 4) at 41SE17.

Sorrow (1966:24) reported 12 *Granbury* points at the Pecan Springs site (41EL11) in Ellis County. All three varieties were present. Two additional specimens were tentatively identified as *Granbury*, but they did not fit the definition of either variety.

Granbury is not included in *Stone Artifacts of Texas Indians* (Turner et al. 2011).

DISTRIBUTION: Its known distribution is described by Perino (1991:90) as "from the Brazos River on the northwest to the Nueces River on the southwest; on the south and east from a line running parallel to, and 50 to 100 miles south and east of the Balcones Escarpment, and on the northwest

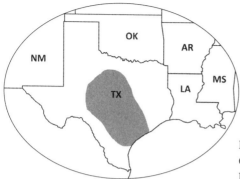

Figure 6.54. Distribution of Granbury points (drafted by Lili Lyddon).

from a line drawn between Young and Edwards counties." According to Prewitt's (1995) distribution and density study, most *Granbury* points are found in Central and South-Central Texas. The most specimens (50 or more) have been reported from Young County in North-Central Texas.

Guadalupe

ORIGINAL RECORDER: Noel D. Justice (2002:231–240) is credited with naming this point.

OTHER NAMES: None reported.

SIMILAR TYPES: *Livermore, Neff.* No reference to *Neff* as a valid type was found.

AGE: Not stated.

DESCRIPTION: No physical description available.

CULTURAL AFFILIATION: Late Prehistoric.

KNOWN SITES: Not stated.

SOURCES FOR ILLUSTRATIONS AND DESCRIPTIONS: Justice (2002:231–240).

COMMENTS: *Guadalupe* is not included in *Stone Artifacts of Texas Indians* (Turner et al. 2011).

Figure 6.55. Guadalupe point (replica by Matt Soultz; photo courtesy of Brian Wootan).

Mallouf (2012:3), writes that "Recently this point style has been lumped within a 'Livermore Cluster' construct and included in a typological subset termed the '*Guadalupe* point' by Justice (2002). In order to separate and clarify the chronological, stylistic, and distributional parameters of a distinctive point style included as '*Guadalupe*' by Justice, the designation, *Guadalupe* arrow point is herein proposed."

Justice (2002:231) incorporates the *Neff* point into his *Guadalupe* point construct, noting that "The *Neff* type is ' . . . well within the overall variation described for *Guadalupe* but it typically exhibits strongly angled shoulders (L-shaped) with straight sides below a narrow blade with serrations which may show progressively smaller serrations moving up the blade."

DISTRIBUTION: Not stated.

Arrow Points | 147

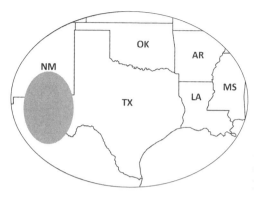

Figure 6.56. Distribution of Guadalupe points (drafted by Lili Lyddon).

Figure 6.57. Guerrero points from 41WH8 (photo courtesy of TARL).

Guerrero

ORIGINAL RECORDER: The *Guerrero* point was named and described by Thomas R. Hester (1977) based on examples found at San Bernard Mission located near the city of Guerrero in Coahuila, Mexico.

OTHER NAMES: Mission points.

SIMILAR TYPES: According to Davis (1995:222), "The Guerrero point resembles Fresno in its general outline." *Fresno* has a more triangular appearance and a straight to mildly concave base, whereas the shape of the *Guerrero*

148 | CHAPTER 6

point is triangular to lanceolate with a basal concavity that is usually deeper (Turner et al. 2011). It is similar to the *Cameron* type described by MacNeish (1958) and Turner, Hester, and McReynolds (2011).

AGE: This point was used in the eighteenth century by mission Indians, and some specimens were made from glass (Turner et al. 2011:194).

DESCRIPTION: Per Turner, Hester, and McReynolds (2011:194), "Most examples are triangular in outline, and distal tips are often reworked." "Some have "very careful parallel flaking." Hester's illustrated examples depict bases that are "straight and slightly to markedly concave. Lateral edges are straight and convex." Dimensions are not given.

CULTURAL AFFILIATION: Historic Stage.

KNOWN SITES: *Mission San José y San Miguel de Aguayo* (41BX3), *San Francisco de la Espada* (41BX4), *Mission San Juan de Capistrano* (41BX5), *Mission San Antonio de Valero* (the Alamo) (41BX6), *Mission Nuestra Señora de la Purísima Concepción de Acuña* (41BX12), *Mission Señora de Rosario* (41GD2), *Mission Presidio la Bahia* (Fort St. Louis) (41VT4), Presidio Nuestra Señora de Loreto de la Bahía del Espíritu Santo (41VT8), *Mission Espíritu Santo de Zuñiga* (41VT11), Shanklin (41WH8), 41DM59, and 41VT38.

SOURCES FOR ILLUSTRATIONS AND DESCRIPTIONS: Davis (1995); Duncan and others (2007); Fox (1979); Fox and Tomka (2006); Hester (1977, 1980, 1989); Hester and Whatley (1992, 1997); Hudgins (1982, 1984); Inman (1999); Lohse (1999); Perino (1991); Ricklis (2000); Tomka (2016); Jelks (1993); Schmeidlin (1997); Turner and Hester (1985, 1993, 1999); and Turner, Hester, and McReynolds (2011).

COMMENTS: This is a historic arrow point that was made by the Coahuiltecan Indians in the 1700s. It is most often found at Spanish Colonial mission sites, ranchos, and native villages.

Turner, Hester, and McReynolds (2011:194) state that "a longer, more lanceolate form found at 41VT11 may have been used by the Aranama Indians."

Daniel E. Fox (1979) discusses this type in his report on lithic artifacts at Spanish Colonial missions. In 1997, Hester and Whatley (1997) mentioned the kinds of archaeological materials found in Southern Texas.

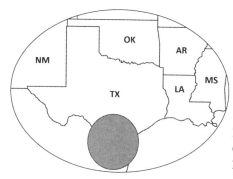

Figure 6.58. Distribution of Guerrero points (drafted by Lili Lyddon).

Mitchell (1980:23) illustrates five *Guerrero* points from Mission San Juan de Capistrano. The complete specimens vary in length from 2.0 cm to 4.0 cm and 1.2 cm to 2.2 cm in width. "Some specimens are completely bifacially thinned to the extent that all original flake surfaces have been obliterated."

Steve A. Tomka (2016:102–103) presents a detailed discussion of the *Guerrero* type based on a study of 283 specimens recovered from controlled excavations at five Spanish missions sponsored by the National Park Service. He describes them as existing in triangular and lenticular forms. The other form consists of two principal variants. He describes the first variant as having a "leaf shape characterized by a contracting stem and a widening blade toward the distal tip." "The second variant is virtually parallel for much of its length." His Figure 4 illustrates his version of how the *Guerrero* point was hafted as compared to the *Fresno* type.

Hester (1980:106) writes that *Guerrero* represents the "survival of chipped stone technology among the missionized Indians of south Texas and northeastern Mexico."

Smitty Schmeidlin (1997) reports a single *Guerrero* point at 41VT38, the presumed third location of Mission Espíritu Santo de Zuñiga (41VT11).

One *Guerrero* point was present at Presidio Nuestra Señora de Loreto de la Bahía del Espíritu Santo (41VT8). "The oblique parallel flaking served to identify this point fragment . . . as *Guerrero*" (Fox and Tomka 2006:102).

DISTRIBUTION: *Guerrero* points are found in Central Texas, Southern Texas, and northern Mexico. Robert J. Mallouf writes that is an infrequent type in the Trans-Pecos Region. Arrow points described as *Guerrero* were found at Mission de los Ais in San Augustine County (Corbin et al.1990).

Figure 6.59. Harrell points (photo courtesy of John Fish).

Harrell

ORIGINAL RECORDER: Jack Hughes (1942) described 78 specimens found at the Harrell site (41YN1) in Young County as triangular points with notches on the sides. An additional 33 points had notches in the base as well. Suhm and Krieger (1954:500) assigned the name *Harrell* to these two groups based on their first appearance at the Harrell site. Bell (1958) believes that the variation in notching represented two separate types, and he proposed *Harrell* for those with side and basal notches and *Washita* for those without basal notches.

OTHER NAMES: *Triple-Notched* point

SIMILAR TYPES: *Washita*

AGE: Suhm and Krieger (1954:500) estimate the age of *Harrell* points in Texas at circa AD 1100 to AD 1500. Elsewhere, it may be considerably older. Turner, Hester, and McReynolds (2011:196) state that it is a Late Prehistoric type that dates to circa AD 1200 to AD 1500. Crook (2017:51) dates it to circa AD 1250 to AD 1600.

DESCRIPTION: Suhm and Krieger (1954:500) describe the type as "Triangular points with edges straight to slightly convex. Two small side notches occur from one-fourth to one-half the distance from base toward tip." They provide the following dimensions:

Length: 1.5 cm to 3.5 cm
Width: 1.2 cm to 2 cm
Notches: 0.2 cm to 0.3 cm deep

CULTURAL AFFILIATION: According to Suhm and Krieger (1954:500), *Harrell* is a major type of the Antelope Focus and one of several types in the Henrietta and Wylie Foci. Duncan and others (2007:57) write that this point is "commonly associated with the Washita River, Turkey Creek, Custer, Paoli and Antelope Creek phases as well as the Edwards Complex and to some extent, the Wheeler Phase in central and western Oklahoma Farmersville Phase" (Crook 2017:51).

KNOWN SITES: Harrell (41YN1), Roark Cave (41BS3), Lubbock Lake (41LU1), 41TG91 (Creel 1990), 41SE17, 41PS194, Esquivel Burial Cache (41CR33), Baker Cave (41VV213), 41CR30, 41CR33, 41GR515, and sites in Possum Kingdom and Texarkana Reservoirs.

SOURCES FOR ILLUSTRATIONS AND DESCRIPTIONS: Bell (1958); Boyd et al. (1989); Davis (1995); Duncan and others. 2007); Krieger (1946); Suhm and Jelks (1962); Suhm and Krieger (1954:500); Kelley (1963); Hester (1980); Turner and Hester (1985, 1993, 1999); Turner and others (2011); Schneider (1966); Perino (1985); Smyers and others (2019); Word and Douglas (1970); and Glasrud and Mallouf (2013).

COMMENTS: Suhm and Krieger (195477:500) state that it appears that two subgroups or subtypes may be valid. There are those with a third notch in the center of the base and those without a basal notch. In Texas, they say that there is no difference in distribution or time between these two subtypes, although a wider study in the Plains and Southwest United States may show significant differences.

Wilson W. Crook III (2017) discusses types of damage to *Harrell* points and other Late Prehistoric types from a sample of 750 specimens.

Three *Harrell* points were found at a burial cache at site 41CR33 in Crane

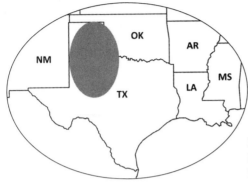

Figure 6.60. Distribution of Harrell points (drafted by Lili Lyddon).

County (Smyers et al. 2019). One specimen has a classic impact fracture. Cindy Smyers (personal communication, October 28, 2022) mentioned that *Harrell* points were found in direct association with *Washita* points at a bison kill site (41CR30).

Four *Harrel* points were found at 41DY17 and only specimen GS-22 is complete It has one pair of lateral notches and a centrally located basal notch. It measures 1.5 cm wide and 2.5 cm long. Two specimens are made from Alibates chert, and two are from Tecovas jasper (Campbell 1970).

Mallouf (personal communication, 2018) informed me of a triple-notched arrow point at 41PS194 that he believes to be a *Harrell*.

DISTRIBUTION: Suhm and Krieger (1954:500) state that Texas specimens are found across the northern part of the state and southward to the Upper Brazos and Trinity River drainages with occasional specimens found to the south. This type occurs widely in the Panhandle-Plains area where no definite complexes have been recognized. It is unknown in eastern Texas except for rare intrusive specimens. Hester (1980:106) writes that *Harrell* points are a rare occurrence in South Texas.

According to Robert J. Mallouf (personal communication, 2018), this type is found in the eastern Trans-Pecos and Big Bend regions, but it is not a common type. Turner and others (2011:196) state that it is found mainly in the Panhandle and Trans-Pecos Regions, and similar forms have been reported over much of North America. Duncan and others (2007) list specific sites in Colorado, Missouri, Oklahoma, and New Mexico where this type has been found.

Figure 6.61. Hayes points from Cherokee County (photo courtesy of TARL).

Hayes

ORIGINAL RECORDER: Newell and Krieger (1949) wrote about the Gibson Aspect in the Caddoan area, and it was in this discussion that this type was first mentioned. It was later described by Suhm and Krieger (1954:502) in *An Introductory Handbook of Texas Archeology*. The type site is George C. Davis (41CE19) in Cherokee County.

OTHER NAMES: *Hayes Barbed Point* (Bell and Hall 1953).

SIMILAR TYPES: Newell and Krieger (1949) write that *Hayes* is similar to *Alba* but is longer and slimmer with needle-like tips and diamond-shaped stems. Suhm and Krieger (1954:502) state that this point is "like *Alba* except for stem shape and 'incut tips' and to *Bonham* except for stem shape and general proportions."

AGE: Suhm and Krieger (1954:502) state that the age of this type "corresponds with the Haley Focus, AD 800 to AD 1200 or the greater part thereof." Turner and others (2011:197) refer to it as Late Prehistoric with no specific date. Webb (2000:15) writes that *Hayes* points in Louisiana "occur chiefly in early Caddo villages and burials, probably from A.D. 800 to 1100 A.D."

154 | CHAPTER 6

DESCRIPTION: Suhm and Krieger (1954:502) describe this type as having a "Slender triangular blade with edges usually concave or recurved, occasionally straight, rarely convex. Some are square shouldered without real barbs, but others have barbs sweeping out laterally rather than pointing downward. Stems are bulb-shaped in some cases but are often featured by a diamond shaped form which tiny protrusions emerge on one or more edges. Blade edges sometimes finely serrated, and tips may be sharply incut. The stems are about one-fourth to one-sixth the total length of the point." They provide the following dimensions:

Length: 3 cm to 5 cm
Width: 1.5 cm to 2 cm
Stem Length: 0.6 mm to 1.0 cm
Stem Width: 0.5 cm to 0.8 cm

CULTURAL AFFILIATION: Krieger (1946) associated it with the Late Gibson Aspect. Suhm and Krieger (1954) say it is a characteristic type of not only the Haley Focus of the Gibson Aspect, but it may occur as a minor type or intrusion in the latter phases of the Alto, Gahagan, and Spiro foci.
KNOWN SITES: In Texas it has been reported from the George C. Davis (41CE19) and A. C. Mackin (41LR39) sites. In Arkansas, specimens have been documented from Crenshaw Mounds (3 MI 0006) and various sites in Pike County. One point identified as *Hayes* was found at Belcher Mound (16 CD 13) in Caddo Parish, Louisiana.

SOURCES FOR ILLUSTRATIONS AND DESCRIPTIONS: Bell (1958); Bell and Hall (1953); Davis (1995); Duncan et al. (2007); Newell and Krieger (1949); Suhm and Krieger (1954); Suhm and Jelks (1962); Turner and Hester (1985, 1993, 1999); Turner and others (2011); Perino (1985); and Webb (1959, 2000).

COMMENTS: Newell and Krieger (1949:162) point out the "near-identity of the *Hayes* points and the common form of the classic Teotihuacan culture in central Mexico" stating that "the only real difference being that the Mexican specimens are almost always obsidian rather than flint."

Webb (2000) writes that the *Hayes* point is a companion to *Alba* and occurred mainly in early Caddo villages and burials.

Arrow Points | 155

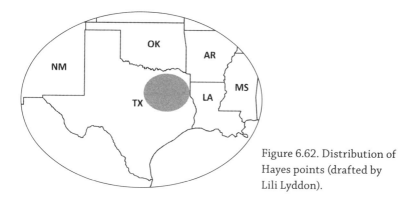

Figure 6.62. Distribution of Hayes points (drafted by Lili Lyddon).

DISTRIBUTION: It is only found in the Great Bend of the Red River in adjacent corners of Texas, Arkansas, Louisiana, and possibly Oklahoma (Suhm and Krieger 1954; Turner, Hester, and McReynolds 2011:197).

Figure 6.63. Homan point (photo courtesy of John Fish).

Homan

ORIGINAL RECORDER: W. Raymond Wood (1963) was the first to describe *Homan* based on examples found at the Crenshaw site in Miller County Arkansas. The origin of its name is not known.

OTHER NAMES: None reported.

SIMILAR TYPES: Turner and Hester (1985:180) believe *Homan* may be a variant of the *Agee* type, but they state that it does not have the needle-like point or the typically flat-tipped barb. Davis (1995:228) states that *Homan* and *Agee* points are similar in general appearance, and they may be part of a continuum. Webb (2000) compares *Homan* to *Alba* because of the triangular body and recurved edges. Its distinguishing feature is the "globular stem." The specimen illustrated here may represent a variation of the *Homan* point. It has the characteristic bulbous stem and recurved edges, but the barbs are squared, reminiscent of *Catahoula*.

AGE: Turner and Hester (1999) estimate its age as AD 1000 to AD 1300. In Louisiana, Webb (2000) dates it to circa AD 800 to AD 900.

DESCRIPTION: Davis (1995:228) describes it as triangular with a subtriangular outline. "The lateral edges are recurved, and the blade becomes wide or convex toward the distal end, tapering to a needle-like tip. The shoulders are strong with flared barbs. The barbs may have a rounded to pointed appearance. The stem is notched near the blade and the deep notches are U-shaped or V-shaped. The stem expands toward the base which is strongly convex giving the stem a bulbous appearance." In Louisiana, they are usually made of novaculite or tan chert (Webb 2000:16).

CULTURAL AFFILIATION: Woodland, Fourche Maline (Bruseth et al. 2009). They date the site to circa AD 800 to AD 900. Webb (2000) associates it with late Coles Creek ceramics in Louisiana.

KNOWN SITES: Turner and Hester (1985, 1993, 1999) do not mention any specific Texas sites. Bruseth and others (2009) illustrate two *Homan* points from the Stallings Ranch site (41LR297). Examples have been found at Crenshaw Mounds (3 MI 0006) in Arkansas and Mounds Plantation (16 CD 12) in Louisiana.

SOURCES FOR ILLUSTRATIONS AND DESCRIPTIONS: Davis (1995); Duncan et al. (2007); Perino (1968, 1985); Turner and Hester (1985, 1993, 1999); Webb (2000); Wood (1963); Turner and Smith (2002); and Bruseth et al. (2009). *Homan* is not included in Turner and others (2011).

COMMENTS: According to Turner and Hester (1985:180), this type is identified by its unusual "flared, fan-shaped" stem. *Homan* is not included in *Stone Artifacts of Texas Indians* (Turner et al. 2011).

Arrow Points | 157

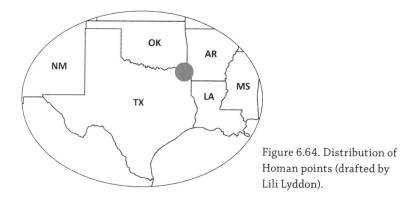

Figure 6.64. Distribution of Homan points (drafted by Lili Lyddon).

Davis (1995) believes that *Homan* may have also functioned as a ceremonial point because it has been found in caches associated with burials.

DISTRIBUTION: Northeastern Texas, Arkansas, Louisiana, and Oklahoma.

Figure 6.65. Kobs Triangular point (no image available).

Kobs Triangular

ORIGINAL RECORDER: The *Kobs* point was first mentioned by Joe Ben Wheat (1953) for examples found at Addicks Reservoir in Harris County.

OTHER NAMES: None.

SIMILAR TYPES: *Perdiz.*

AGE: Late Prehistoric.

CHAPTER 6

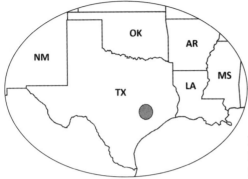

Figure 6.66. Distribution of Kobs points (drafted by Lili Lyddon).

DESCRIPTION: Wheat (1953:203) describes this provisional type as follows: The blade is "Usually concave from base to mid-blade, convex to tip; a few are straight to convex, sometimes serrated; basically triangular. The base is usually convex." He provides the following dimensions: length: 45 mm; width: 22 mm; thickness: 4 mm.

CULTURAL AFFILIATION: Unknown.

KNOWN SITES: Kobs (41HR7).

SOURCES FOR ILLUSTRATIONS AND DESCRIPTIONS: Wheat (1953:203, Plate 35).

COMMENTS: Joe Ben Wheat (1953) referred to the *Kobs Triangular* point as a provisional type.

The *Kobs Triangular point* is not included in *Stone Artifacts of Texas Indians* (Turner et al. 2011).

DISTRIBUTION: This type has only been reported at sites within the Addicks Basin Reservoir in Harris County.

Figure 6.67. Livermore points (photo courtesy of TARL).

Livermore

ORIGINAL RECORDER: J. Charles Kelley, T. N. Campbell, and Donald J. Lehmer (1940) described this point and named it for Mount Livermore in the Davis Mountains where a large cache of more than 1,200 points was found by Susan M. Jones.

It was later described and illustrated by Suhm and Krieger (1954:502–503). The find is now known as the Livermore Cache.

OTHER NAMES: *Livermore Barbed.*

SIMILAR TYPES: *Perdiz* (Greer 1968a) and *Sabinal.*

AGE: Suhm and Krieger (1954:502) estimate its age at AD 800 to AD 1200 According to Turner and others (2011:198), this is one of the earliest arrow points yet documented in the eastern Trans-Pecos region, and its age is estimated at AD 800 to AD 1350. J. Charles Kelley (1957:51) believes "that the Livermore Focus was "best developed in the Texas Trans-Pecos region during the period circa A.D. 900 to A.D. 1200 with the possibility of a still earlier appearance and a somewhat later survival in the Pecos River drainage."

DESCRIPTION: The following information is paraphrased from Davis (1995:230) who describes it as a "small to large arrow point that looks somewhat like a cross as the stem and blade are quite narrow with laterally barbed shoulders that often jut out at a ninety-degree angle to the blade

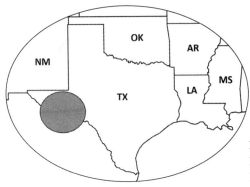

Figure 6.68. Distribution of Livermore points (drafted by Lili Lyddon).

axis. The lateral edges vary from straight or convex to concave, and they are frequently serrated. The narrow stem may be straight, contracting, or expanding toward the base that is sometimes straight to pointed or rounded with a bulbous appearance. In contrast, the stem of the *Sabinal* point expands slightly toward a relatively straight base when compared to the pointed or strongly convex basal area of the *Livermore* point. The workmanship on the *Sabinal* point is considered to be better." He does not provide dimensions.

CULTURAL AFFILIATION: Suhm and Krieger (1954:502) state that *Livermore* is a major type of the Livermore Focus, and it also extends intrusively into the Jornada Branch (Mesilla Phase) in New Mexico.

KNOWN SITES: Livermore Cache (41JD66), Wolf Den Cave (41JD191), Tall Rockshelter (41JD10), Midden Circle site (no trinomial), Roark Cave (41BS3), Squawteat Peak (41PC14), Ram's Head (41PC35), Perro Salvaje (41PC2), John Z. and Exa Means Cache (41JD212).

SOURCES FOR ILLUSTRATIONS AND DESCRIPTIONS: Bell (1960); Davis (1995); Kelley, Campbell, and Lehmer (1940); Suhm and Jelks (1962); Suhm and Krieger (1954); Kelley (1963); Greer (1968a); Turner and Hester (1985, 1993, 1999); Perino (1985); Katz (1978); Young (1981a, 1982); Jelks (1993); Jarvis and Crawford (1974); Hedrick (1989); Young (1982b); and Turner and others (2011).

COMMENTS: Many *Livermore* and *Toyah* arrow points made of local material indicating that this is a core area for Kelley's (1957) Livermore Focus.

Greer (1968b) writes about excavated ring midden sites in the Lower Pecos and Trans-Pecos regions. He refers to a type that he names *Perdiz/Livermore but* does not describe it in detail.

A possible *Livermore* point was found at 41GR33 (Boyd et al. 1989:310).

DISTRIBUTION: Suhm and Krieger (1954:502) state that it is found mainly in the central part of the Trans-Pecos region. Robert J. Mallouf (personal communication, 2018) reports *Livermore* is a type commonly found in the eastern Trans-Pecos and Big Bend regions.

Figure 6.69. Lott point (replica by Matt Soultz; photo courtesy of Brian Wootan).

Lott

ORIGINAL RECORDER: The first known reference to this type was by Ronnie Shawn (1975) who described a single specimen found at the Blue Hill site in Midland County. It was not complete, and he described it as a triangular point with convex lateral edges and a concave base. F. E. Green (1962) found the basal tang of a *Lott* point at the Lubbock Reservoir site (a.k.a. Lubbock Lake site) that was known at the time as an "informally named

162 | CHAPTER 6

point." Although the name *Lott* appeared in earlier reports, Frank A. Runkles and E. D. Dorchester (1986) are credited with officially naming and describing this point in honor of John Lott, the owner of the Lott site in Garza County.

OTHER NAMES: None reported.

SIMILAR TYPES: According to Davis (1995:232), "the *Lott* point and the *Garza* point are similar in general appearance. However, *Garza* lacks shoulders while the *Lott* point sometimes has weak barbs."

AGE: Turner, Hester, and McReynolds (2011:199) estimate its age at AD 1350 to AD 1500. Boyd (2001) places this type as protohistoric.

DESCRIPTION: Davis (1995:232) describes *Lott* as "A small point with a triangular outline. The lateral edges are straight or slightly convex and may exhibit miniature serrations. The shoulders range from weak to slightly barbed. The bifurcated stem expands toward the base and has a deep basal notch. The flared basal corners range from square to pointed. This point may be widest at the shoulders but more often at the base when the basal corners are flared." Dimensions are not given.

CULTURAL AFFILIATION: Unknown.

KNOWN SITES: Lott (41GR56), Lubbock Lake (41LU1), Floydada Country Club (41FL1), Blue Mountain Rockshelter (41RK4), Pete Creek site (41CB63), 41GR56, 41CC131, and the Wooden Bow Burial site in Floyd County (no trinomial listed).

SOURCES FOR ILLUSTRATIONS AND DESCRIPTIONS: Davis (1995); Johnson et al. (1977); Runkles and Dorchester (1986); Shawn (1975); Turner and Hester (1985, 1993, 1999); and Turner, Hester, and McReynolds (2011).

COMMENTS: Per Johnson and others (1977:88), "*Lott* points were associated with *Garza* points in the upper two occupation levels at Blue Mountain Rock Shelter."

Turner and Hester (1985:182) describe and illustrate *Lott* as a "distinctive triangular point that has an expanding stem and a central basal notch."

Fifty-six examples were found at the Lott site (Runkles and Dorchester 1986:92–93). Most of the specimens are thin and finely made from local

Arrow Points | 163

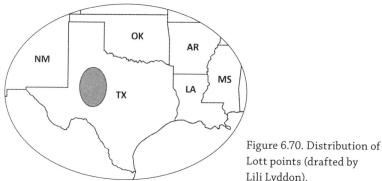

Figure 6.70. Distribution of Lott points (drafted by Lili Lyddon).

chert and flint. The points from this site cover the range of *Lott* varieties, and these variations are illustrated in Runkles and Dorchester (1986). They say that Specimen "C" in Figure 7 represents a typical *Lott* point.

Boyd (2001:11) maps the distribution of *Garza* and *Lott* points in the Texas Panhandle-Plains. He labels the Lott site as a bison kill site and hunting camp.

Lott points had also been found with *Garza* points in the upper two occupation levels at the Pete Creek site (Parsons 1967). Parker (1982) briefly discussed this point in his report on the Wooden Bow Burial site in Floyd County.

DISTRIBUTION: It is found at sites in the Llano Estacado and the rolling plains of North-Central Texas. According to Robert J. Mallouf (personal communication, 2018), this type is infrequently found in the eastern Trans-Pecos and Big Bend regions. Boyd (2001:Figure 5) depicts the distribution of *Garza* and *Lott* points in the Texas Panhandle-Plains.

Lozenge

ORIGINAL RECORDER: This point was named by James E. Corbin for examples found in the Coastal Bend area of Texas. It was formally described by Ellen Sue Turner and Thomas R. Hester (1985:182).

OTHER NAMES: None reported.

Figure 6.71. Lozenge point (photo courtesy of TARL).

SIMILAR TYPES: None reported.

AGE: *Lozenge* was in use from AD 700 to AD 1600 (Davis 1995:232).

DESCRIPTION: Turner and Hester (1985:183, 2011:200) describe *Lozenge* as "A distinctive point that is characterized by an elongated, oval to diamond-shaped outline. One-half of the point is bifacially worked, resulting in a lenticular cross-section; the opposite end is alternately beveled, usually on the right. It is not always clear which end is the distal, and which is the proximal, or if the beveling is the result of resharpening." No dimensions are given.

CULTURAL AFFILIATION: Unknown

KNOWN SITES: Kent-Crane (41AS2), McGloin Bluff (41SP11), Mitchell Ridge (41GV66).

SOURCES FOR ILLUSTRATIONS AND DESCRIPTIONS: Corbin (1974); Hester (1980); Davis (1995); Turner and Hester (1985, 1993, 1999); and Turner, Hester, and McReynolds (2011)

Arrow Points | 165

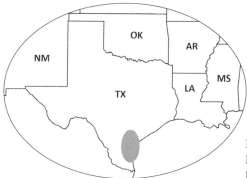

Figure 6.72. Distribution of Lozenge points (drafted by Lili Lyddon).

COMMENTS: According to Davis (1995), this point was probably hafted and used as an arrow point or hafted and used for etching or drilling. He recommends microwear analysis to make a formal determination.

Hester (1980:106) says, "They are in no way related to the lozenge-shaped *Desmuke* points of Archaic times" [sic].

DISTRIBUTION: Gulf Coast–Baffin Bay to Corpus Christi Bay (Turner et al. 2011:200).

McGloin

ORIGINAL RECORDER: James E. Corbin (1963) discusses his surveys along the northern shore of Corpus Christi Bay that yielded numerous artifacts. Six specimens did not appear to him to be examples of a defined type. They are discussed and illustrated in his Figure 1. Specimens E–G may be examples of the *McGloin* type, but they are not named as such. Ellen Sue Turner and Thomas R. Hester (1985) formally described it, and they may have named it as well. This point is named for the McGloin Bluff site where Corbin found his examples.

OTHER NAMES: None reported.

SIMILAR TYPES: According to Davis (1995), *McGloin* is similar to the *Turney* and *Maud* types. All three have a triangular outline. *McGloin*,

166 | CHAPTER 6

Figure 6.73. McGloin point (photo courtesy of TARL).

however, does not usually exhibit the very fine flaking found on the blades of *Maud* and *Turney* points.

AGE: This type has an approximate age of AD 700 to AD 1550 (Davis 1995).

DESCRIPTION: Turner, Hester, and McReynolds (2011:202) describe *McGloin* as a "triangular point that almost always has a distinctively concave, V-shaped base." No dimensions are given.

CULTURAL AFFILIATION: Unknown.

KNOWN SITES: McGloin Bluff (41SP11), Kent-Crane (41AS2), and Mud Bridge (41NU27). Possible examples were found at 41JW8 (Black 1986:64) and the Bert Johnson site (41AS1).

SOURCES FOR ILLUSTRATIONS AND DESCRIPTIONS: Martin (1930); Corbin (1974); Hester (1980); Davis (1995); Perino (1991); Turner and Hester (1985, 1993, 1999); Jelks (1993); Campbell (1952); Randall (2010); and Turner and others (2011).

COMMENTS: The Kent-Crane site is discussed by Campbell (1952) who also reported on the Johnson site (believed to be 41AS1) where possible examples of this type may have been found.

Arrow Points | 167

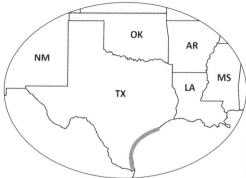

Figure 6.74. Distribution of McGloin points (drafted by Lili Lyddon).

The specimens illustrated by Perino (1991) were found by William C. Valentine of Blossom, Texas, on a beach where they were exposed by shifting sands. Other types found by him at this site include *Cameron*, *Fresno* (plain and serrated), *Lozenge*, *Padre*, *Perdiz* (plain and serrated), *Scallorn* (plain and serrated), *Starr*, and a glass arrow point (Perino 1991).

Martin (1930) illustrates a point from the Mud Bridge site on the Callo del Oso in Nueces County that resembles the *McGloin* type.

DISTRIBUTION: This type is primarily found in the Coastal Bend region of Texas, especially in the Corpus Christi Bay area.

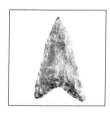

Figure 6.75. Maud point (photo courtesy of TARL).

Maud

ORIGINAL RECORDER: It was described and illustrated by Suhm and Krieger (1954). They named it for the town of Maud in Bowie County. No type site was mentioned.

OTHER NAMES: None reported.

168 | CHAPTER 6

SIMILAR TYPES: Suhm and Krieger (1954:504) state that *Maud* is similar to *Talco* "except for excessive depth of base, and the edges are usually straight rather than recurved." According to Davis (1995), *Maud* is similar in general appearance to *McGloin* and *Turney*.

AGE: Suhm and Krieger (1954:504) estimate its age at "A.D. 1300 to A.D. 1500 or the greater part thereof." Webb (2011:15) writes that *Maud* points "may occur with *Basset* points" and "are probably of the same time period."

DESCRIPTION: Suhm and Krieger (1954:504) describe this type as "Slender triangular points with edges usually straight, sometimes recurved with constriction near middle. Bases deeply concave to deeply V-shaped. Commonly very finely chipped, thin, flat, with edges minutely serrated." Webb (2000:15) states that the *Maud* point in Louisiana was typically made from flakes of local materials. He says that they are not as frequent in Louisiana as in East Texas. They provide the following dimensions:

Length: 2.0 cm to 5.5 cm
Width: 1.0 to 1.5 cm
Basal Concavity: 0.3 cm to 0.7 cm

CULTURAL AFFILIATION: This is a common type in the Belcher and Texarkana foci, and it extends to the easternmost components of the Titus Focus and all of the Fulton Aspect (Suhm and Krieger 1954).

KNOWN SITES: Jones Hill (41PK8), 41CS87, 41CS91, Tuck Carpenter (41CP5), Williams site (41CP10), Alex Justiss (41TT13), Gilbert (41RA13), Dan Holdeman (41RR11), Roitsch, formerly Sam Kaufman (41RR16), Goldsmith (41WD208), GG site (41UR136), 41SE17, and Lake Monticello. In Oklahoma, examples have been recovered from the A. W. Davis site (34MC6) and Roden (34MC253). Webb (1959:162) illustrates a *Maud* point from Belcher Mound (16 CD 13) in Caddo Parish, Louisiana.

SOURCES FOR ILLUSTRATIONS AND DESCRIPTIONS: Allen et al. (1967); Bell (1958); Davis (1995); Duncan et al. (2007); Suhm and Jelks (1962); Suhm and Krieger (1954); Perino (1985); Tully (1986); Turner and Hester (1985, 1993, 1999); Turner, Hester, and McReynolds (2011); and Webb (1959, 1963, 2000); McCormick (1973); Jelks (1993); and Turner and Smith (2002).

Arrow Points | 169

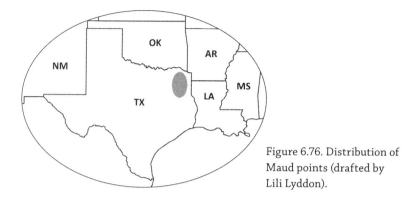

Figure 6.76. Distribution of Maud points (drafted by Lili Lyddon).

COMMENTS: *Maud* predates *Talco* where they are found associated with burials. Davis also states that this type was used as a grave offering in the Caddoan culture (Davis 1995:236).

Thurmond (1985:189–191) writes that *Maud* is often associated with arrow point types *Bassett*, *Reed*, and *Talco*. It does not appear in Turner, Hester, and McReynolds (2011).

DISTRIBUTION: It is found in the northeastern corner of Texas and adjacent corners of Arkansas and Louisiana (Suhm and Krieger 1954). Webb (2000) says that this type is less common in Louisiana than in Eastern Texas.

Means

ORIGINAL RECORDER: Robert J. Mallouf (2013) described and named this point for twenty-two specimens found at the John Z. and Exa Means Cache and eight specimens in private collections. This type was named for the landowners, Alfred and Ruth Means of Valentine, Texas.

OTHER NAMES: *Scallorn* variants.

SIMILAR TYPES: None reported.

AGE: The *Means* point is believed to date to sometime within the Late Prehistoric period (circa AD 700 to AD 1350). This statement is based on average size, thickness, stylistic parameters, and its direct association with

170 | CHAPTER 6

Figure 6.77. Means points from the Trans-Pecos (no image available).

Livermore and *Toyah* points in the John Z. and Exa Means Cache (Mallouf 2013). Corrick (2000) and Cloud (2001) document radiocarbon dates for *Toyah* points, and they propose that this type was most commonly used circa AD 1150 to AD 1350. They suspect that the terminal age for *Means* points is within that span.

DESCRIPTION: Mallouf (2013:198) describes it in the following: "*Means* arrow points typically have long, narrow blades with moderately to strongly serrated lateral edges. Lateral blade edges, which are typically straight but may also be recurved, are in some instances strongly beveled to obtain the desired narrow configuration. Distal blade tip beveling is common, sometimes resulting in a tiny, perforator-like tip, but with no evidence of use wear. Base width of the blade at its juncture with the barbs roughly equates to neck width below the barbs but may be slightly wider or slightly narrower. Well-defined barbs project laterally at roughly right angles to the long axis of the point. Specimen width at the barbs roughly equates with the maximum width of the stem. In rare instances, strong shoulders may supplant true barbs. Stem necks are short and fairly wide relative to the overall length of the point, with neck width roughly equivalent to the basal blade width. Stems expand quickly and strongly from the stem neck, and basal edges of stems are commonly straight, but may be slightly convex or slightly concave. Width of the basal stem edge often approximates specimen width at the barbs." This point is lenticular in cross-section. Mallouf (2013:200) provides the following dimensions:

Length: 22.3 mm to 36.1 mm
Width: 10.0 mm to 14.5 mm
Thickness: 2.3 mm to 4.4 mm

Arrow Points | 171

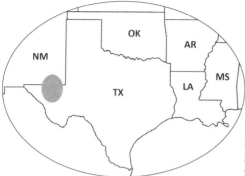

Figure 6.78. Distribution of Means points (drafted by Lili Lyddon).

CULTURAL AFFILIATION: The occurrence of *Means* points in direct association with *Livermore* and *Toyah* in the John Z. and Exa Means Cache suggests cultural affiliation with the Livermore Phase of the Late Prehistoric period. Because *Means* points were absent from the Livermore Cache and from Livermore assemblages at Wolf Den Cave and Tall Rockshelter, more research is needed before this type can definitely be considered to be associated with the Livermore Phase. This information was taken from Mallouf (2013).

KNOWN SITES: John Z. and Exa Means Cache (41JD212), Wolf Den Cave (41JD191), and Tall Rockshelter (41JD10).

SOURCES FOR ILLUSTRATIONS AND DESCRIPTIONS: Wheaton (2009); Mallouf (2012, 2013); and Turner, Hester, and McReynolds (2011).

COMMENTS: Wheaton (2009) illustrates three specimens identified by him as "*Scallorn* variants" that he considers are good examples of *Means* points. All are from mixed midden components containing ceramics in the vicinity of the southern Guadalupe Mountains.

DISTRIBUTION: This point occurs primarily in the central and northern areas of the eastern Trans-Pecos region and probably northward into southeastern New Mexico. More specifically, they are known to occur in the Davis and Guadalupe Mountains, Lobo Valley, Salt Basin, Glass Mountains, and areas north to the Toyah Basin. One specimen was found in Big Bend National Park. The western extent of distribution is currently unknown. This information was taken from Mallouf (2013).

Figure 6.79. Metal points (photo courtesy of Michael Boutwell).

Metal

ORIGINAL RECORDER: Not applicable.

Names for Metal Points: Under the umbrella of metal points, several types have been identified from sites in Texas. They include *Benton, Harbison, Fillinger,* and *Lipantitlan,* and possibly *Watson*. There may be others, but I did not find them. A metal point known as *Claremore* point has been identified in Oklahoma.

Benton

The namesake for this point is the late Joe Benton, a pioneer cattle and oil man of Nocona, Texas, who was an avid collector of artifacts from the Spanish Fort sites in Montague County, Texas, and Jefferson County, Oklahoma. It has been found in sites along the Arkansas, Brazos, Red, Sabine, and Trinity Rivers in Texas and also in Oklahoma and Louisiana.

Perino (1968:10) writes that this type is based on 600 specimens from these sites. It dates to the Norteño Focus that lasted from the middle of the eighteenth century to the middle of the nineteenth century.

Nine metal arrow points were found at the Gilbert site (41RA13) in Rains County. They are described and illustrated by Harris and others (1967:Figure 25). "Some of the types are like others found at Norteño Focus sites that a name was considered to be warranted. Three were designated as *Benton Type A* and *Benton Type B*. The remainder are referred to as miscellaneous. Three of the points from the Gilbert site were made from scrap pieces of brass from kettles, while two were worked from decorated gun fittings such as trigger guard bows, side plates, or butt plates The most unique metal point in the sample was made from the engraved brass butt plate finial of a trade gun" (Harris et al. 1967). *Benton* points were generally made locally using scrap iron as opposed to commercially made specimens used as trade goods by Europeans (Taylor 1989:18). Bell and Cross (1980:101) write that *Benton* points were made by the protohistoric Wichita in southern Oklahoma and northern Texas. Perino (1968:10–11) discusses and illustrates five Type A *Benton* points and five Type B *Benton* points from sites in Oklahoma and Texas.

Harbison

This point was found on the surface as an isolated find in Medina County. It was named by C. K. Chandler (1993) in honor of Ray Harbison who found it. It is made of thin iron and was cut out with a chisel. There is no evidence of notching on the stem edges.

Fillinger

This point was found on the surface as an isolated find in Medina County. It was named by C. K. Chandler (1993) in honor of Tom Fillinger who found it. Its dimensions are:

46 mm (length)
18 mm (width)
2.4 mm to 3 mm (thickness)
21 mm (stem length)
25 mm (blade length)
8.5 mm (base width)

174 | CHAPTER 6

It weighs 5.8 g and is made of iron that appears to have been cut with metal shears. There is no evidence of notching on the stem edges.

Lipantitlan

Lipantitlan was first reported by Skip Kennedy and Jim Mitchell (1988) for a type found in the vicinity of Fort Lipantitlan in Nueces County. The preform for this type was chiseled from sheet iron scrap or barrel hoops. It was made by the Lipan Apache during the 1830s. These points may have been traded to the Indians for meat from their hunts. It is illustrated and described by Kennedy and Mitchell (1988) and Perino (1991).

SIMILAR TYPES: Other metal points.

AGE: Historic Period. Paul R. Katz and Paul D. Lukowski (1981) write that the use of metal implements in the Trans-Pecos area of Texas began circa AD 1500. The metal point at 41PS16 was associated with ceramics believed to date sometime after AD 1650. Bell and Cross (1980:101) state that "In general, the Oklahoma metal arrow points date after AD 1750, and they were commonly used for perhaps 100 years or more after that date." Metal points continued to be used until the early part of the twentieth century even after firearms were adopted. Specimens were recovered from the site of the Custer battle at the Little Big Horn in Montana and other military engagements with Indians.

CULTURAL AFFILIATION: Metal arrow points were widely used by Indian tribes in Texas during the historic period. The Apache and Comanche (McReynolds and Kumpe 2008) and the Tonkawa (Jones 1969) are perhaps the best known and documented bands during this time.

KNOWN SITES: 41BI34, 41BX5, 41CB29, 41ME74, 41ML38, Ayers site (41MU12), 41MU16, 41NU14, 41NU54, 41NU209, 41PS16, Gilbert site (41RA13), 41SE17, 41SF18, 41TA29, 41TA58, 41WH8, 41PR92, and 41TV1405. Brass arrow points have been reported at sites with *Leon Plain* sherds (Chandler 1986:29).

SOURCES FOR ILLUSTRATIONS AND DESCRIPTIONS: Baker and Campbell (1959); Bauman (1988, 1989, 1991); Bell and Cross (1980); Brown and Taylor (1989); Chandler (1984b, 1986, 1989, 1993); Chandler and Kumpe (1994);

Collins and Collins (1990); Davis (1995); Fox (1982); Goebel and others (1987); Greer (1967); Gregory (1982); Harris et al. (1967); Hester (1968, 1970a, 1980); Jelks (1967); Johnson (1987); Kennedy and Mitchell (1988); McReynolds (1982); McReynolds and Kumpe (2008); Mitchell (1974, 1980); Mitchell and Highley (1982); Mounger (1959); Parker (1978, 1983, 1985); Perino (1968, 1971, 1985); Randall (1970); Runkles (1982); Schuetz (1969); Smith (1984); Walters and Rogers (1975); Thompson (1980); Saner et al. (2004); Taylor (1989); Word and Campbell (1962); and 41TV1405.

COMMENTS: Texas Indians began to use metal for arrow points once Europeans introduced this material. Many of the metal points were made available to tribes as trade goods. Points manufactured by the Indians were made from any form of scrap metal available such as sheet iron, copper, files, door hinges, and cuperous metals such as brass cartridge cases. Barrel hoops were the preferred raw material when it was available (Parker 1983). McReynolds and Kumpe (2008) discuss various historic Indian groups in Texas that probably used metal points.

Metal arrow points can be found in various types of metal, sizes, and shapes. Regarding trade points, Hester (1980:108) writes: "The most common form has a long narrow blade and a rectangular stem with notching on both edges."

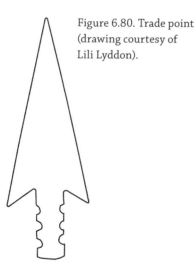

Figure 6.80. Trade point (drawing courtesy of Lili Lyddon).

176 | CHAPTER 6

The methods used to fashion points from metal are unlike knappers working with stone or glass. Metal points were commonly made by local blacksmiths and Indians who had learned the trade.

The Smithsonian Institution published *Notes on the History and Material Culture of the Tonkawa Indians* authored by William K. Jones (1969). Among the collection of artifacts are several bows and arrows with metal points. They are described in the chapter titled "Object Description" (Jones 1969:74–75). Arrows and bows are illustrated in figures 2–5 (pages not numbered). Three complete arrows with fletching are illustrated in Figure 2 and described as: "Three arrows were in the quiver." "The top arrow is 67.2 cm long and 0.73 cm in diameter. Its metal head is 4.45 cm long and has a serrated shank. The arrowhead is lashed to the shaft with sinew." "The feathers are turkey (*Meleagris pt. gallopavo*) and turkey vulture (*Cathartes aura septentrionalis*)." The middle arrow has a point 4.3 cm long and a plain shank. It was attached to the shaft with sinew. The bottom arrow has a point 3.59 cm long with a plain shank. It was also attached to the shaft with sinew. A Tonkawa arrow housed at the Peabody Museum in Salem, Massachusetts, is illustrated in Figure 3. A Tonkawa bow and five arrows are illustrated in Figure 5 (USNM negative 2053-H).

A. J. Taylor (1989) conducted an extensive study of metal arrow points. In all, she has described over 700 specimens from Texas and other states. Her unpublished manuscript is on file at TARL and titled "A Preliminary Study of Metal Arrow Points." She presents a thorough discussion of the methods of manufacture of metal points, their dispersal through trade, and discussions of variations by regions of North America. It is well illustrated.

Taylor (1989:28) writes that shears were likely used to "cut a metal strip uniformly into roughly formed points." Some were shaped by chisels. Once a piece of metal has been cut to the desired shape, the stem and/or blade were sometimes altered to create fine, irregular cut marks that were probably made with a knife or some other sharp instrument such as a saw blade. These alternations are referred to by Baker and Campbell (1959:51) as "hack marks." Taylor (1989:4) prefers the term "serrated" and writes that the notches may have been created by filing or a chisel. Asymmetrical points are believed by some to have been made by Indians rather than Europeans.

An article by Brown and Taylor (1989) is the only published account by Ms. Taylor that I am aware of. Apparently, the article was a revision of a class paper she wrote that reviewed published reports of historic North American metal arrow points.

Grinnell (1962:71) mentions the practice of sharpening of iron points with a file.

Jean Louis Berlandier (1969:48) wrote about the Indians he encountered between AD 1828 and AD 1829. Regarding the manufacture of metal points, he writes that "The natives make most of their own weapons.... In the villages they buy iron barrel hoops which they cut and work into heads for their arrows."

Robert J. Mallouf photographed a large collection of metal points collected by James Davis in Sterling County. Some are too large to have functioned as arrow points.

Carl P. Russel (1967) presents historical accounts of the manufacture and trade of metal arrow points throughout North America as well as illustrations of certain specimens. It is his opinion that conformity to tribal tradition was evidenced by markings on the arrow shaft and fletching rather than the shape of the point. He (Russel 2004) also describes four metal arrow points from South Central Texas.

As stated, many metal points used by the Indians of North America were maintained through trade. In some cases, the manufacturer's trademark appears on the blade. Examples of known trademarks are "H. Murphy, Harvard, Mass.," J. Ward, Riverside," and J. Russel & Co." (Taylor 1989: Figure 7).

Baker and Campbell (1959) have stated that it is difficult at times to distinguish between metal points made by Europeans and Indians. They discuss a collection of 53 metal arrow points found in the Texas and Oklahoma panhandles. Fifty-one are made of iron, while the remainder are brass and copper. The collection is available for viewing at No Man's Land Historical Museum in Goodwell, Oklahoma. They assigned 46 specimens to four morphological categories and identified the remainder as "miscellaneous forms." Their study is provided in detail in Taylor's (1989) unpublished manuscript. She also illustrates the collection. Metal arrow points were also produced by commercial cutlery firms and local blacksmiths (Brown and Taylor 1989).

178 | CHAPTER 6

In Corbin's (1974:47) article titled "A Model for Cultural Succession for the Coastal Bend Area of Texas," he does not mention metal arrow points per se, but he discusses the importance of European objects obtained by the local Indians. "It has been mentioned that there are sites in this vicinity which contain aboriginal materials mixed with the remains of European manufactured goods. Thus, at this point in time (circa A.D. 1700) we are dealing with the cultural remains of a people who were beginning to obtain goods from the French and the Spanish (either in person or from shipwrecks) and these contacts should be recorded to some extent in the historical record."

In 1999, Heinz W. Pysczyk published *Historic Period Metal Points and Arrows, Alberta, Canada: A Theory for Aboriginal Arrow Design on the Great Plains*. It is a useful source with information relevant to Texas. The utility and design of metal points are compared to their stone counterparts. He states in his abstract that "This Study considers whether the design and performance of the Aboriginal arrow on the Great Plains changed after the arrival of the Europeans." "On the northern Great Plains, Aboriginal people used metal projectile points that were shaped differently, were larger (longer and wider), and weighed more than Late Prehistoric stone projectile points. Some differences in projectile point attributes were related to differences in other parts of the arrow between the two periods. Despite these differences in the size, balance and design of arrows from the two periods, their basic performance and that of the respective bows from which they were shot were remarkably similar."

Hester's (1980:160–164) book, *Digging into South Texas Prehistory: A Guide for Amateur Archaeologists*, presents a discussion of the historic period, in which he writes, "Up to the present, few clearly identifiable Indian occupation sites of the Historic era have been found. There have been a few sites at which metal arrow points or glass trade beads have been discovered, but these have not been linked to occupational remains that were also present."

In southern Texas, metal arrow points are primarily associated with missions. Taylor (1989:28) writes that "Each presidio and many of the missions in Texas and in New Mexico as well, had its own blacksmith to make and repair metal tools, weapons, and ornaments."

Greer (1967) reports on a metal arrow point from the Alamo in Bexar County, Texas.

Jimmy Mitchell (1980) authored an article on five metal points from *San Juan de Capistrano*. Four are arrow points, and one is a spear point made of copper believed to be Indian made. An iron arrow point was found that Schuetz (1969:49) believes to be of Towakoni origin. It is strikingly similar to a stemmed point found in Lamb County (Randall 1970).

T. N. Campbell (1988) and Thomas R. Hester (1989) discuss the life of the mission Indians and their material culture on the border of South Texas and northeastern Mexico.

Hester and Eaton (1983) present a guide to literature on northern Mexico and the American Southwest. This source contains information relevant to the subject of this book.

Bell and Cross (1980:101) write that "Most of the metal points [in Oklahoma] were made from scrap pieces of metal that were cut and shaped by the Indians. They are commonly of iron or steel although scraps of brass from gun parts were sometimes used. The metal iron hoops were especially useful for making points as they were thin and required less effort in their manufacture. In later times, metal arrow points were being manufactured and sold by Indian traders." They state that "There is considerable variation in the outline and size of the metal arrow points. The size range tends to fall between 35 mm and 95 mm with most examples measuring around 60 mm."

Metcalf (1963) also noted a change in the size of metal points as the historic period progressed. His findings were based on the excavation of an Arikara Indian village in North Dakota. He writes that they became larger and heavier over time. He also mentioned that some weighed more than their stone counterparts.

Clinton L. Smith and Jefferson D. Smith (2002) are the authors of *The Boy Captives*, the story of two brothers who were captured by a band of Comanches in 1869 near San Antonio and lived as Indians for several years. Clinton Smith discusses the use of metal points in the following: "Here we met with another party of Mexicans, with their trading clothes on. This time they brought with them all kinds of paint, knives, steel with which to make arrow points and other trinkets" (Smith and Smith 1977:64). "One

180 | CHAPTER 6

of the Indians happened to have a file which he used in making arrows" (Smith and Smith 1977:147). "Many people have asked me if we used stone arrow spikes. We knew nothing about this kind of arrowhead, for they belonged to tribes of a former age. The Mexican traders also brought in iron or steel arrow spikes ready-made" (Smith and Smith 1977:159).

Bauman (1988) found a brass arrow point near the Bluntzer site in Nueces County, and he mentions the possibility of a very active trade relationship between the local Indians and settlers based on the manufacture of metal arrow points. He cites three possible places where this could have taken place, a blacksmith shop at Fort Lipantitlan, a possible shop at the Bluntzer site, and one in the town of San Patricio. This statement is based, in part, on the fact that twelve metal arrow points had been found in this area.

A metal arrow point was found at site 41BI34 in the MacKenzie Reservoir (Willey and Hughes 1978). This stemmed iron arrow point was found on the surface. Its edges are beveled, and the stem edges have been sawed to form "toothed" notches.

One of the more interesting finds is a metal arrow point embedded in a log house in Travis County (Collins and Collins 1990). The point was discovered during restoration of the Moore-Hancock house (41TV1405). Archival research suggests that the arrow with this point was fired at the house sometime between the 1840s and 1850s.

Three unfinished metal points and three cut metal fragments were found at site 41CB29 in Crosby County just off the rim of the caprock in the southern part of the county (Parker 1983). The size of the three points is identical except two are missing the distal tip. Parker believes they may have been manufactured by the Comanche between AD 1750 and AD 1875. He says that there were three groups in the area at the time that could have made and used these points. They are the Comanche, Lipan Apache, and Mexican Comancheros who were known to have traded metal points to the Indians.

Parker (1978, 1985) also reported 24 iron arrow points and one lance blade as surface finds in Crosby County and vicinity.

Mitchell (1980:20) writes that "At least three other metal points were recovered at Juan de Capistrano." These specimens are thought to be of Apache origin. This is because this mission was attacked by the Apache. One point was embedded in a human vertebra, and this suggests violence associated with a raid against the mission (Mitchell 1980). These three points conform to the shapes and styles of the area known as Apachería as defined by Thompson (1980).

Schuetz (1969) states that metal points were found at Fort Belknap on the Brazos River where the Towakoni and other tribes were held in the 1840s and 1850s. One metal point has been typed as *Lipantitlan* (see previous discussion) based on examples found at or near this fort in Nueces County (Kennedy and Mitchell 1988). The Coastal Bend Archaeological Society recovered seven metal arrow points from the site of the fort. Kennedy and Mitchell (1988) report the finding of eight points. It has been suggested that the metal points from the fort date to the early period of the fort (1831–1835) and were probably manufactured there for trade with the Lipan Apache.

Baker and Campbell (1959) state that the criteria for distinguishing between metal points made by Europeans and Indians are very inexact. An in-depth article describing the probable method of manufacture of metal arrow points was authored by Brown and Taylor (1989).

David Keller found and recorded an arrow point made of a cuperous metal, either brass or copper in 1938 at the Coppenbarger site in Presidio County on the surface of a badly eroded surface that was first documented as a site by J. Charles Kelley. This is a site rich in ceramics. Kelley collected approximately 3,800 sherds, some of which dated to sometime after AD 1650. The site is on private property, and the artifacts are in the personal collection of the landowners. The specimen described above was temporally curated at the Center for Big Bend Studies in Alpine, Texas, at the time of this writing.

Seven metal points reportedly found opposite the mouth of Live Oak Creek on the west side of the Pecos River are illustrated by Walters and Rogers (1975). A large metal point from the same area is depicted in Walters and Rogers (1975) who also found three metal points near Iraan, Texas, in Crockett County.

At site 41SE17 in Stephens County, a point made from a sheet of copper or brass was found in a small fire pit with a small snub-nosed end-scraper of clear glass. This feature is described by Forrester (1987b:13) as "at least a minor occupation in the Historic period."

Saner and others (2004) published an article titled "Four Metal Pro-

182 | CHAPTER 6

jectile Points from the Hill Country of South Central Texas" in *Ancient Echoes*, the journal of the Hill Country Archeological Association. They describe and illustrate examples from Kerr, Kimble, and Real Counties. The four points were measured and examined under a 40X microscope and weighed [weights not given.]

Bob Bennett (1956) authored a history of Kerr County in which he described a raid near Kerrville by a group of Indians in 1857 who were believed to be Comanches. Bennett (1956:178) recounts the unfortunate events that caused a Mr. Kelso to suffer a wound from an arrow for twenty years. "When Kelso drew the arrow from the wound during the fight and threw it down, he did not notice that the spike failed to come out with the shaft. For twenty years the wound did not heal until by an operation the iron arrowhead was discovered and removed."

Jim Mitchell and Lynn Highley (1982:21–23) mention a metal point they examined in a local collection belonging to Bromley F. Cooper. It is believed that this specimen was found in the early 1900s by Theo Buhler Jr. in Victoria County. The exact location of the find was not disclosed to the authors who point out the significance of reporting on private collections. It weighs 4 grams, and its dimensions are provided in the following:

Total length: 4.6 cm (part of tip missing)
Maximum width: 1.8 cm
Thickness: 0.15 cm
Width of stem at neck: 0.8 cm
Width of stem at base: 0.5 cm

Chandler (1993:29–32) discusses four metal points in Medina County. Three are arrow points, and the other one is believed to have functioned as a lance based on its size. All four are made of iron and illustrated in his Figure 1. Specimen "A" came from the surface of 41ME74 and is not named as a type. Specimen "B" was an isolated find by Tom Fillinger and is referred to as the *Fillinger* type. Specimen "C" is an example of the *Harbinger* type. It was found on a high bank above Seco Creek as an isolated find by Ray Harbison. The lance point was a surface find in a cultivated field in 1992 by Malcom Watson. When Chandler plotted the locations of these points, he concluded that they appear to follow one of the earliest roads from Mexico to Texas.

Arrow Points | 183

He (Chandler 1984b:13–16) discusses and illustrates two metal points from Central Texas with expanding and straight stems. Both are in private collections. The expanding stem point was a surface find by John Scott in Comanche County between Rush Creek and the Leon River. Chandler (1984:13) describes it as "made from thin sheet metal and appears to have been cut to shape with some form of metal chisel working against an anvil." "The expanding stem and sharp barbs of this point make it fairly unusual and thus unusual to document. Most Texas metal arrow points are relatively straight stemmed, some with rounded bases and some with straight bases; an example of the latter type is a point from the Meyer collection." It weighs 6 grams. Its dimensions are as follows:

Length: 55 mm
Maximum width: 17 mm
Maximum thickness: 1.75 mm

The second point is made of iron and has a straight stem. Armin Elmendorf is credited with finding it on the banks of the Pedernales River. "The stem is 23 mm long and 8 mm wide. Both stem edges have several small, shallow notches, six on one side and seven on the other. Both blade edges have been thinned (sharpened) from both faces and this appears to have been done with a file." The blade edges exhibit irregularities due to erosion. Its other dimensions are as follows:

Length: 52 mm
Width: 17 mm
Thickness: 2 cm

Site 41PR92 is a lithic scatter in Parker County. Two metal points were found at this site (Glasgow 2011:47). The landowner found a brass arrow point that was shallowly buried (specimen a). It measures 68 mm long, 19 mm wide, and 3 mm thick. Marvin Glasgow visited the site and found a metal point on the surface (specimen b). Its dimensions are 44 mm long and 16 mm at its widest point. Thickness not determined.

A complete iron metal point was found at site 41BI34 in Briscoe County. It is described by Hughes and Willey (1978:262) as "asymmetrical." "From tip to shoulder the point is 28 mm, from base to shoulder 12 mm, maximum stem width 7 mm, and minimum stem width 6 mm." The authors

184 | **CHAPTER 6**

illustrate it in Figure 94c. The two edges have been bifacially beveled. The stem edges are notched.

Patsy Goebel, Robert Goebel, and Jim Mitchel (1987) describe and illustrate an unusual metal arrow point from McCulloch County found on a ridge near the San Saba River. It is part of a collection of lithic artifacts that included a *Scallorn* arrow point and some earlier Archaic types. The site of the find is known locally as "Comanche Hill." The shape of the point when found is described by the authors as a "stemless triangular blade made of iron." It has an irregular basal notch that is somewhat off center. The authors conclude that it is "likely that the point was originally a stemmed form since a close examination of the notch reveals chisel cut marks on the base of the blade, but not in the basal notch. The point was probably formed by chiseling it from a thin, flat sheet of iron; there are no hammer marks which would indicate it had been flattened (as from a barrel hoop or other curved form)."

Ray Smith (1984) documents and illustrates three metal arrow points reportedly found in Uvalde County in the 1950s by Billy Evans. The provenience is not known and, at the time of Smith's article, they were in a private collection. Smith (1984:28) writes: "The three specimens are all heavily rusted iron points with various degrees of serration on the stem." The largest specimen (Figure 2a) "appears to have been made from a flat metal sheet; it shows very slight sharpening of the blade edges toward the point and notches have been filled into the stem, presumably to facilitate hafting. The base appears to be snapped off. The surfaces of the point are heavily rusted, and an irregular hole is obvious in the central portion of the blade. This hole measures 7 mm by 6.5 mm; it is not clear whether this hole was eroded through or was intentionally punched." Its other dimensions are as follows:

Length: 78 mm
Maximum blade width: 20.5 mm
Blade length: 63 mm
Stem length: 15 mm
Stem width: 9.5 mm

"The second specimen (Figure 2b) is smaller and damaged at the tip, where the metal was first bent and then broken off" [*sic*]. "The upper edges of the blade evidence a slight sharpening, and the stem appears to have been chisel cut and snapped off. There are slight horizontal hack marks on both side of the stem for notching. . . . The point is not entirely flat in cross-section suggesting that the metal was beaten flat from some other shape." Dimensions are as follows:

Length: 48.5 mm
Maximum blade width: 18 mm
Blade length: 38.5 mm
Stem length: 10 mm
Stem width: 7 mm

"The third specimen (Figure 2c) is the smallest of the three." "This specimen was made from a flat piece of metal; the base appears to have been snapped off; and the shoulders were chisel cut. This specimen also has a hole in the blade but, unlike the first specimen, the hole is very regular in outline (a square shape with rounded corners) and appears to be punched out. The hole is 4.5 mm in diameter. The stem of this iron point has hack marks which are angled; this notching or serration occurs on both sides of the stem, presumably to aid the securing of hafting." Dimensions are as follows:

Length: 41 mm
Maximum blade width: 18 mm
Blade length: 33 mm
Blade thickness: 1 mm
Stem length: 8 mm
Stem width: 8 mm
Thickness: 1.5 mm

Malcolm Johnson (1987:37–39) describes and illustrates two metal points at the site of the old community of Osage in Colorado County in the 1930s by a local resident. Both points, according to the author, appear to have been made from flat pieces of scrap iron. Because the thickness of the points is not equal, the assumption is made that they were created from separate pieces of iron. The creator of these points is not clear. Specimen "Figure 2a" is believed to have been cut with a chisel against an anvil or stone "as the cuts are fairly clean." "Apparently, it was first cut into a

186 | CHAPTER 6

triangular shape, and then the basal corners were cut away, to leave the forward sloping shoulders, and more or less straight-sided stem with a square base. Then the blade was bifacially sharpened along both lateral edges, either with a metal file or a coarse grinding stone."

"The second point (Figure 2b) exhibits a different style of workmanship. In the center of the base is a portion of a drilled or punched hole for a rivet or small bolt. The hole measured approximately 6 mm (7/32 inch) diameter." The material it was made from was not determined, but the metal bands from a large trunk or chest is considered a possibility. The author also states that "it is not clear if the cutting was done by a chisel or some combination of chiseling and sawing. The corners of the square shoulders appear to have been slightly rounded off. The distal tip was fashioned to a bluntly rounded shape instead of to a sharp point. This shaping of the blade seems to have been accomplished by heavy drilling or grinding, but only unifacially. The opposite or bottom side of this point is flat and is not ground or sharpened."

Los Adaes was the capital of Tejas (now Texas) on the frontier of New Spain from 1729 to 1770. The area included Mission San Miguell de Cuellar de Los Adaes and Presidio Nuestra Señora del Pilar de Los Adaes. The name *Adaes* refers to the Indigenous Indians who were associated with the mission. It is now a historic site open to visitors. George Avery (1995) summarizes the historical and archaeological components of the previous investigations at the site by Hiram F. Gregory (1980, 1982) in 1979 and 1981–1982. Pertinent to this report is the finding of two iron arrow points. They are not discussed in detail, and only one is illustrated (Avery 1995:Figure 15).

A complete iron metal point was found at site 41BI34 in Briscoe County. It is described by Hughes and Willey (1978:262) as "asymmetrical." "From tip to shoulder the point is 28 mm, from base to shoulder 12 mm, maximum stem width 7 mm, and minimum stem width 6 mm." The authors illustrate it in Figure 94c. The two edges have been bifacially beveled. The stem edges are notched

Dwain Rogers of Temple, Texas, has a large collection of metal points from Texas and other states. Of special interest is a trade point that bears the trademark Remington (personal observation, July 13, 2022).

Arrow Points | 187

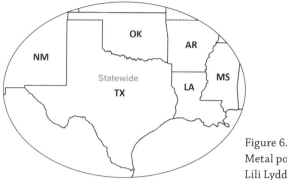

Figure 6.81. Distribution of Metal points (drafted by Lili Lyddon).

A copper arrow point is on display at the Bullock Texas State History Museum in Austin as part of a loan by TARL.

A metal knife was found at Presidio Nuestra Señora de Loreto de la Bahía del Espíritu Santo (Fox and Tomka 2006:Figure 26). Despite the fact that no metal arrow points were present, the technology existed for their production.

DISTRIBUTION: Metal points have been documented throughout Texas in the following counties: Aransas, Atascosa, Bell, Bexar, Briscoe, Burnet, Coke, Colorado, Comanche, Crockett, Crosby, Dimmit, Floyd, Garza, Gillespie, Goliad, Hardeman, Hood, Kendall, Kerr, Lamb, Live Oak, McCulloch, McMullen, Medina, Menard, Milam, Montague, Nueces, Parker, Presidio, Rains, San Patricio, Shackelford, Stephens, Sterling, Taylor, Terrell, Travis, Uvalde, Val Verde, Victoria, Wharton, Young, and Zapata. Examples are also known from sites in the adjacent states of Arkansas, Louisiana, New Mexico, and Oklahoma.

Moran

ORIGINAL RECORDER: *Moran* was named by Robert E. Forrester (1987a) for specimens found at the Salt Prong Burial site near Moran, Texas, in Shackelford County.

OTHER NAMES: None reported.

188 | CHAPTER 6

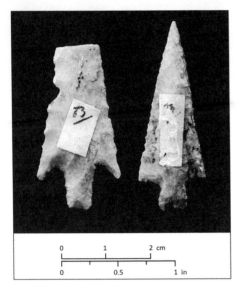

Figure 6.82. Moran points (photo courtesy of TARL).

SIMILAR TYPES: *Moran* is similar to *Bonham* but is bigger, has larger serrations, and does not have the strongly recurved sides found in some of the *Bonham* examples. They are often found with *Chadbourne* points.

AGE: According to Turner, Hester, and McReynolds (2011:204), this point is believed to have been used from circa AD 700 to AD 1200 based on the presence of "*Scallorn*-like" points found in association with *Moran* points in burials at the Salt Prong site (41SF18).

DESCRIPTION: Turner and others (2011:204) describe this point as "slender, exceptionally well made, and often have straight, serrated lateral edges. The shoulders are sometimes squared but occasionally have small barbs. The stem is narrow (5 to 7 mm in width), parallel edged, and 4 to 9 mm long. The base is straight."

CULTURAL AFFILIATION: Unknown.

KNOWN SITES: Salt Prong Burial site (41SF18) and 41TA58

SOURCES FOR ILLUSTRATIONS AND DESCRIPTIONS: Forrester (1951, 1987a), Perino (1991), Shafer (1969), Turner and Hester (1993, 1999), and

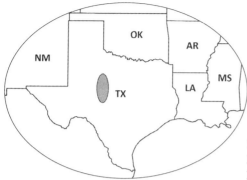

Figure 6.83. Distribution of Moran points (drafted by Lili Lyddon).

Turner and others (2011). Ray (1929) illustrates two points that closely resemble *Moran*, but they are not named.

COMMENTS: The Indian group associated with *Moran* points is unknown.

DISTRIBUTION: It has been reported in Callahan, Coke, Fisher, Jones, Mitchell, Nolan, Runnels, Scurry, Shackelford, and Taylor Counties.

Morris

ORIGINAL RECORDER: It was named by Robert E. Bell and Roland S. Hall (1953) for specimens found at the Morris site (Ck-39) in eastern Oklahoma.

OTHER NAMES: None reported.

SIMILAR TYPES: *Cuney, Edwards*, and *Haskell*.

AGE: Perttula (1997:47) discusses the Middle Caddo period in the Red River valley in northeast Texas and places *Morris* points in that period with an estimated date of circa AD 1100 to AD 1300/1350. The Dan Holdeman site (41RR11) yielded a radiocarbon date from remains in a grave to a 1-sigma range of AD 1410 to AD 1460 (beta-75060 calibrated).

DESCRIPTION: A small side-notched point with a flattened cross section. Some examples have what appears to be corner notches. The blades are typically incurvate with fine serrations. The shoulders are primarily

Figure 6.84. Morris point (replica by Matt Soultz; photo courtesy of Brian Wootan).

horizontal, but some are slightly barbed. Bases are mostly straight, but some specimens are notched.

CULTURAL AFFILIATION: Perttula (1997:47) assigns this type to the Sanders Phase of the Middle Caddoan period.

KNOWN SITES: Morris (Ck-39) in Oklahoma is the type site. *Morris* points have been reported at the Dan Holdeman site (41RR11) and sites in the Red River valley of northeastern Texas (Perttula 1997).

SOURCES FOR ILLUSTRATIONS AND DESCRIPTIONS: Bell (1958); Bell and Hall (1953); Brown (1976, 1996); Perttula (1997); and Perino (1968, 1995).

COMMENTS: This type has been found in burial contexts at several sites. Perino (1995:56) mentions the presence of *Morris* points interred as grave offerings at the Dan Holdeman site. Nineteen examples were associated with "Burial 2." Two were side-notched, and three resemble *Scallorn*. A single *Morris* point was recovered in the grave fill of Burial 7. It was made of gray to tan siltstone. Burial 18 produced three *Morris* points. Two were made of Battiest chert and siltstone. The third specimen is identified as made from an unidentified white chert.

Other articles pertaining to the Middle Caddo period are present in

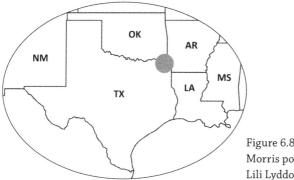

Figure 6.85. Distribution of Morris points (drafted by Lili Lyddon).

issues 9 and 10 of the *Journal of Northeast Texas Archaeology*, edited by Timothy K. Perttula (1997).

Morris is not included as a valid Texas type by Turner and Hester (1985, 1993, 1999) and Turner and others (2011).

DISTRIBUTION: Duncan and others (2007) report that *Morris* points occur primarily in Oklahoma, Arkansas, and Missouri. They have also been documented at sites in Northeast Texas.

Padre

ORIGINAL RECORDER: First mentioned by T. N. Campbell in 1963 for examples found on Padre Island (Davis 1995:242). Formally described by Turner and Hester (1985:186).

OTHER NAMES: None reported.

SIMILAR TYPES: According to Davis (1995), *Padre* is similar to the *Young* type. Both have a subtriangular to leaf-shaped appearance with convex bases, but the *Young* point is usually larger and wider and exhibits cruder flaking. Turner and Hester (1985:186) liken it to *Cameron* and *Fresno*.

AGE: Davis (1995) believes this type dates to sometime between AD 700 and AD 1600.

Figure 6.86. Padre points (photo courtesy of TARL).

DESCRIPTION: Turner and Hester (1985:186) refer to this type as a "small, triangular, unstemmed point that has convex lateral edges and a rounded base." No dimensions are given.

CULTURAL AFFILIATION: Unknown.

KNOWN SITES: McGloin Bluff (41SP11), Kent-Crane (41AS2), and Presidio Nuestra Señora de Loreto de la Bahia del Espíritu Santo (41VT8).

SOURCES FOR ILLUSTRATIONS AND DESCRIPTIONS: Corbin (1974); Hester (1980); Prewitt and others (1987); Davis (1995); Turner and Hester (1985, 1993, 1999); Fox and Tomka (2006); and Turner and others (2011).

COMMENTS: Davis (1995) believes that *Padre* points probably represent a continuum with the *Abasolo* and *Catán* dart points. No dimensions were found.

DISTRIBUTION: Padre Island and the central part of the Texas coast.

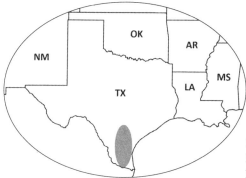

Figure 6.87. Distribution of Padre points (drafted by Lili Lyddon).

Perdiz

ORIGINAL RECORDERS: J. Charles Kelley, T. N. Campbell, and Donald J. Lehmer (1940) were the first to illustrate this type, but they did not name it. It was named *Perdiz Pointed Stem* by Kelley (1947b), and the name was shortened to *Perdiz* by Suhm and Krieger (1954) during the writing of *An Introductory Handbook of Texas Archeology*. This point was named for Perdiz Creek in Presidio County. The Lehman Rock Shelter (41GL1) is the type site (Duncan et al. 2007).

OTHER NAMES: *Foyle Flake Point, Perdiz Stemmed,* and *Perdiz Pointed Stem*. Greer (1968b:40) refers to a type that he calls *Perdiz/Livermore,* but he does not describe it in detail.

SIMILAR TYPES: Per Davis (1995), *Alba, Bonham,* and *Cuney* resemble *Perdiz* in general outline. Turner and others (2011:206) state that *Perdiz* preforms or poorly made specimens have sometimes been identified as *Cliffton*.

AGE: Suhm and Krieger (1954:504 say that *Perdiz* is a late type, and they estimate its age at AD 1000 to AD 1500. Prewitt (1981) calls it Neo-Archaic. Turner, Hester, and McReynolds (2011:206) estimate its age at AD 1200 to AD 1700. Crook (2017:51) dates it to the Farmersville Phase, circa AD 1250 to

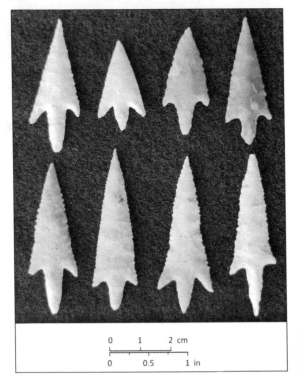

Figure 6.88. Perdiz points (photo courtesy of John Fish).

AD 1600. Webb (2000:15) believes that they were used from circa AD 1000 to AD 1300 in Louisiana and are probably older than *Bassett*. Arnn (2012:47) writes that "*Perdiz* points are representative of the Late Prehistoric transition to the Protohistoric."

DESCRIPTION: Suhm and Krieger's (1954:504) description of *Perdiz* is based on a broad sample from various sites in the state. "Triangular blade with edges usually quite straight but sometimes slightly convex or concave. Shoulders sometimes at right angles to stem but usually well barbed. Stem contracted, often quite sharp at base, but may be somewhat rounded. Occasionally specimens may be worked on one face only, or mainly one face." I collected a probable *Perdiz* point from 41GM40 that was unifacially worked.

Suhm and Krieger (1954:504) provide the following dimensions: length: 1.5 cm to 6 cm; width: 1.2 cm to 3 cm; stems: 0.5 cm to 1.5 cm. Selden and Dockall (2023:2) write that *Perdiz* may vary in outline within a particular region as well as in other parts of the state. They point out that this type has a greater range of variation in shape and size than most arrow points in Texas. Schmiedlin (1993:38) divides *Perdiz* points from 41KA101 (Karnes County) into seven groups.

Group 1 is characterized by having well defined barbs that angle sharply downward.

Group 2 is characterized by short, slightly downward sloping barbs and short rounded stems.

Group 3 is characterized by barbs that are barely recognizable, and the blades are not well made. The stems are slightly tapered and somewhat rounded.

Group 4 is characterized by serrated edges on the blades and broken barbs that may have been reworked.

Group 5 is characterized by serrated edges on the blades. These points have been reworked to the point that the barbs stick out at right angles.

Group 6 is classified as a rough *Perdiz* preform with only a "slight hint of a stem and little flaking."

Group 7 is described as probable "*Perdiz* blanks with minimal shaping to partially shape the flake."

Baskin (1981:264, Figure 32) places *Perdiz* points from the George C. Davis site (41CE19) into the following categories: Contracting Stem Edge Group, Form 3 (pointed base) and Contracting Stem Edge Group, Form 4 (platform base).

"Perdiz arrow points generally follow two manufacturing trajectories—one that enlists flakes, and the other, blade flakes, and are known to encompass a greater range of variation and shape than most arrow point types in Texas" (Selden and Dockall 2023:2). This type is sometimes found in large numbers at a single site. Mallouf (1987) reports a burial cairn in northern Chihuahua that contained 180 *Perdiz* points, and more than 100 arrow points classified as *Perdiz* were recovered from 41JW8. "The

196 | CHAPTER 6

collection of stone tools from the Buckhollow site contains 70 finished Perdiz-style arrow points and fragments and 15 Perdiz preforms" (Johnson 1994:66). His report contains the most thorough discussion of this type I have found with twenty pages devoted solely to *Perdiz*. A prehistoric semisubterranean cairn burial in the western portion of Big Bend National Park yielded 73 arrow points and point fragments. All but one was classified as *Perdiz*. "The association of Perdiz points and a burial offers a glimpse of the mortuary customs practiced by the makers and users of the ubiquitous Perdiz arrow point" (Cloud 2002:Abstract). At 41HE114, 20 *Perdiz* points were recovered, and 9 were from a single feature. Sixteen were made from chert, three from quartzite, and one from silicified wood (Shafer 1981). Perttula, Nelson, and Walters (2009:185) illustrate two *Perdiz* points made of quartzite from Nacogdoches County. Greer (1968b:40) writes that *Perdiz* points were found scattered about the surface of two ring middens in Sutton County. He also refers to a type that he describes as *Perdiz/Livermore*, but he does not describe it in detail.

CULTURAL AFFILIATION: The manufacture and utilization of the *Perdiz* point took place during the post-Archaic at a time archaeologists refer to as the Late Prehistoric (formerly Neo-American) era of Texas prehistory. The earliest reference to the cultural affiliation of *Perdiz* was proposed by J. Charles Kelley (1947a, 1944b) on the basis of technological and morphological differences in material culture during the Toyah Phase. He opined that its emergence occurred sometime between the Protohistoric and preceding Austin Phase of the Late Prehistoric period. Two years later, Newell and Krieger (1949) considered it to be later than the Alto Focus at the George C. Davis site. Suhm and Krieger (1954:504) referred to *Perdiz* as a common type in many Neo-American complexes in Texas. It has been assigned to the Cielo Complex by (Cloud and Mallouf 1996) and the Dunlap Complex by James Word (1971). They (Suhm and Krieger 1954:504) further divided its existence into the Bravo Valley and Central Texas aspects and the Frankston, Galveston Bay, Henrietta, Rockport, and Wylie foci. William J. Shackelford (1955:262) posits that *Perdiz* has a closer affinity with Toyah than the Brazos Valley Aspect. His conclusion is based on analysis of *Perdiz Stemmed* points at the Polvo site. Turner and others (2011:206) state that *Perdiz* is a key element of the Toyah Phase tool kit. This statement is echoed by Selden and Dockall (2023:1) in the following: "Perdiz arrow points are considered the epitome of the Late Prehistoric Toyah lithic assemblage in Texas." Prewitt (1981) presents a detailed discussion of the Toyah Phase in his article titled "Cultural Chronology in Central Texas," where he mentions the presence of *Perdiz* points at bison kill sites. Selden and Dockall (2023:1) comment this association in the following: "This technological assemblage is typically attributed to groups of highly mobile bison hunters and has been documented across the geographic extent of Texas."

KNOWN SITES: Attaway (41HE114), Devil's Mouth (41VV188), Oblate (41CM1), Kyle (41HI1), Sam Hemby (41KA101), Buckhollow (41KM16), Ernest Rainey (41BN33), Hinojosa (41JW8), Sam Roberts (41CP8), Lott (41GR56), Lehman Rock Shelter (41GL1), Smith Rock Shelter (41TV42), Baker Cave (41VV213), Mellon (41RF21), Roark Cave (41BS3), Wunderlich (41CM3), Mission San Lorenzo de la Santa Cruz in Real County (Tunnell and Newcomb 1969), Peerless Bottoms (41HP175), Washington Square Mound (41NA49), Mitchell Ridge (41GV66), Polvo (41PS21), Jetta Court (41TV151), Rough Run Burial (41BS844), Brawley Cave (41BQ20), Upper Farmersville (41COL34), and sites 41DL148, 41DL149, 41DL184, 41GL19, 41VT38, 41DM59, 41JW8. 41GM40, and 41VV1991.

SOURCES FOR ILLUSTRATIONS AND DESCRIPTIONS: Bell (1960); Bell and Hall (1953); Davis (1995); Duncan and others (2007); Jelks (1953, 1993); Hester (1980); Hester and Whatley 1992); Mallouf (1987); Miller and Jelks (1952); Stephenson (1952); Suhm and Krieger (1954); Kelley (1963); Turner and Hester (1985, 1993, 1999); Shafer (1981); Ricklis and Collins (1994); Turner and others (2011); Perino (1985); Perttula and others (2009); Black (1986); Tunnell and Tunnell (2015); Roberts and Alvarado (2011); Johnson (1994); Shackelford (1955); Moore (1988a); Wesolowsky and others. (1976); Word and Douglas (1970); Cloud (2002); Cloud and Mallouf (1996); Olds (1965); Story (1981); Schmeidlin (1993, 1997); Crook (2008–2009); Glasrud and Mallouf (2013); Black (1986); and Selden and Dockall (2023).

COMMENTS: Selden and Dockall (2022) conducted a pilot study intended to assess whether metrics collected for *Perdiz* arrow points (length, width,

198 | CHAPTER 6

thickness, and such) can be viewed as indicators of regional shape boundaries for ceramics in Caddoan burial sites in the same behavioral region or across different regions or boundaries. Their sample was based on 67 complete *Perdiz* points recovered from Caddo burial contexts in Camp, Nacogdoches, and Shelby Counties. They concluded that "This study demonstrated that linear metrics and shape variables collected for Perdiz arrow points support the shape boundary posited in recent social network and geometric morphometric analyses, and that those same metrics can be used to predict regional membership" (Selden and Dockall 2023:10). They (Selden and Dockall 2023:2) tested their hypothesis that the shape of the *Perdiz* point is a function of time (a.k.a. protean). Factors that affect shape are time, raw material, and context in burials. Their hypothesis was tested using geometric morphometrics.

Damage to *Perdiz* points is discussed by Cox and Smith (1989) and Wilson W. Crook III (2017).

Stephen L. Black (1986:61) presents evidence that suggests *Perdiz* points were hafted. "The hafting modification [stems] and presence of stem grinding, and occasional stem edge and facial polish strongly support the idea that *Perdiz* points were hafted. The most prevalent blade use wear patterns are edge and facial flake ridge rounding and polish. The light irregular nature of the polish is consistent with use by hide or meat."

Twenty *Perdiz* points were recovered from the Sam Hemby site (41KA101). They were "predominantly made from bifacial thinning flakes as evidenced by the curvature of the unifacial blades, while some show a definite 'arris' that may indicate blade technology" (Schmiedlin 1993:37). All but one is made from what Schmiedlin believes to be locally obtained chert. The single exception was made from greenish-gray agate. Two are described as flake preforms. Schmiedlin (1993:Table 1) provides measurements for each point and divides them into groups based on recognizable differences.

Grant D. Hall (1981) conducted one of the major archaeological surveys in the lower Brazos River valley of Texas (Austin County). A variety of arrow points and dart points was recovered, along with numerous burials and occupational features. In addition to illustrations of each type, he provides dimensions, provenience (vertical and horizontal), and color taken

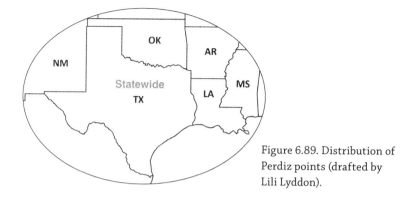

Figure 6.89. Distribution of Perdiz points (drafted by Lili Lyddon).

from the Munsell soil color chart. One specimen identified as *Perdiz* was found at 41AU37, and five were found at 41AU38.

Late stage unfinished *Perdiz* points are discussed and illustrated in Ricklis and Collins (1994:214).

Perdiz points have been found in open sites and rockshelters such as Brawley's Cave where the stem of a *Perdiz*, var. *whitney* embedded in a wooden foreshaft was recorded (Olds 1965:114, Figure 1).

Jelks (1962) describes and illustrates a similar foreshaft with a *Perdiz* fragment encased and a *Perdiz* fragment that had been repurposed as a drill.

Although *Perdiz* is considered to be a prehistoric arrow point, overlap into historic times must be considered a possibility. Two examples are presented here.

Smitty Schmeidlin (1997) reported a single *Perdiz* point at 41VT38, the presumed third location of Mission Espíritu Santo de Zuñiga (41VT11).

Davis and Skiles (1999) mention a possible *Perdiz* point at 41VV890. It was found beneath the northeast corner of a historic rock structure that was built circa 1879. Collett (1993) believes it predates construction of the building.

DISTRIBUTION: Suhm and Krieger (1954:504) say it is found in "Most of Texas from Rio Grande in extreme west to Neches River Valley on the east; from Red River Valley in both Texas and Oklahoma southward to eastern and central parts of Gulf Coast."

CHAPTER 6

Aten (1983) places it in the region he calls the Upper Texas Coast. It also occurs into the border area of the Rio Grande and into northern Chihuahua.

According to Robert J. Mallouf (personal communication, 2018), this type is commonly found in the Eastern Trans-Pecos and Big Bend region and is the most common arrow point found in Big Bend National Park.

Greer (1968b:40) writes that *Perdiz* points were found scattered about the surface of two ring middens in Sutton County. He also refers to a type that he refers to as *Perdiz/Livermore*, but he does not describe it in detail.

Turner and others (2011:206) and Webb (2000) refer to *Perdiz* as a Texas type occasionally found in Louisiana.

Pinwah

ORIGINAL RECORDER: Unknown. The points illustrated here are part of a private collection.

OTHER NAMES: None

SIMILAR TYPES: *Perdiz*

AGE: Late Prehistoric

DESCRIPTION: This description is based on a sample of several hundred examples by Thomas Oakes (personal communication, June 25, 2022). Many are serrated, and most are very well made. Oakes describes the shape as "elongated bell." He repeated to me that "The stem is always contracting and small compared to the overall point length. The ears are usually horizontal, but some have a slight downward angle. The average size is about 1 inch to 1 ¼ inches. Exceptions are ¾ inch, and one specimen is more than 2 inches in length."

CULTURAL AFFILIATION: Late Prehistoric

KNOWN SITES: None reported.

SOURCES FOR ILLUSTRATIONS AND DESCRIPTIONS: Thomas Oakes of Bossier City, Louisiana, has a large private collection.

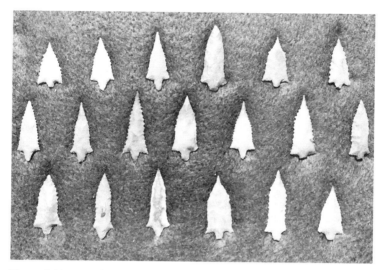

Figure 6.90. Pinwah points (photo courtesy of Thomas Oakes).

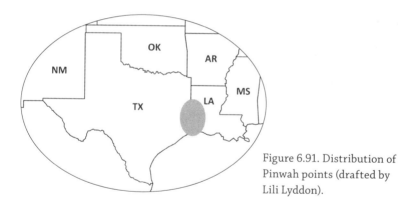

Figure 6.91. Distribution of Pinwah points (drafted by Lili Lyddon).

COMMENTS: *Pinwah* is not included in *Stone Artifacts of Texas Indians* (Turner et al. 2011). It is mentioned here because of the large number of specimens with similar morphology.

DISTRIBUTION: They are most commonly found in Beauregard, Calcasieu, and Vernon Parishes, Louisiana. Specimens have been reported from extreme east and southeast Texas (John Fish, telephone conversation on June 4, 2023).

No Image Available

Figure 6.92. Ray point (no image available).

Ray

ORIGINAL RECORDER: First identified as a provisional type during the 1991–1992 TAS field school in Lamar and Red River Counties (Perttula et al. 2001). The type site is 41LR1034.

OTHER NAMES: None reported.

SIMILAR TYPES: None reported.

AGE: Late Prehistoric.

DESCRIPTION: "The points are triangular with convex lateral edges and have parallel to slightly expanding stems. Their most diagnostic trait is that they are crudely made by retouching the lateral margin of small flakes. *Ray* points tend to be small, with most less than 2 cm in length. They are made from a variety of local and nonlocal cherts" (Perttula et al. 2001:203).

CULTURAL AFFILIATION: Caddoan.

KNOWN SITES: Ray (41LR135) and Stallings Ranch (41LR297).

SOURCES FOR ILLUSTRATIONS AND DESCRIPTIONS: Perttula and others (2001); Unpublished Appendix by Elton R. Prewitt for the 1991–1992 TAS field school report.

COMMENTS: No image suitable for publication was available during this study, and no dimensions were found.

DISTRIBUTION: Known examples are from sites in Lamar and Red River Counties.

Arrow Points | 203

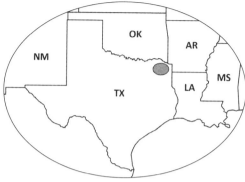

Figure 6.93. Distribution of Ray points (drafted by Lili Lyddon).

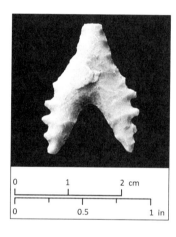

Figure 6.94. Revilla point (photo courtesy of TARL).

Revilla

ORIGINAL RECORDER: The first detailed description of the *Revilla* point was published in *La Tierra* by Don Kumpe and others (2000). They state that *Revilla* was the original name, but they describe it as *Form 4*. Turner and others (2011) prefer the term *Revilla*. This point was named for the Spanish Colonial town of *Revilla* (a.k.a. *Guerrero Viejo*) now submerged under the waters of Falcon Reservoir.

OTHER NAMES: *Form 4*.

SIMILAR TYPES: None reported.

204 | CHAPTER 6

AGE: This type dates to the Late Prehistoric period, but since the distributional center for this type is in the vicinity of a former Spanish mission it may have also been used during historic times. Since no specimens have been found in a databale context, its exact age is not known.

DESCRIPTION: Turner and others (2011:207) describe this point in the following: "These are very thin, finely made arrow points of excellent quality chert. They are generally triangular in outline with distinctly deep (at least 4 mm) concave bases. Bases have a rounded apex and convex lateral edges. Prominent serrations begin at the basal corners, usually three to seven per side." Dimensions are not given.

CULTURAL AFFILIATION: Unknown.

KNOWN SITES: 41ZP8, 41ZP83, and 41ZP154.

SOURCES FOR ILLUSTRATIONS AND DESCRIPTIONS: Kumpe and others (2000) and Turner and others (2011).

COMMENTS: This type was first found at 41ZP154 in 1971. By 1983, seven more specimens had been found at sites 41ZP83 and 41ZP154. Don Kumpe took several examples to a Southern Coastal Corridor Palaver in Corpus Christi, and the consensus of other archaeologists was that this is a type that had not been found elsewhere in the state. Later, the water levels of the lake dropped drastically, and 15 specimens were added to the list of known types (Kumpe et al. 2000).

Revilla points were found in association with *Carcara, Form 1, Fresno, Perdiz, Scallorn, Starr, and Toyah* at sites 41ZP83 and 41ZP154 (Kump et al. 2000).

DISTRIBUTION: It occurs along the old channel of the Rio Grande between Chapote Creek and Arroyo Clareno in Zapata County, and Tamaulipas, Mexico (Turner et al. 2011:207), The distribution of this point is based on a small sample. All Texas specimens were found within the normal conservation pool of Falcon Reservoir, and not one has been documented from an inland site. The limited distribution and small number of specimens suggests to the authors that this type may have had a short life span.

Arrow Points | 205

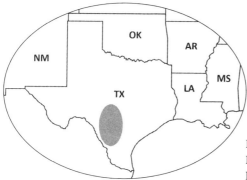

Figure 6.95. Distribution of Revilla points (drafted by Lili Lyddon).

Figure 6.96. Rockwall point (photo courtesy of John Fish).

Rockwall

ORIGINAL RECORDER: This point was named and described by J. B. Sollberger (1970) for examples found in Rockwall County, Texas.

OTHER NAMES: None reported.

SIMILAR TYPES: Crook (personal communication, 2017) does not believe that "there is much of a difference between the *Rockwall* type and the variation seen within the *Scallorn* type."

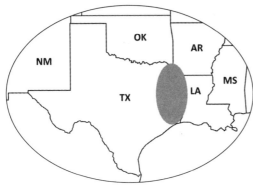

Figure 6.97. Distribution of Rockwall points (drafted by Lili Lyddon).

AGE: W. W. Crook III (personal communication, 2017) believes the best current date for this type is circa AD 900 to AD 1250. Davis (1995), relying on dates presented by others, dates the *Rockwall* point at circa AD 700 to AD 1400.

DESCRIPTION: Davis (1995:246) describes this point in the following: "A small point with a triangular outline. The shoulders are strongly barbed but do not extend to the base of the point. The stem expands toward the base and the base may be straight or slightly convex." No dimensions are given.

CULTURAL AFFILIATION: Unknown.

KNOWN SITES: Lower Rockwall (41RW1) is assumed to be the type site.

SOURCES FOR ILLUSTRATIONS AND DESCRIPTIONS: Davis (1995); Duncan and others (2007); Perino (1971, 1985); and Sollberger (1970).

COMMENTS: Davis (1995:246) states that "*Rockwall* and *Scallorn* are similar in general outline. Both types have barbs and stems that expand toward the base. The main difference is that *Scallorn* has a more pronounced expanded base that is often as wide as the shoulders."

This type is not mentioned in any of the type books by Suhm and Krieger (1954), Suhm and Jelks (1962); Turner and Hester (1985, 1993, 1999); or Turner and others (2011).

DISTRIBUTION: *Rockwall* points are found in north central and eastern Texas with less frequency in adjacent areas (Davis 1995:246).

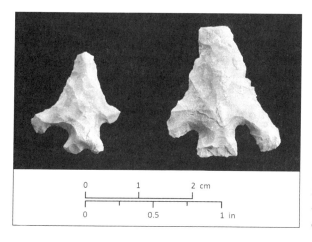

Figure 6.98. Sabinal points from 41BU17 (photo courtesy of TARL).

Sabinal

ORIGINAL RECORDER: This type was named and described by Thomas R. Hester (1971) for examples found at the La Jita site (41UV21) in northwestern Uvalde County. He named it for the Sabinal River where the type site is located.

OTHER NAMES: None reported.

SIMILAR TYPES: Davis (1995:248) states that *Sabinal* and *Catahoula* points "are quite similar in general outline. Both types have concave to recurved lateral edges with long barbs that are often bulbous at the ends. The barbs are usually wider and more bulbous on the Catahoula type and the blade of the Sabinal appears narrower." *Sabinal* points are found in southern or southwestern Texas, while the *Catahoula* point occurs in eastern Texas and Louisiana.

AGE: According to Turner, Hester, and McReynolds (2011:208), this is a Late Prehistoric point that dates to circa AD 1120 to AD 1250.

DESCRIPTION: Turner and others (2011:208) describe the *Sabinal* point in the following: "A long, narrow triangular point that has deeply concave to recovered lateral edges and heavy barbs that flare outward and curve upward. The stem is produced by deep, narrow basal notches and expands moderately." No dimensions are given.

208 | **CHAPTER 6**

CULTURAL AFFILIATION: Unknown.

KNOWN SITES: La Jita (41UV21), Anthon (41UV60), Ernest Rainey (41BN33), Montell Rockshelter (41UV3), 41UV20, 41ZV226, 41BX1, Rough Enough Rockshelter (41VV1987), J. W. Sparks in Real County, 41DM59, 41HR269, and 41VV1991.

SOURCES FOR ILLUSTRATIONS AND DESCRIPTIONS: Beasley (1978), Coleman and others (2000), Davis (1995), Hall and others (1982), Henderson (2001), Hester (1971), Hester and Whatley (1992), Lukowski (1987), Mauldin and others (2004), Mitchell (1982), Perino (1991), Turner and Hester (1985, 1993, 1999), Turner and others (2011), Stillwell (2011), Calame (2017–2018), Roberts and Alvarado (2011), Fields (1988), and Weir and Doran (1980).

COMMENTS: The new type was proposed based on seven specimens found in one of the four burned rock middens that make up the La Jita site. It was found to be present throughout the late occupation of the site. Private collections with *Sabinal* points were observed near Utopia in northwestern Uvalde County.

Sabinal points from the J. W. Sparks site in Real County and one specimen from the Montell Rockshelter in Uvalde County are housed at TARL.

"A number of Texas archaeological reports have wrongly used the 'Sabinal' label in areas great distances from its area" (Turner et al. 2011:208).

Henderson (2001) writes that *Sabinal* is a "short lived type" that was in use between *Edwards* and *Scallorn*. This statement is based on work at the Ernest Rainey site (41BN33) in Bandera County.

DISTRIBUTION: Turner and others (2011) state that this point was initially found in a small area in the southwestern part of the Edwards Plateau. Similar specimens have been reported from the Lower Pecos and southern Texas.

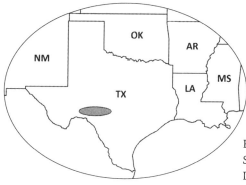

Figure 6.99. Distribution of Sabinal points (drafted by Lili Lyddon).

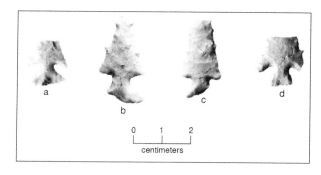

Figure 6.100. Scallorn points from 41BU13 (photo courtesy of Tanner Singleton).

Scallorn

ORIGINAL RECORDER: The *Scallorn* point was first recognized by J. Charles Kelley (1947b) as *Scallorn Stemmed*. Suhm and Krieger (1954) shortened it to *Scallorn*. It was named for the town of Scallorn in Mills County.

OTHER NAMES: Ford and Willey (1940) referred to this type as "fir-tree" before Kelley (1947b) named it *Scallorn Stemmed*.

SIMILAR TYPES: *Eddy* (Corbin 1963); *Edwards* (Davis 1995).

AGE: Suhm and Krieger (1954) estimate its age at somewhat older than *Perdiz*, circa AD 700 to AD 1500. Prewitt (1981) refers to it as Neo-Archaic. According to Turner, Hester, and McReynolds (2011), this is a Late Prehistoric

CHAPTER 6

type that has been dated at AD 830 ± 50 BP at 41FB255 and 800 BP to 1250 BP at the Buckhollow site. Radiocarbon dates from the stratified Ernest Rainey (sinkhole) site overlap with *Scallorn* but occur later in time. Crook and Hughston (2015b:34–35) were able to get radiometric data from a femur at the Lower Rockwall site that contained *Scallorn* points. The results were reported as 1240 ± 30 BP. The 1-sigma calibration is AD 715 to AD 775, and the 2-sigma calibration is AD 680 to AD 880. In a later article, Crook (2017:53) dates this type to circa AD 700 or AD 800 to AD 1250.

DESCRIPTION: Suhm and Jelks (1954:506) describe this point in the following: "Broad to slender triangular blades with edges straight to convex. Shoulders may be squared but usually well barbed. Stem formed by notching into corners at various angles, making it expand from a broad wedge shape to rounded extremities as wide as the shoulders Base straight, concave, and convex. Blade edges are often finely serrated." Louisiana specimens are made from many materials (Webb 2000). The following measurements were taken from Suhm and Krieger (1954:506):

Length: 2.5 cm to 4.5 cm
Width: 1.5 cm to 2.0 cm
Stems: One-third to one-seventh of total length

CULTURAL AFFILIATION: Miller and Jelks (1952) refer to it as one of the main types of the Austin Focus. According to Suhm and Krieger (1954), this is a common type of the Central Texas Aspect, and it also occurs in sites attributed to the Henrietta Focus and maybe the Rockport Focus. Prewitt (1981) and Turner and others (2011) place it in the Austin Phase. Crook (2017:53) dates this type as part of the Wylie Phase, circa AD 700 or AD 800 to 1250. In Louisiana, "it occurs with Coles Creek and possibly Troyville cultures into early Caddoan Alto period in this area" (Webb 2000:16). According to Robert J. Mallouf (personal communication, 2018), this type is sometimes found in the Eastern Trans-Pecos and Big Bend regions. Aten (1983) refers to it as a type found in the Upper Texas Coast. Perino (1985:334) refers to *Scallorn* as a Late Woodland point, circa AD 500 to AD 900. Schiffer and House (1975:32) place it in northeast Arkansas circa AD 1200.

KNOWN SITES: Baker Cave (41VV213), Smith Rockshelter (41TV42), Evoe Terrace (41BL104), Love-Fox (41WM230), Frisch Auf (41FY42), Blue Bayou (41VT94), Buckhollow (41KM16), Dan Holdeman (41RR11), Perry (41FT193), Ernest Rainey (41BN33), High Bluff (no trinomial), Red Ochre Burials (41PR12), Lower Rockwall (41RW1), Jetta Court (41TV151), Tankersley Creek (41TT108), Pecan Springs (41EL11), Upper Farmersville (41COL34), 41BL22, 41BL23, 41BL58,4 1GM40, 41DL148, 41DL149, 41DL184, 41SP11, 41VV1991, 41VT38, 41BT6, and sites at Belton Reservoir (Shafer et al. 1964). Webb (1959:162) illustrates two *Scallorn* points found at the Belcher Mound (16 CD 13) in Caddo Parish, Louisiana.

SOURCES FOR ILLUSTRATIONS AND DESCRIPTIONS: Bell (1960), Bell and Hall (1953), Davis (1995), Duncan et al. (2007), Kelley (1947b), Miller and Jelks (1952), Suhm and Jelks (1962), (Jelks 1993), Saunders and Hester (1993), Suhm and Krieger (1954), Shafer et al. (1964), Aten (1983), Turner and Hester (1985, 1993, 1999), Ricklis and Collins (1994), Turner and others (2011), Webb (2000), Hester (1980, 2004), Collins (2004), Crook (2008–2009), Boyd (2004), Fields (1988, 2004), Perttula (2020), Ricklis (2004), Wesolowsky and others (1976), Young (1981b, 1982a), Word and Douglas (1970), Schmeidlin (1997), Sorrow (1966), and Tunnell and Tunnell (2015). Flinn and Flinn (1968) illustrate *Scallorn,* var. *coryell* and Scallorn, var. *sattler* from the High Bluff site in Stephens County near the county line with Young County.

COMMENTS: At 41SP11, James E. Corbin (1963) describes three fragmentary specimens that may be *Scallorn*, var. *eddy.* According to Turner and others (2011), *Scallorn* points are often found with *Chadbourne* points. The following is a quote from Turner and others (2011:209): "During the Austin Phase, of which Scallorn points are chronological hallmarks, they are often found with burials (grave goods) and in burials (as in cause of death). Indeed, the best evidence for warfare among ancient groups in central, south, and coastal Texas comes from Scallorn-related woundings and death."

Prewitt (1981) presents a detailed discussion of the Austin Phase in his article titled "Cultural Chronology in Central Texas."

Scallorn is the most common type found at sites in the Belton Reservoir

212 | CHAPTER 6

area (Bell and Coryell Counties) with eighty-four specimens reported (Shafer et al. 1964). The authors reported a wide range of *Scallorn* varieties or subtypes and listed them as *brangus, coryell, eddy,* and *sattler* based on variations of the stem. These varieties are illustrated in Shafer et al. (1964). They were recovered from sites 41BL22, 41BL23, and 41BL58.

Wilson W. Crook III (2017) discusses types of damage to *Scallorn* points and other Late Prehistoric types from a sample of 750 examples. He does not believe that "there is much of a difference between the *Rockwall* type and the variation seen within the *Scallorn* type."

Perttula (2020) illustrates two *Scallorn* points found in the chest region of burial 2 at the Red Ochre Burial site. Both specimens exhibit breaks in the distal area due to impact with the body.

A *Scallorn* and *Scallorn*-like point made from Alibates chert were found at 41OC93 by Office of the State Archeologist Steward Doug Wilkins (TARL site form).

Saunders and Hester (1993:22–31) discuss side-notched arrow points from the Falcon Lake region of Texas and Mexico. Their discussion of *Scallorn* includes examples of this type that points out the similarities between *Caracara* and *Scallorn*.

Frederick et al. (1994:38) conducted a chert patination study of 105 *Scallorn* points from sites at Fort Hood. Thirty-one of the specimens lacked patina, and the authors report "the results of this study suggest that it is unlikely that chert patination will ever develop into a reliable dating method.

Some *Fresno* points may represent a stage in the production of *Scallorn* points (Jelks 1993:12).

Grant D. Hall (1981) conducted one of the major archaeological surveys in the lower Brazos River valley of Texas (Austin County). A variety of arrow and dart points were recovered, along with numerous burials and occupational features. In addition to illustrations of each type, he provides dimensions, provenience (vertical and horizontal), and color taken from the Munsell soil color chart. Three specimens identified as *Scallorn* were found at 41AU37, and eleven were found at 41AU38.

Sorrow (1966:24–27, Figure 14) reported 26 *Scallorn* points at the Pecan Springs site (41EL11) in Ellis County. Four varieties were present.

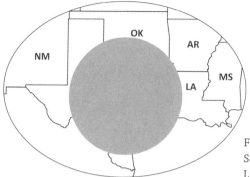

Figure 6.101. Distribution of Scallorn points (drafted by Lili Lyddon).

Smitty Schmeidlin (1997) reports two *Scallorn* points at 41VT38, the presumed third location of Mission Espíritu Santo de Zuñiga (41VT11).

Four artifacts described as *Fresno* were recovered at Presidio Nuestra Señora de Loreto de la Bahia del Espíritu Santo (41VT8). Two are complete, and two are fragments. Their provenience and metric data are found in Fox and Tomka (2006:Table 15). "Technologically, two lack the fine edge-pressure retouch found on finished Scallorn points, and therefore, may be late stage Scallorn preforms. Another reason to support this interpretation is that they consistently occur with Scallorn" (Fox and Tomka 2006:102, Figure 35).

DISTRIBUTION: Suhm and Krieger (1954:506) plot its distribution as "More or less a broad central belt through Texas from Red River valley to Gulf Coast but absent in East Texas and eastern and southern extremities of coast." Conversely, Turner and others (2011) say it is found over much of Texas. Webb (2000:16) says it is frequently found throughout Louisiana. McGahey (2000:202) extends its range into Mississippi. Jelks (1993) writes it has been reported from northern Mexico into the central plains and eastward as far as Illinois and the Ohio River valley.

Figure 6.102.
Conch columella shell points
(photo courtesy of TARL).

Shell

ORIGINAL RECORDER: Not applicable.

OTHER NAMES: None reported.

SIMILAR TYPES: None reported.

AGE: Late Prehistoric

DESCRIPTION: No standard description.

CULTURAL AFFILIATION: Brownsville Complex.

DISTRIBUTION: Gulf Coast and Rio Grande Delta.

KNOWN SITES: None.

SOURCES FOR ILLUSTRATIONS AND DESCRIPTIONS: A. E. Anderson (1932:21–22); Hester (1980:121–122, Figure 5–20).

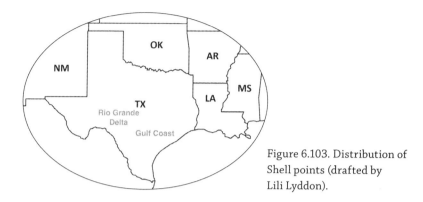

Figure 6.103. Distribution of Shell points (drafted by Lili Lyddon).

COMMENTS: Evidence of arrow points made from shell has mainly been documented from sites on the Texas coast. Examples of shell projectile tips made from the *columella* (a.k.a. central column) of the conch shell have been found at sites in the Rio Grande Delta as part of the Brownsville Complex).

A. E. Anderson (1932:21:Plate 7) illustrates conch shell points and other tools. He writes that "Chipped projectile points of conch shell, similar in form to the triangular points occur but are quite rare."

DISTRIBUTION: Suhm and Krieger (1954:506) plot its distribution as "More or less a broad central belt through Texas from the Red River valley to Gulf Coast but absent in East Texas and eastern and southern extremities of coast." Conversely, Turner, Hester, and McReynolds (2011) say it is found over much of Texas. Webb (2000:16) says it is frequently found throughout Louisiana. McGahey (2000:202) extends its range into Mississippi. Jelks (1993) writes it has been reported from northern Mexico into the central plains and eastward as far as Illinois and the Ohio River valley.

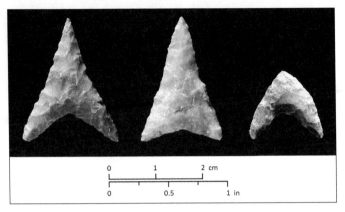

Figure 6.104. Starr points from Northern Mexico (photo courtesy of TARL).

Starr

ORIGINAL RECORDER: This type was named and described by Dee Ann Suhm and Alex D. Krieger (1954) during the writing of *An Introductory Handbook of Texas Archeology*. It was named for the town of Starr in Starr County near the area where the first examples were found. The type site was not identified.

OTHER NAMES: None reported.

SIMILAR TYPES: Suhm and Krieger (1954:506) say that *Starr* may be a variation of the *Fresno* type. Davis (1995:252) believes *McGloin*, *Maud*, and *Turney* are also similar.

AGE: Suhm and Krieger (1954:506) state that the age of this Late Prehistoric point is about the same as *Fresno* (AD 800 or AD 900 to AD 1600 or later).

DESCRIPTION: Suhm and Krieger (1954:506) describe this type in the following: "Simple triangular points with both edges and base concave." No dimensions are given.

CULTURAL AFFILIATION: Brownsville and Mier foci (Suhm and Krieger 1954). Newton (1968) illustrates the relative position of this type to known types of the earlier Falcon Focus.

Arrow Points | 217

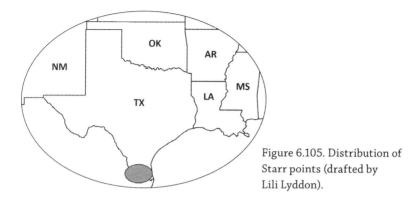

Figure 6.105. Distribution of Starr points (drafted by Lili Lyddon).

KNOWN SITES: In Texas, this type has been found at 41HG4, 41HG5, 41HG6, 41KL13, and McGloin Bluff (41SP11). Three possible examples were found at 41JW8. In Mexico, it has been reported from the *Cueva de la Zona de Derrumbes* rockshelter in *Nuevo Leon*.

SOURCES FOR ILLUSTRATIONS AND DESCRIPTIONS: Corbin (1963); Davis (1995); Duncan and others (2007); Gunter (1985); Hester (1969, 1980); Kelly and Graves (1980); Steele and Mokry (1983); Suhm and Jelks (1962); Suhm and Krieger (1954); McClurkan (1966); Newton (1968); Fields (1995); Turner and Hester (1985, 1993, 1999); Perino (1985); Mallouf et al. (1977); Ricklis (2004); Turner and others (2011); Saunders (1985); and Jelks (1993).

COMMENTS: Davis (1995) believes that *Starr* may be part of a continuum with *McGloin*. Turner and others (2011:210) state "These points are highly restricted in their geographical distribution and should not be used as a 'niche' for similar points found at great distances from this distribution."

DISTRIBUTION: This type is most common in the coastal portion of the state and in Southwest Texas (Suhm and Krieger 1954). According to Davis (1995:250), this is primarily a type found in the lower Rio Grande Valley and extending up the southern portions of the Texas Gulf Coast with less frequency in adjacent areas of Texas.

Figure 6.106. Steiner point (replica by Matt Soultz; photo by Brian Wootan)

Steiner

ORIGINAL RECORDER: According to Story (1965), *Steiner* was originally named by J. Charles Kelley (1947a) and called *Steiner Serrated*. It was briefly described and illustrated by Perry H. Newell and Alex D. Krieger (1949, 2002). Dee Ann Story (1965) "tentatively revived" this type with the suggestion that its name be shortened to *Steiner*. Her description is based on points found at Cedar Creek Reservoir in Henderson and Kaufman Counties.

OTHER NAMES: *Steiner Serrated*.

SIMILAR TYPES: Story (1965:183) writes, "The shoulders [of the Steiner type] are prominent and occasionally extend laterally in a manner somewhat similar to the Catahoula type." Davis (1995:254) says, "The Steiner point and the Friley point are probably the most similar in general outline." He states that the primary difference is the "*Friley* type has strong barbs that usually curve upward toward the distal end which distinguishes it from the *Steiner* point." J. B. Sollberger (1970) defined a type that he called *Rockwall* that is very similar to *Steiner*.

AGE: Story (1965) did not offer a date for this type. Crook and Hughston (2015b:34–35) were able to get radiometric data from a femur at the Lower Rockwall site (41RW1) that contained *Steiner* points. The results were reported as AD 1240 ± 30 BP. The 1-sigma calibration is AD 715 to AD 775, and the 2-sigma calibration is AD 680 to AD 880. Davis (1995) estimates its age at AD 800 to AD 1400.

DESCRIPTION: Davis (1995:254) describes *Steiner* as "A small point with a triangular outline. The lateral edges may be straight, concave, or convex and exhibit strong serrations at right or odd angles. Shoulders are strong on these points and flare outward with one shoulder often being more pronounced than the other. The short stems may expand or contract toward the base. The base may be straight, concave, or convex."

CULTURAL AFFILIATION: Possible *Steiner* points have been found at Wylie Focus sites. Kelley (1947a) places it within the time frame of the Clear Fork Focus.

KNOWN SITES: George C. Davis (41CE19), Upper Farmersville site (41COL34), Lower Rockwall (41RW1), and 41DL240. Story (1965) reports that possible *Steiner* points have been found at the Limerick site (41RA8), Forney Reservoir, and Wylie Focus sites. Fields (2004) illustrates specimens from Cooper Lake and Jewett Mine. Crook (2011) reports three *Steiner* points at 41DL406 that were made of quartzite.

SOURCES FOR ILLUSTRATIONS AND DESCRIPTIONS: Duffield (1961, 1963); Newell and Krieger (1949); Story (1965); Turner and Hester (1985, 1993, 1999); Pertttula and others (1976); Perino (1985); Fields (2004); Crook (2008–2009); Crook and Hughston (2009b, 2015a, 2015b); Crook (2011); and others (2011).

COMMENTS: Story (1965:185) states that "Unlike most of the arrow point types, Steiner is based primarily on blade characteristics rather than on stem features."

Newell and Krieger (2002:162–163) discuss *Steiner Serrated* points found at the George C. Davis site (41CE19) in the following: "This type is recognized by J. Charles Kelley as most common in the middle Brazos River

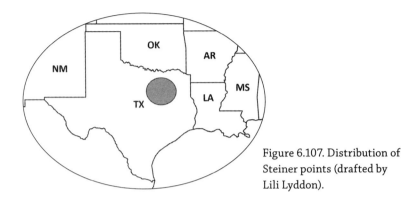

Figure 6.107. Distribution of Steiner points (drafted by Lili Lyddon).

valley in the vicinity of Waco, Texas. The blade edges are featured by numerous tiny protrusions jutting out at regular intervals or irregularly at different angles. Four specimens were found, one in the plow zone, three in Zones 14 and 15 (Figure 56, o–q). All are petrified wood and possibly were made locally, but the general absence of this type in eastern Texas cultures indicates their presence was due to trade or a visit to the Davis site toward the end of occupation." Specimen "q" does not resemble *Steiner* in my opinion.

DISTRIBUTION: This type is primarily found in eastern Texas with fewer numbers found at sites in adjacent areas.

Talco

ORIGINAL RECORDER: *Talco* was first described and named by Dee Ann Suhm and Alex D. Krieger (1954:508) during the writing of *An Introductory Handbook of Texas Archeology*. It was named for the town of Talco in Titus County.

OTHER NAMES: None reported.

SIMILAR TYPES: *Fresno, Maud,* and *Turney*.

AGE: Suhm and Krieger (1954:508) estimate its age at AD 1200 to AD 1500, and they say it may continue with minor changes into the *Turney* type into

Figure 6.108. Talco points from 41MX4 and 41FK1 (photo courtesy of TARL).

historic times, circa AD 1600 to AD 1700. Turner, Hester, and McReynolds (2011:212) estimate its age at AD 1450 to AD 1700. Thurmond (1985:189–191) dates *Talco* points to sometime in the Late Caddoan period, AD 1500 to AD 1700.

DESCRIPTION: Suhm and Krieger (1954:508) describe *Talco* in the following: "Slender triangular points with edges occasionally almost straight but usually recurved with constriction approximately in middle. Bases almost always concave. Workmanship extremely fine, blades thin and flat. Edges commonly minutely serrated, tips often slimmed down to needle-like point." They provide the following dimensions:

Length: 2.0 cm to 5.5 cm
Width: 1.0 to 1.8 cm
Basal concavity: 0.1 cm to 0.4 cm

CULTURAL AFFILIATION: This is a common type in the Titus Focus, Fulton Aspect (Suhm and Krieger 1954). Thurmond (1985:189–191) writes that *Talco* points are one of the dominant types in the Titus Phase. The others are *Bassett*, *Maud*, and *Reed*.

KNOWN SITES: Culpepper (41HP1), Q. Miller (41DT98), Tuck Carpenter (41CP5), Williams site (41CP10), Gilbert (41RA13), Peerless Bottoms

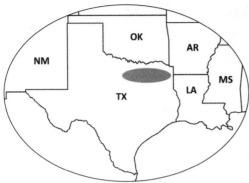

Figure 6.109. Distribution of Talco points (drafted by Lili Lyddon).

(41HP175), Roitsch formerly Sam Kaufman (41RR16), Alex Justiss (41TT13), 41MX4 and 41FK1.

SOURCES FOR ILLUSTRATIONS AND DESCRIPTIONS: Allen and others (1967); Bell (1958); Thurmond (1985); Davis (1995); Duncan and others (2007); Suhm and Jelks (1962); Suhm and Krieger (1954); Goldschmidt (1935); Fields (2004); Turner and Hester (1985, 1993, 1999); Jelks (1993); Turner and Smith (2002); and Turner and others (2011).

COMMENTS: According to Davis (1995), *Talco* points are often found in association with burials as grave offerings containing *Ripley Engraved* ceramics.

Goldschmidt (1935:94, Plate 11) illustrates examples of the *Talco* type before the name was assigned. He refers to the arrow points in Plate 11 as "flint arrowheads."

The *Talco* point at the Roitsch site (41RR16) was found associated with "burial 3" in the terrace area.

Thurmond (1985:189–191) writes that *Talco* is often associated with arrow point types *Bassett, Maud,* and *Reed*. The *Reed* point does not appear in Turner and others (2011).

DISTRIBUTION: Northeastern Texas, especially in the upper drainage system of the Sabine and Sulphur Rivers and to the Red River.

Figure 6.110. Toyah points (photo courtesy of John Fish).

Toyah

ORIGINAL RECORDER: J. Charles Kelley, T. N. Campbell, and Donald J. Lehmer (1940) were the first to recognize the *Toyah* point, but they did not describe it in detail. Later, Kelley (1947b) described it and named it *Piedras Triple Notched*. Suhm and Krieger (1954:508) described and illustrated it and changed the name to *Toyah*. This name was chosen because Kelley believed that this type is associated with the Toyah Focus. Walter W. Taylor (1966) described this type as the *Sierra Madre* point.

OTHER NAMES: *Piedras Triple Notched, Toyah Triple Notched,* and *Sierra Madre.*

SIMILAR TYPES: Kelley (1947b) describes similar types and named them *Saragosa Notched-Serrate, Frisco Base-Notched,* and *Saucia Split Base,* but he does not describe them in detail. Suhm and Krieger (1954:508) state that *Toyah* is similar to *Harrell* but smaller and more modified in the blade and around the corners by notching, incutting, and serration. Johnson (1994) compares it to *Harrell* and *Lott*.

AGE: Suhm and Krieger (1954:508) and Turner and others (2011), and McReynolds (2011:213) refer to it as Late Prehistoric and possibly early

224 | CHAPTER 6

historic with no specific dates. Cloud et al. (1994) mentions that *Toyah* points were found in a feature at the Polvo site that yielded a date of AD 1190 to AD 1280. Davis (1995) estimates its age at AD 1400 to AD 1650.

DESCRIPTION: Suhm and Krieger (1954:508) describe *Toyah* points as follows: "Small triangular blades with two side notches anywhere from near base to about middle. Bases originally straight to concave but strongly modified in most cases with a large third notch in center of base. Blade edges often strongly serrated and narrowed above notches." They provide the following dimensions: Length: 1.5 cm to 2.5 cm. Width: 1.0 cm to 1.5 cm.

CULTURAL AFFILIATION: Kelley (1947b) assigns this type to the Toyah Focus, a division of the Central Texas Aspect that he relates to the Jumano Indian occupation of west-central and Trans-Pecos Texas. These points have also been associated with the Bravo Valley Aspect and Livermore Focus of the Texas Big Bend-northern Chihuahua region (Kelley, Campbell, and Lehmer 1940) and the Jora Complex of central Coahuila (Taylor 1966).

KNOWN SITES: Baker Cave (41VV213), Devil's Mouth (41VV188), Parida Cave (41VV187), Roark Cave (41BS3), Buckhollow Encampment (41KM16), Polvo (41PS21), and 41BS188.

SOURCES FOR ILLUSTRATIONS AND DESCRIPTIONS: Bell (1960); Cloud (2001); Cloud and others (1994); Crook (2009); Corrick (2000); Davis (1995); Duncan and others (2007); Kelley (1947b); Kelley and others (1940); Suhm and Krieger (1954); Suhm and Jelks (1962); Hester (1980); Johnson (1964, 1994); Turner and Hester (1985, 1993,1999); Hedrick (1989); Word and Douglas (1970); Kenmotsu and Boyd (2012); and Turner and others (2011).

COMMENTS: According to Cloud et al. (1994:126), "Stratigraphic information from the Polvo site suggests that the Toyah type slightly predates Perdiz, that the two types were contemporaneous over an unknown length of time, and that the Perdiz style persisted somewhat later than Toyah."

Artifacts from 41BS188 in Big Bend National Park include fragments, preforms, and complete *Toyah* points. Many of the artifacts were broken during manufacture, and this has allowed some insight into how they were made. A radiocarbon sample was obtained from direction association of

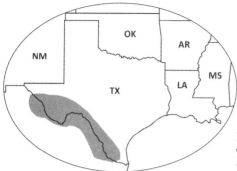

Figure 6.111. Distribution of Toyah points (drafted by Lili Lyddon).

Toyah points in a hearth and provided much-needed information for this type in the Big Bend (Corrick 2000).

Crook (2009) describes a *Toyah*-like point with multiple notches found in a cache at the Upper Farmersville site (41COL34).

I found no evidence of *Saragosa Notched-Serrate*, *Frisco Base-Notched*, and *Saucia Split Base*, as discussed by Kelly (1947b) being proposed as valid types.

LeRoy Johnson (1994) illustrates a probable *Toyah* point, but he refers to it as follows: "Stylistically, this arrowpoint is halfway between the so-called Harrell and Lott." His report, *The Life and Times of the Toyah Folk Culture: The Buckhollow Encampment, Site 41IKM16, Kimble, County Texas*, is a major source for information during the Toyah Focus.

Piedras Triple Notched and *Toyah Triple Notched* arrow points were found at the Polvo site in Presidio County (Shackelford 1955).

Boyd (2001:Figure 6) presents a map of the classic Toyah culture area, general Toyah culture area, and shared area. This map is a modification of one by Johnson (1994:Figure 105).

Four *Toyah* points were recovered from the Devil's Mouth site (41VV188). Johnson (1964:58) list their measurement as 15 mm to 25 mm (length) and 10 mm to 14 mm (width at the base).

DISTRIBUTION: According to Turner and others (2011:213), this point is found in southern and western Texas, the Lower Pecos, and less frequently in central Texas. According to Robert J. Mallouf (personal communication, 2018), it is commonly found in the Eastern Trans-Pecos and Big Bend regions.

Figure 6.112. Turner point (photo courtesy of John Fish).

Turner

ORIGINAL RECORDER: According to Perino (1991) and Hoffman (1971), most of the points illustrated by Clarence B. Moore (1912) from the Haley site are of the *Turner* variety.

OTHER NAMES: *Crickett*.

SIMILAR TYPES: Perino (1991) believes it is a variety of the *Hayes* type.

AGE: circa AD 1100 in northeastern Texas.

DESCRIPTION: No description available.

CULTURAL AFFILIATION: Caddoan culture.

KNOWN SITES: Haley (trinomial not found).

SOURCES FOR ILLUSTRATIONS AND DESCRIPTIONS: Perino (1991).

COMMENTS: *Turner* is not included in *Stone Artifacts of Texas Indians* (Turner and others 2011).

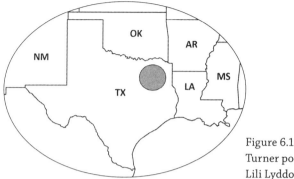

Figure 6.113. Distribution of Turner points (drafted by Lili Lyddon).

DISTRIBUTION: The primary range of this type is southwestern Arkansas, but it has been reported at sites in Louisiana, Oklahoma, and northeastern Texas.

Turney

ORIGINAL RECORDER: Dee Ann Suhm and Alex D. Krieger (1954) were the first to illustrate and describe the *Turney* point. The origin of this name is not known.

OTHER NAMES: None reported.

SIMILAR TYPES: According to Suhm and Krieger (1954:510), the "shorter specimens are very similar to *Talco* points but are constructed above the base rather than recurved with the constriction near the middle and the bases are more V-shaped." Davis (1995:260) claims *Turney* is similar in general appearance to *Maud*. The primary difference between the two is that the basal corners of *Maud* slope downward, and the basal corners of *Turney* tend to flare more outward.

AGE: Suhm and Krieger (1954:510) estimate the age of this Late Prehistoric arrow point at AD 1600 to AD 1800.

DESCRIPTION: Suhm and Krieger (1954:510) describe *Turney* points as follows: "Slender triangular blade, edges cut inward just above base, then

228 | CHAPTER 6

Figure 6.114. Turney points from 41NA206 (photo courtesy of Timothy K. Perttula).

straight to tip. Base a broad 'V' rather than concave, so that basal tips somewhat like barbs rather than ordinary corners. Very finely chipped, thin, flat, with edges serrated in most cases." They provide the following dimensions: length: 3.0 cm to 6.0 cm; width: 1.1 cm to 1.8 cm.

CULTURAL AFFILIATION: Suhm and Krieger (1954:510) write that this type is a diagnostic type of the Allen Focus of the Fulton Aspect, Historic Stage.

KNOWN SITES: Jim Allen (41CE12), Peerless Bottoms (41HP175), Spradley (41NA206), Gilbert (41RA13), and DeShazo (41NA27).

SOURCES FOR ILLUSTRATIONS AND DESCRIPTIONS: Davis (1995); Duncan and others (2007); Fields (2004); Perino (1985); Suhm and Jelks (1962); Suhm and Krieger (1954); Turner and Hester (1985, 1993, 1999); and Turner and others (2011).

COMMENTS: Davis (1995) says that *Turney*, *Maud*, and *Talco* are all found in eastern Texas, and this makes positive identification by type difficult. The *Turney* points in Figure 6–114 above are from a historic Allen Phase component at 41NA206 (Tim Perttula, personal communication, 2022).

DISTRIBUTION: Found in the central part of the Neches River valley of eastern Texas and mainly in Cherokee County (Suhm and Krieger 1954:510).

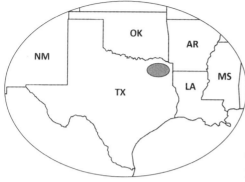

Figure 6.115. Distribution of Turney points (drafted by Lili Lyddon).

Figure 6.116. Washita point (replica by Matt Soultz; photo courtesy of Brian Wootan).

Washita

ORIGINAL RECORDER: Alex D. Krieger (1946) was the first to describe it, but he did not name it. When Dee Ann Suhm and Alex D. Krieger (1954) wrote *An Introductory Handbook of Texas Archeology*, they included it as a subtype of the *Harrell* point. Robert E. Bell (1958) suggested the name *Washita* for one of the subtypes originally included with *Harrell*. This name was taken from the Washita River in Oklahoma.

OTHER NAMES: Washita var. *norris* (Perttula 2020).

SIMILAR TYPES: *Harrell*.

230 | CHAPTER 6

AGE: Davis (1995:262) estimates the age of this Late Prehistoric arrow point at AD 1100 to AD 1600. Crook (2017:51) dates it to circa AD 1250 to AD 1600.

DESCRIPTION: Davis (1995:262) describes *Washita* as a small point with triangular blades. "The stem is formed by side notches. The base is usually straight but may be slightly concave. The basal corners are usually the widest part of this point, and the large basal area has a unique square appearance."

CULTURAL AFFILIATION: This point is a diagnostic artifact of the Washita Focus in Oklahoma. Crook (2017:51) associates it with the Farmersville Phase.

KNOWN SITES: Sam Kaufman (41RR1), A. C. Mackin (41LR39), Bell Camp (41PR107), Greenbelt (41DY17), Upper Farmersville (41COL34), 41PR126 (Private Collection), 41SE17, 41DL406, 41CR33, and 41YN1.

SOURCES FOR ILLUSTRATIONS AND DESCRIPTIONS: Bell (1958); Crook (2008–2009, 2011, 2017); Davis (1995); Duncan and others (2007); Forrester (1987b); Kehoe (1966); Krieger (1946); Perino (1985, 1991); Perttula (2020); Suhm and Krieger (1954); Shawn (1975); Parker (1982); Turner and Hester (1985, 1993, 1999); and Turner and others (2011).

COMMENTS: Perino (1991) illustrates and discusses a northern variety of the *Washita* point that is found from northern Kansas to west-central Canada.

This type is described in more detail by Thomas F. Kehoe (1966). Forrester (1987b) mentions 16 *Washita* points at 41SE17.

Wilson W. Crook III (2017) discusses types of damage to *Washita* points and other Late Prehistoric types from a sample of 750 examples.

At the Gilkey Hill site (41DL406), *Washita* is represented by three specimens—two of chert and one of quartzite (Crook 2011:Table 1).

A single *Washita* point made from Alibates chert was found at 41OC93 in Ochiltree County.

Fifty-one *Washita* points were collected at the Greenbelt site (41DY17) Campbell (1970:44) describes two of the specimens as a multiple notch

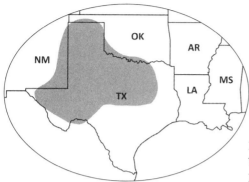

Figure 6.117. Distribution of Washita points (drafted by Lili Lyddon).

variety. Forty-one points are Alibates material, nine are Tecovas jasper, and one is from unidentified chert.

Cindy Smyers (personal communication, October 28, 2022) mentioned that *Washita* points were found in direct association with *Harrell* points at a bison kill site (41CR33) in Crane County.

DISTRIBUTION: In Texas, it is found in the Panhandle-Plains, North-Central Texas, and the Northeast Texas subregion. Bell (1958) states that this type is found in Oklahoma, parts of the Great Plains, the Mississippi River valley, and the Southwest. According to Robert J. Mallouf (personal communication, 2018), it is infrequently found in the Eastern Trans-Pecos and Big Bend Region.

Young

ORIGINAL RECORDER: Alex D. Krieger (1946) was the first to recognize and describe the *Young* point. When Dee Ann Suhm and Alex D. Krieger (1954) wrote *An Introductory Handbook of Texas Archeology*, they described and illustrated it and named it for Young County where many specimens have been found. Example is from 41PP63.

OTHER NAMES: None reported.

SIMILAR TYPES: *Cliffton* and *Padre*.

Figure 6.118. Young point from 41PP62 (photo courtesy of TARL).

AGE: AD 1200 to AD 1500 Sum and Krieger (1954:510).

DESCRIPTION: "Crudely triangular to leaf-shaped, edges occasionally almost straight but usually strongly convex and often asymmetrical. Made from thin, curved flakes with little modification on either side, usually not enough to flatten the artifacts. Bases straight to convex, seldom concave, often crooked" (Suhm and Krieger 1954:510). They describe the following dimensions: Length: 2.5 cm to 4.5 cm; width: 1.5 cm to 2.5 cm.

CULTURAL AFFILIATION: A common type in Henrietta Focus sites and rare in the Central Texas Aspect (Suhm and Krieger 1954).

KNOWN SITES: Kyle (41HI1), Smith Rockshelter (41TV42), Greenshaw (41HY29), Wunderlich (41CM3), Live Oak Point (41AS2), and 41SE17.

SOURCES FOR ILLUSTRATIONS AND DESCRIPTIONS: Campbell (1956); Bell (1960); Davis (1995); Krieger (1946); Perino (1985); Suhm and Jelks (1962); Suhm and Krieger (1954); Hester (1980); Turner and Hester (1985, 1993, 1999); Watt (1967); and Turner, Hester, and McReynolds (2011).

COMMENTS: Weir (1979:24) writes, "A type now thought to be a preform rather than finished form."

Arrow Points | 233

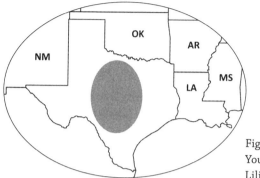

Figure 6.119. Distribution of Young points (drafted by Lili Lyddon).

DISTRIBUTION: Concentrated in Young County, the upper Brazos River valley, and North-Central Texas with a few specimens reported in the northern part of Central Texas.

Zapata

ORIGINAL RECORDER: The *Zapata* point was first described as *Form 1* based on examples found by Don Kumpe at Falcon Reservoir in Zapata County. The first published description of this type appears in an article by Don Kumpe et al. and C. K. Chandler (2000). Turner and others (2011) state that the name had been changed to *Zapata* to reflect the county where the first specimens were found.

OTHER NAMES: *Form 1.*

SIMILAR TYPES: *Maud.*

AGE: Turner and others (2011) refer to this type as Late Prehistoric, but they do not offer any specific dates.

DESCRIPTION: Turner and others (2011:217) describe *Zapata* as "triangular to unstemmed arrow points. Specimens have slightly to markedly convex lateral edges near the base, which usually has the widest measurement. The stem and basal areas are slightly to moderately concave and have a 'bowlegged' appearance. The points are usually made on flakes and may

Figure 6.120. Zapata point from Northern Mexico (photo courtesy of TARL).

retain much of the original flake surface. Some specimens appear to have been sharpened while hafted, thus altering the original flake form above the hafted area." No dimensions are given.

CULTURAL AFFILIATION: Unknown.

KNOWN SITES: 41ZP83 and 41ZP154.

SOURCES FOR ILLUSTRATIONS AND DESCRIPTIONS: Kumpe (1993); Kumpe and others (2000); and Turner and others (2011).

COMMENTS: According to Turner and others (2011:217), "these points are usually made on flakes and sometimes retain much of the original flake surface. Some appear to have been hafted, and this alters the original flake form above the hafted area."

Kumpe and others (2000) state that the quantity of broken specimens may be an indication that they are preforms that broke during manufacture. Only seven of the 26 specimens in the senior author's collection are complete. The authors suggest that breakage may be a result of the thinness and length of some *Form 1* points. The frequency of this type in local

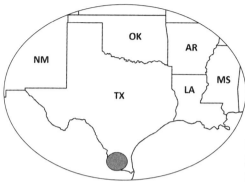

Figure 6.121. Distribution of Zapata points (drafted by Lili Lyddon).

collections is probably underestimated because collectors usually only keep complete specimens, and some collectors refer to this type as *Maud*.

This point is not included in *Prehistoric Artifacts of the Texas Indians: An Identification and Reference Guide* (Davis 1995).

DISTRIBUTION: According to Kumpe and others (2000:43), this type "occurs in substantial numbers in sites in the northern portion of Falcon Reservoir." They also say that "They [*Form 1* points] appear to be absent from the southern portion of the lake." "In Zapata County, they are seldom found farther than a few hundred yards from the normal conservation pool of the lake."

Zavala

ORIGINAL RECORDER: Turner and Hester (1985:197) state that *Zavala* points were found at the Honeymoon site in Zavala County. Only four arrow points were found at this site (Hill and Hester 1971), and each one is described as *Scallorn* or a variation of *Scallorn*. It is, therefore, assumed that one or more of these points were later named *Zavala*. In the typology book by Turner and others (2011), the Honeymoon site is no longer mentioned as a site where *Zavala* points have been found.

OTHER NAMES: None reported.

CHAPTER 6

Figure 6.122. Zavala point (replica by Matt Soultz; photo courtesy of Brian Wootan).

SIMILAR TYPES: *Zavala* and the *Figueroa* point are quite similar. Davis (1995:266) states that the shoulders om *Figueroa* are usually stronger than *Zavala*, and the basal width is wider than those on *Zavala*. *Figueroa* is classified as a dart point, and *Zavala* is an arrow point.

AGE: According to Turner and others (2011:218), this is a transitional Archaic arrow point that was used circa 200 BC to AD 600 or later.

DESCRIPTION: Turner and others2011:218) describe this point as "small, stubby, and thick." No dimensions are given.

CULTURAL AFFILIATION: Unknown.

KNOWN SITES: Devil's Mouth (41VV185), Wunderlich (41CM3), Honeymoon (41ZV34), Coontail Spin (41VV82), 41BS66, and 41BS402.

SOURCES FOR ILLUSTRATIONS AND DESCRIPTIONS: Lukowski (1987); Davis (1995); Hill and Hester (1971); Hester (1974, 1980); Hafernik (1984); Turner and Hester (1985, 1993, 1999); and Turner and others (2011).

COMMENTS: Davis (1995:266): states that *Zavala* points were probably used with the bow and arrow weaponry system, and it is equally possible that the earlier ones were darts used with the atlatl.

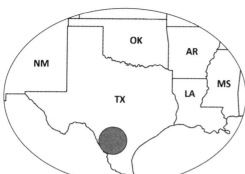

Figure 6.123. Distribution of Zavala points (drafted by Lili Lyddon).

It is assumed that this type is named for Zavala County where the first examples were found.

DISTRIBUTION: This type is found primarily in southern Texas, especially in the Nueces River–Rio Grande River corridor. Specimens may occur in the Lower Pecos and central Texas.

CHAPTER 7

Final Thoughts

THE LATE Prehistoric and Early Historic periods are well represented in Texas in terms of arrow point types. Numerous types have been identified, while others remain questionable. Overlapping shapes are sometimes interpreted as variations of a known type or a type yet to be identified. Types of materials available are also abundant and, in some cases, widespread across the state. Within these materials is a variability in quality that affects the outcome of the finished product. A point that may be defined as crudely made should not necessarily be considered to have been knapped by someone with poor skills, as some archaeologists have posited. Factors such as type of raw material and expediency may have been the main contributors. Valid conclusions drawn from the examination of arrow points are based on empirical data and not speculation and untested hypotheses. Diaries of early explorers have provided a wealth of information about the lifeways of the Indigenous peoples of Texas, but they offer little insight to arrow point production. Artificial boundaries have no meaning in terms of the separation of different groups and their material culture. Arrow points such as *Catahoula* were first identified in Louisiana, and it has been found to be a common type in much of East Texas. Arrow points found in Texas and adjacent states are listed in Appendix B. Those appearing in figures are housed in public and private collections (Appendix F).

Although it is true that large numbers of artifacts are removed legally from private property and illegally from public lands by persons interested solely in enhancing their personal collections, not all collecting is as detrimental as claimed by professionals. Of course, the preference among the archaeological community is for no sites to be collected by relic hunters. However, the reality is that there is a divide between professionals and some collectors regarding the right to collect. Many archaeological sites are on private land where collecting is legal, and it is unlikely that archaeologists will ever have a reason or permission to visit these sites. Therefore, cooperation with collectors can be very productive, especially those who can identify the source of their collections and are willing to share information. Albeit, artifacts found on the surface of a plowed field, or otherwise disturbed sites yield less data than those collected under controlled conditions, they still provide useful information in terms of site location, material used, types present, and associated artifacts and features such as a burial. Archaeological sites are rapidly disappearing due to vandalism, erosion, and development. Consequently, pristine sites are rare.

The intended audience for this book is professional archaeologists and nonprofessionals such as avocational archaeologists as well as persons with an interest in learning more about Texas prehistory. There are numerous informative online sources (e.g., glossaries) that provide lists of archaeological terms and their definitions.

In Texas, there are archaeological societies at the local, regional, and state level. These groups are open to membership of persons interested in learning about their collections and have a desire to educate themselves about Texas prehistory. Regular meetings and supervised field trips provide members with opportunities to learn how to properly collect and document their finds. The critically acclaimed books on stone artifacts of Texas Indians by Turner and Hester (1985, 1993, 1999) and Turner and colleagues (2011) provide lists of these societies with contact information. There are times when nonprofessionals want to report their finds but are not sure who to reach out to. Turner and colleagues (2011:Appendix V) provide contact information for state and federal agencies that have professional archaeologists on their staffs.

The Boy Scouts of America has a long tradition of interest in Indian lore, and many present-day archaeologists got their start in this manner. In the formative years of the Boy Scouts, the interest in Indian lore unfortunately resulted in instances of indiscriminate collecting resulting in the destruction of numerous sites throughout the country. This phenomenon was discussed by the renowned Texas archaeologist J. E. Pearce (1936:46): "All over the country, archeologists are having trouble with Boy Scouts whose surplus time and energies have been misdirected by ill-informed leaders into making 'Indian Collections.' Once they get started at this, they often become more destructive than all other agencies combined." S. Alan Skinner is a well-known Texas archaeologist who was acutely aware of these practices. He was instrumental in the development of the popular archaeology merit badge for the Boy Scouts of America as an incentive to educate our youth on the importance of the documentation and preservation of archaeological sites.

To be fair, many archaeologists (including me) have personal collections of Indian artifacts obtained during their younger days. The artifacts I collected were never mixed, and I kept records of site locations and obtained site numbers, when possible, from TARL. Later, I documented much of my work as articles in professional journals. My professional career spanned more than 40 years. Hopefully, this treatise will be of some benefit to those who follow after me.

EPILOGUE

HE NUMBER of intact prehistoric archaeological sites in Texas and elsewhere is disappearing at an alarming rate. This loss of cultural resources is the result of several factors such as land alteration by development, erosion, subsidence, and artifact collectors. An integral part of interpreting these sites is a reliable and consistent system of identifying artifacts by a name that is recognizable by professionals. Projectile point typology is not exact and is often confusing due to variations of specific types. My purpose in writing this book is to discuss arrow points found in Texas and adjacent areas that have been assigned to types based on credible evidence. This text also is an attempt to summarize the bulk of many disparate resources often used by both professional and avocational archaeologists to interpret archaeological assemblages. Archaeologists do not always agree regarding certain types, and I make no judgment as to the validity of the those discussed herein.

Appendix A

County Abbreviations

County	Abbreviation
Anderson	AN
Andrews	AD
Angelina	AG
Aransas	AS
Archer	AR
Armstrong	AM
Atascosa	AT
Austin	AU
Bailey	BA
Bandera	BN
Bastrop	BP
Baylor	BY
Bee	BE
Bell	BL
Bexar	BX
Blanco	BC
Borden	BD
Bosque	BQ
Bowie	BW
Brazoria	BO
Brazos	BZ
Brewster	BS
Briscoe	BI
Brooks	BK
Brown	BR

County	Abbreviation
Burleson	BU
Burnet	BT
Caldwell	CW
Calhoun	CL
Callahan	CA
Cameron	CF
Camp	CP
Carson	CZ
Cass	CS
Castro	CAS
Chambers	CH
Cherokee	CE
Childress	CI
Clay	CY
Cochran	CQ
Coke	CK
Coleman	CN
Collin	COL
Collingsworth	CG
Colorado	CD
Comal	CM
Comanche	CJ
Concho	CC
Cooke	CO
Coryell	CV

246 | Appendix A

County	Abbreviation
Cottle	CT
Crane	CR
Crockett	CX
Crosby	CB
Culberson	CU
Dallam	DA
Dallas	DL
Dawson	DS
Deaf Smith	DF
Delta	DT
Denton	DN
De Witt	DW
Dickens	DK
Dimmitt	DM
Donley	DY
Duval	DV
Eastland	EA
Ector	EC
Edwards	ED
Ellis	EL
El Paso	EP
Erath	ER
Falls	FA
Fannin	FN
Fayette	FY
Fisher	FS
Floyd	FL
Foard	FD
Fort Bend	FB
Franklin	FK
Freestone	FT

County	Abbreviation
Frio	FR
Gaines	GA
Galveston	GV
Garza	GR
Gillespie	GL
Glasscock	GC
Goliad	GD
Gonzales	GZ
Gray	GY
Grayson	GS
Gregg	GG
Grimes	GM
Guadalupe	GU
Hale	HA
Hall	HL
Hamilton	HM
Hansford	HF
Hardeman	HX
Hardin	HN
Harris	HR
Harrison	HS
Hartley	HT
Haskell	HK
Hays	HY
Hemphill	HH
Henderson	HE
Hidalgo	HG
Hill	HI
Hockley	HQ
Hood	HD
Hopkins	HP

County Abbreviations | 247

County	Abbreviation
Houston	HO
Howard	HW
Hudspeth	HZ
Hunt	HU
Hutchinson	HC
Irion	IR
Jack	JA
Jackson	JK
Jasper	JP
Jeff Davis	JD
Jefferson	JF
Jim Hogg	JH
Jim Wells	JW
Johnson	JN
Jones	JS
Karnes	KA
Kaufman	KF
Kendall	KE
Kenedy	KN
KENT	KT
KERR	KR
Kimble	KM
King	KG
Kinney	KY
Kleberg	KL
Knox	KX
Lamar	LR
Lamb	LA
Lampasas	LM
La Salle	LS
Lavaca	LC

County	Abbreviation
Lee	LE
Leon	LN
Liberty	LB
Limestone	LT
Lipscomb	LP
Live Oak	LK
Llano	LL
Loving	LV
Lubbock	LU
Lynn	LY
Madison	MA
Marion	MR
Martin	MT
Mason	MS
Matagorda	MG
Maverick	MV
McCulloch	MK
McLennan	ML
McMullen	MC
Medina	ME
Menard	MN
Midland	MD
Milam	MM
Mills	MI
Mitchell	MH
Montague	MU
Montgomery	MQ
Moore	MO
Morris	MX
Motley	MY
Nacogdoches	NA

Appendix A

County	Abbreviation
Navarro	NV
Newton	NW
Nolan	NL
Nueces	NU
Ochiltree	OC
Oldham	OL
Orange	OR
Palo Pinto	PP
Panola	PN
Parker	PR
Parmer	PM
Pecos	PC
Polk	PK
Potter	PT
Presidio	PS
Rains	RA
Randall	RD
Reagan	RG
Real	RE
Red River	RR
Reeves	RV
Refugio	RF
Roberts	RB
Robertson	RT
Rockwall	RW
Runnels	RN
Rusk	RK
Sabine	SB
San Augustine	SA
San Jacinto	SJ
San Patricio	SP

County	Abbreviation
San Saba	SS
Schleicher	SL
Scurry	SC
Shackelford	SF
Shelby	SY
Sherman	SH
Smith	SM
Somervell	SV
Starr	SR
Stephens	SE
Sterling	ST
Stonewall	SN
Sutton	SU
Swisher	SW
Tarrant	TR
Taylor	TA
Terrell	TE
Terry	TY
Throckmorton	TH
Titus	TT
Tom Green	TG
Travis	TV
Trinity	TN
Tyler	TL
Upshur	UR
Upton	UT
Uvalde	UV
Val Verde	VV
Van Zandt	VN
Victoria	VT
Walker	WA

County Abbreviations | 249

County	Abbreviation
Waller	WL
Ward	WR
Washington	WT
Webb	WB
Wharton	WH
Wheeler	WE
Wichita	WC
Wilbarger	WG
Willacy	WY

County	Abbreviation
Williamson	WM
Wilson	WN
Winkler	WK
Wise	WS
Wood	WD
Yoakum	YK
Young	YN
Zapata	ZP
Zavala	ZV

Appendix B

Texas Arrow Points Found in Other States and Mexico

Arkansas

Agee, Bassett, Bonham, Hayes, Homan, Howard, Maud, Metal, Morris, Rockwall, Scallorn, Talco

Louisiana

Agee, Alba, Bassett, Bonham, Catahoula, Friley, Hayes, Homan, Howard, Maud, Metal, Rockwall

Mexico

Ahumada, Caracara, Form 2, Garza, Guerrero, Metal, Perdiz, Revilla, Scallorn, Starr, Toyah, and Zapata

New Mexico

Deadman's, Fresno-like, Garza, Harrell, Livermore-like, Metal, Perdiz, Toyah, Washita

Oklahoma

Agee, Alba, Bassett, Bonham, Deadman's, Fresno, Garza, Harrell, Hayes, Homan, Howard, Maud, Metal, Morris, Perdiz, Rockwall, Scallorn, Talco, Washita

Appendix C

Shapes of Arrow Points

AS STATED EARLIER, most projectile points were created from a triangular template with numerous variations in overall appearance. This is a necessary plan because a pointed tip is required for penetration. Some specimens have tips that are somewhat rounded as opposed to the majority that exhibit a pronounced point. This can be the result of use, reworking, or this tip was considered suitable for that type. A factor that should not be overlooked is the intended purpose of the finished artifact. Overwhelmingly, the artifacts described and illustrated in this book are considered to have been created to function as an arrow point, and this is probably true for the majority. However, while hafted, they could have also been used for other tasks such as cutting. I believe this is more likely with the larger dart points, some of which are too large and heavy for atlatl use. The basic parts of a triangular-shaped point are illustrated here.

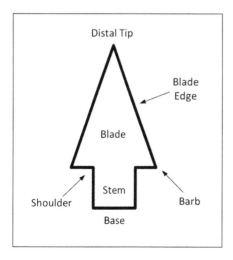

Figure C1. Parts of a projectile point (drafted by Lili Lyddon).

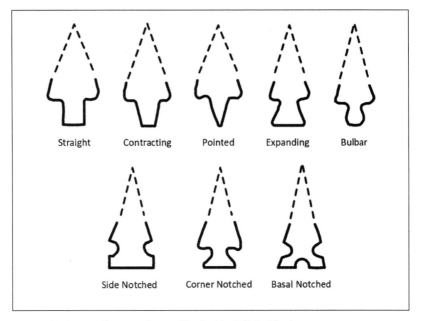

Figure C2. Projectile point shapes (drafted by Lili Lyddon).

Triangular points, for example, have no stems, shoulders, notches, or barbs. Others have elongated blades that culminate in what is referred to as a "needle nose," and some types have serrated edges, often to the point of being described as eccentric. Others were reworked to function as a drill or perforator. In the past, it was not unusual for unidentified artifacts to have been identified as ceremonial or as objects used for trade.

Even though the edge of a point can be a valuable determinant in point classification, it is the stem and base that are the most diagnostic features. The examples depicted here illustrate the most common configurations.

Appendix D

Sites with Manning Fused Glass

Cherokee County
41CE19, 41CE49, and 41CE54

Houston County
41HO4, 41HO7, 41HO11, 41HO13, 41HO15, and 41HO17

Limestone County
41LT58

Nacogdoches County
41NA27

Polk County
41PK1

Rusk County
41RK9, 41RK10, 41RK11, 41RK13, 41RK16, 41RK17, 41RK19, 41RK20, 41RK21, 41RK23, 41RK26, 41RK30, 41RK32, 41RK36, 41RK39, and 41RK47

Trinity County
41TN11, 41TN31

Walker County
41WA1, 41WA52, 41WA71, 41WA72, 41WA65, 41WA66, and 41WA74

Appendix E

Counties in the Planning Regions

Eastern Planning Region

Prairie-Savanna

Bosque, Collin, Cooke, Dallas, Denton, Ellis, Falls, Freestone, Grayson, Hill, Hood, Hunt, Johnson, Kaufman, Leon, Limestone, McLennan, Madison, Montague, Navarro, Parker, Robertson, Rockwall, Somervell, Tarrant, and Wise.

Southeast Texas

Brazoria, Brazos, Chambers, Fort Bend, Galveston, Grimes, Hardin, Harris, Jasper, Jefferson, Liberty, Montgomery, Newton, Orange, Polk, San Jacinto, Tyler, Walker, and Waller.

Northeast Texas

Anderson, Angelina, Bowie, Camp, Cass, Cherokee, Delta, Fannin, Franklin, Gregg, Harrison, Henderson, Hopkins, Houston, Lamar, Marion, Morris, Nacogdoches, Panola, Rains, Red River, Rusk, Sabine, San Augustine, Shelby, Smith, Titus, Trinity, Upshur, Van Zandt, and Wood.

Central and Southern Planning Region

Central Texas

Bandera, Bastrop, Bexar, Blanco, Burnet, Caldwell, Comal, Concho, Crockett, Edwards, Gillespie, Guadalupe, Hays, Irion, Kendall, Kerr, Kimble, Kinney, Lampasas, Lee, Llano, McCulloch, Mason, Medina, Menard, Mills, Real, San Saba, Schleicher, Sutton, Tom Green, Travis, Uvalde, and Williamson.

Central Coastal Plains

Austin, Colorado, DeWitt, Fayette, Gonzales, Guadalupe, Karnes, Lavaca, Washington, and Wilson.

Coastal Corridor

Aransas, Bee, Calhoun, Cameron, Goliad, Jackson, Kennedy, Kleberg, Nueces, Matagorda, Refugio, San Patricio, Victoria, Wharton, and Willacy.

Lower Pecos

Crockett and Val Verde.

Rio Grande Plains

Atascosa, Brooks, Dimmit, Duval, Frio, Hidalgo, Jim Hogg, Jim Wells, Kinney, La Salle, Live Oak, McMullen, Maverick, Medina, Uvalde, Starr, Webb, Zapata, and Zavala.

Plains Planning Region

Northern Panhandle

Armstrong, Carson, Collingsworth, Dallam, Deaf Smith, Donley, Gray, Hansford, Hartley, Hemphill, Hutchinson, Lipscomb, Moore, Ochiltree, Oldham, Potter, Randall, Roberts, Sherman, and Wheeler.

Unnamed

Andrews, Archer, Bailey, Baylor, Borden, Briscoe, Brown, Callahan, Castro, Childress, Clay, Cochran, Coke, Coleman, Comanche, Cottle, Crane, Crosby, Dawson, Dickens, Eastland, Ector, Erath, Fisher, Floyd, Foard, Gaines, Garza, Glasscock, Hale, Hall, Hardeman, Haskell, Hockley, Howard, Jack, Jones, Kent, King, Knox, Lamb, Loving, Lubbock, Lynn, Martin, Midland, Mitchell, Motley, Nolan, Palo Pinto, Parmer, Reagan, Runnels, Scurry, Shackelford, Stephens, Sterling, Stonewall, Swisher, Taylor, Terry, Throckmorton, Upton, Yoakum, Young, Ward, Wichita, Wilbarger, and Winkler.

Trans-Pecos Planning Region

Brewster, Culberson, El Paso, Hudspeth, Jeff Davis, Pecos, Presidio, Reeves, and Terrell.

References Cited

Agogino, George A., and Phillip Shelly

1988 Could Gar Scales Have Been Used as Projectile Points in the Southern United States and Northern Mexico? *The Artifact* 26(1):29–31.

Allen, G. L., Jr., Pauline Allen, Joe F. Cochran, Lathel F. Duffield, R. E. Forrester Jr., Elbert D. Helm, Isabelle R. Lobdell, David Lubell, Roy E. Padgett, and Robert L. Tapscott

1967 Stone Tools: In the Gilbert Site, A Norteño Focus Site in Northeastern Texas. *Bulletin of the Texas Archeological Society* 37:191–219.

Anderson, Andrew Elliot

1932 Artifacts of the Rio Grande Delta Region. *Bulletin of the Texas Archeological and Paleontological Society* 2:29–31. Page numbers are from the 2009 reprint edition.

Anthony, Dana

1991 Lithic Analysis. In *Prairie Hinterland: The Archaeology of Palo Creek, Phase II: Testing, Palo Duro Reservoir, Hansford County, Texas,* edited by John Peterson, pp. 255–327. Archaeological Research, Inc. Austin.

Arakawa, Fumiyasu

2013 Gendered Analysis of Lithics from the Central Mesa Verde Region. *Kiva* 78(3):279–312.

Arnn, John Wesley, III

2012 Defining Hunter-Gatherer Sociocultural Identity and Interaction at a Regional Scale. In *The Toyah Phase of Central Texas: Late Prehistoric Economic and Social Processes,* edited by Nancy A. Kenmotsu and Douglas K. Boyd, pp. 44–75. Texas A&M University Press, College Station.

Asaro, Frank, and Fred H. Stross

1994 Mexican Provenience of Two Obsidian Artifacts from Willacy County, Texas. Report submitted to Thomas R. Hester, June 9, 1994.

Aten, Lawrence E.

1979 *Indians of the Upper Texas Coast: Ethnohistorical and Archeological Frameworks.* PhD dissertation, Department of Anthropology, the University of Texas at Austin.

1983 *Indians of the Upper Texas Coast.* Academic Press, New York.

260 | References Cited

Avery, George

1995   More Friend Than Foe: Eighteenth Century Spanish, French, and Caddoan Interaction at Los Adeas, a Capital of Texas Located in Northwestern Louisiana. *Louisiana Archaeology* 22:163–193.

Bacha-Garza, Roseann, Juan L. Garza, Christopher L Miller, and Russell K. Skowronek

2022   From a Tabula Rasa to the Governor's Award for Historic Preservation: How the CHAPS Program Brought Archaeology to Deep South Texas. *Public Historian* 44(4):169–189.

Bailey, Gail, L.

1988   *Archeological Bibliography for the Southern Coastal Corridor Region of Texas.* Office of the State Archeologist, Special Report 29. Texas Historical Commission. Austin. With contributions by Helen Simons and Patricia A. Mercado-Allinger.

Bailey, Gail L., Ross C. Fields, Gary DeMarcay, Michael B. Collins, and Jack M. Jackson

1988   Analysis of Previous Collections. In *Cultural Resources Investigations along Whiteoak Bayou, Harris County, Texas.* Reports of Investigations 62, pp. 97–210. Prewitt & Associates, Inc. Austin.

Baker, William E., and T. N. Campbell

1959   Metal Projectile Points from the Oklahoma Panhandle and Vicinity. *Bulletin of the Oklahoma Anthropological Society* 7:51–54.

Baker, William E., and Clarence H. Webb

1976   Catahoula Type Projectile Points. *Louisiana Archaeology* 3:225–251.

Banks, Larry

1990   From Mountain Peaks to Alligator Stomachs: A Review of Lithic Resources in the Trans-Mississippi South, the Southern Plains, and Adjacent Southwest. Oklahoma Anthropological Society, *Memoir* 4.

Banks, Larry, and Joe Winters

1975   *The Bentsen-Clark Site, Red River County, Texas: A Preliminary Report.* Special Publication No. 2. Texas Archeological Society. Austin.

Barnes, Virgil E.

1979   *Geologic Atlas of Texas.* Emory Peak Presidio Sheet. Bureau of Economic Geology, University of Texas at Austin.

Baskin, Barbara J.

1981   Lithic and Mineral Artifacts. In *Archeological Investigations at the George C. Davis Site, Cherokee County, Texas: Summers of 1979 and 1980.* Texas Archeological Research Laboratory, Occasional Papers No. 1. Austin.

Basso, Keith H., editor

1971   *Western Apache Raiding and Warfare: From the Notes of Greenville Goodwin.* University of Arizona Press, Tucson.

References Cited | 261

Baugh, T. G., and F. W. Nelson Jr.

1987   New Mexico Obsidian Sources and Exchange on the Southern Plains. *Journal of Field Archaeology* 14(3):313–329.

Bauman, Jerry L.

1988   A Brass Arrow Point from Nueces County, Texas. *La Tierra* 15(4):34–39.

1989   A Brass Arrow Point from San Patricio County, Texas. *La Tierra* 16(4):26–28.

1991   Two Metal Arrow Points from Nueces County, Texas. *La Tierra* 18(3):27–29.

Beasley, Tom S.

1978   A Site with Edwards Points in Banderas County, Texas. *La Tierra* 5(4):23–31.

Bell, Robert E.

1962   Indian Arrowheads. *Archeological Newsletter* 3(1):1–12.

1958   *Guide to the Identification of Certain American Indian Projectile Points.* Special Bulletin No. 1. Oklahoma Anthropological Society, Norman.

1960   *Guide to the Identification of Certain American Indian Projectile Points.* Special Bulletin No. 2. Oklahoma Anthropological Society, Norman.

Bell, Robert E., and Roland Scott Hall

1953   Selected Projectile Points of the United States. *Bulletin of the Oklahoma Anthropological Society* 1:1–16.

Bell, Robert E., and George Lynn Cross

1980   *Oklahoma Indian Artifacts.* Contributions from the Stovall Museum No. 4. University of Oklahoma, Norman.

Bennett, Bob

1956   *Kerr County, Texas: 1856–1956.* Naylor, San Antonio.

Bennett, Wendall C., and Robert M. Zingg

1976   *The Tarahumara: An Indian Tribe of Northern Mexico.* Rio Grande Press, Glorieta, New Mexico. Reprint of the original published in 1935 by the University of Chicago Press.

Berlandier, Jean Louis

1969   *The Indians of Texas in 1830.* Edited by John C. Ewers. Smithsonian Institution Press, Washington, DC.

Biesaart, Lynne A., Wayne R. Roberson, and Lisa Clinton Spotts

1985   *Prehistorical Archeological Sites in Texas: A Statistical Overview.* Office of the State Archeologist, Special Report 28. Texas Historical Commission, Austin.

Black, Stephen L.

1986   *The Clemente and Herminia Hinojosa Site, 41JW8: A Toyah Horizon Campsite in Southern Texas.* Center for Archaeological Research, Special Report No. 18. University of Texas at San Antonio.

262 | References Cited

Blitz, J. H.
1988 Adoption of the Bow in Prehistoric North America. *North American Archaeologist* 9:123–145.

Boisvert, Richard
1985 A Technological Analysis of Lithic Assemblages from Guadalupe Mountains National Park, Texas. *Bulletin of the Texas Archeological Society* 54:1–104.

Bolton, Herbert Eugene
1970 *Athanase de Mezieres and the Louisiana-Texas Frontier, 1768–1780* (Vol. 1), Kraus Reprint. Original published by Arthur H. Clarke, Cleveland 1914.

Boyd, Douglas K.
1995 The Palo Duro Complex: Redefining the Early Ceramic Period in the Caprock Canyonlands. *Bulletin of the Texas Archeological Society* 66:461–518.
2001 *Querechos* and Texas: Protohistoric Hunters and Gatherers in the Texas Panhandle-Plains, A.D. 1540–1700. *Bulletin of the Texas Archeological Society* 72:5–22.
2004 The Palo Duro Complex. In *The Prehistory of Texas*, edited by Timothy K. Perttula, pp. 296–330. Texas A&M University Press, College Station.

Boyd, James Bryan
1997 A Late Prehistoric Burial from 41ZP85, Old Zapata, Zapata County, Texas. *La Tierra* 24(3):8–14.

Boyd, Douglas K., Martha Doty Freeman, Michael D. Blum, Elton R. Prewitt, and J. Michael Quigg
1989 *Phase I Cultural Resources Investigations at the Justiceburg Reservoir on the Double Mountain Fork of the Brazos River, Garza and Kent Counties, Texas.* Reports of Investigations 66, Vol. 1, Prewitt and Associates, Inc., Austin.

Boyd, James Bryan, and D. E. Wilson
1999 A Cremation Burial from the Arroyo Salinillas, Falcon Reservoir. *La Tierra* 26(5):4–7.

Boyd, James Bryan, and Timothy K. Perttula
2000 On the Association of Caracara Arrow Points with Late Prehistoric Burials in the Falcon Reservoir Area. *La Tierra* 27(4):5–14.

Brockmoller, Sunny
1987 The Identification and Classification of Projectile Points from the Plateau Complex, Van Horn, Texas. *The Artifact* 25(1):1–48.

Brown, C.
1985 The Tale of Two Sites: A (41LU34) and B (41LU29). *Transactions of the 20th Regional Archeological Symposium for Southeastern New Mexico and Western Texas*, pp. 143–155.

References Cited | 263

Brown, James A.

1976 *Spiro Studies: The Artifacts*. University of Oklahoma Research Institute, Vol. 4. University of Oklahoma, Norman.

1996 The Spiro Ceremonial Center: The Archaeology of Arkansas Valley Caddoan Culture in Eastern Oklahoma. *Memoirs*, No. 29, Museum of Anthropology, University of Michigan, Ann Arbor.

Brown, Kenneth M.

1976 Fused Volcanic Glass from the Manning Formation. *Bulletin of the Texas Archeological Society* 47:189–207.

Brown, Kenneth M., and A. J. Taylor

1989 A Comment on Metal Arrow Points. *La Tierra* 16(4):10–22.

Browne, Jim

1938 Antiquity of the Bow. *American Antiquity* 3(4):358–359.

1940 Projectile Points. *American Antiquity* 5(4):209–213.

Bruseth, James E., and Timothy K. Perttula (editors)

1995 *Advances in Texas Archeology: Contributions from Cultural Research Management*. Texas Historical Commission, Austin.

Bruseth, Jim, Jeff Durst, Richard Proctor, Larry Banks, and Bill Pierson

2009 Investigations at the Gene and Ruth Ann Stallings Ranch Site (41LR297). *Bulletin of the Texas Archeological Society* 80:194–205.

Bryan, Frank

1936 Geological Sketch of Moffat-Whitehall Pendleton Area. *Bulletin of the Central Texas Archeological Society* 2:28–29.

Buck, B. A.

1982 Ancient Technology in Contemporary Surgery. *Western Journal of Medicine* 136(3):265–269.

Button, Van Tries

1989 The Byrd Mountain Lithic Cache (34GR149): A Find of Edwards Chert from Greer County, Southwestern Oklahoma. *Bulletin of the Texas Archeological Society* 60:209–216.

Byrd, Clifford L.

1971 *Origin and History of the Uvalde Gravels of Central Texas*. Bulletin No. 20, Baylor Geological Studies, Waco.

Calame, David L., Sr.

2017–18 Sabinal Points from Northern Uvalde County, Texas. *La Tierra* 42:121–130.

Cambron, James W., and David C. Hulse

1964 *Handbook of Alabama Archaeology: Part I, Point Types*. Archaeological Research Institute of Alabama.

1975 *Handbook of Alabama Archaeology: Part I, Point Types*. Archaeological Research Institute of Alabama. Reprinted in 1975. Available as eBook #3974.

264 | References Cited

Campbell, Thomas Jefferson
1970 The Greenbelt Site: An Example of Variation among Prehistoric Village Sites in the Texas Panhandle. Unpublished master's thesis, Department of Anthropology, Texas Tech University, Lubbock.

Campbell, T. N.
1947 The Johnson Site: Type Site of the Aransas Focus of the Texas Coast. *Bulletin of the Texas Archeological Society* 18:40–75.
1956 Archaeological Material from Five Islands in the Laguna Madre, Texas Coast. *Bulletin of the Texas Archeological Society* 27:7–46.
1958 Archeological Remains from the Live Oak Point Site, Aransas County, Texas. *Texas Journal of Science* 10(4):423–442.
1960 Archeology of the Central and Southern Sections of the Texas Coast. *Bulletin of the Texas Archeological Society* 29:145–175.
1979 *Ethnohistoric Notes on Indian Groups Associated with Three Spanish Missions at Guerrero, Coahuila.* Center for Archaeological Research, University of Texas at San Antonio, Archaeology and History of the San Juan Bautista Mission Area, Coahuila and Texas, Report No. 3.
1988 *The Indians of Southern Texas and Northeastern Mexico: Selected Writings of Thomas Nolan Campbell.* Texas Archeological Research Laboratory, with the cooperation of the University of Texas at Austin.

Carmichael, David L.
1986 Archaeological Survey of the Southern Tularosa Basin, New Mexico. *Historic and Natural Resources Report,* No. 3. Cultural Resources Branch, Environmental Management Division, Directorate of Environment, United States Army Air Defense Artillery Center, Fort Bliss, Texas.

Carpenter, Stephen M., Kevin A. Miller, Mary Jo Galindo, Brett A. Houk, Charles D. Frederick, Mercedes C. Cody, John Lowe, Ken Lawrence, Kevin Hanselka, and Abby Peyton
2013 *The Siren Site and the Long Transition from Archaic to Late Prehistoric Lifeways on the Eastern Edwards Plateau of Central Texas.* Texas Antiquities Permits 3834 and 3938. SWCA Cultural Resources Report 12–93. Texas Department of Transportation Archeological Studies Program Report 142. Texas Department of Transportation, Austin.

Cattelain, Pierre
1997 Hunting during the Upper Paleolithic: Bow, Spearthrower, or Both? In *Projectile Technology,* edited by H. Knecht, pp. 213–240. Plenum Press, New York.

Chandler, Charles K.
1984a Lithic Resources of the Texas Coastal Bend. *La Tierra* 11(1):26–27.
1984b Two Metal Projectile Points from Central Texas. *La Tierra* 11(3):13–16.
1986 Notes on a Metal Projectile Point from Bexar County, Southcentral Texas. *La Tierra* 13(3):28–31.

References Cited | 265

1989   A Metal Arrow Point from Terrell County, Texas. *La Tierra* 16(4):23–24.

1993   Metal Projectile Points from Medina County, Texas. *La Tierra* 20(4):29–32.

Chandler, Charles K., and Leo Lopez

1992   A Quarry in Western Duval County. *La Tierra* 19(2):12–13.

Chandler, Charles K., and Don Kumpe

1994   Metal Arrow Points from South Texas and Tamaulipas, Mexico. *La Tierra* 24(4):38–41.

Christenson, Andrew L.

1986   Projectile Point Size and Projectile Aerodynamics: An Exploratory Study. *Plains Anthropologist* 31:109–128.

Cliff, Maynard B.

1997   The Middle Caddoan Period in the Lower Sulphur River Area. In *Journal of Northeast Texas Archaeology*, edited by Timothy K. Perttula, No. 9, pp. 9–16. Friends of Northeast Texas Archaeology, Austin and Pittsburg, Texas.

Cloud, William A.

2001   Toyah Arrow Points in the Big Bend. *La Vista de la Frontera* 14(1):8.

2002   The Rough Run Burial: A Semi-Subterranean Cairn Burial from Brewster County, Texas. *Journal of Big Bend Studies* 14:33–84.

2004   *The Arroyo de la Presa Site: A Stratified Late Prehistoric Campsite along the Rio Grande, Presidio County, Trans-Pecos, Texas.* Reports in Contract Archeology 9, Center for Big Bend Studies, Sul Ross State University.

Cloud, William A., Robert J. Mallouf, Patricia A. Mercado-Allinger, Cathryn A. Hoyt, Nancy A. Kenmotsu, Joseph M. Sanchez, and Enrique R. Madrid

1994   *Archeological Testing at the Polvo Site, Presidio County, Texas.* Office of the State Archeologist, Report 39. US Department of Agriculture and Soil Conservation Service and Texas Historical Commission, Austin.

Cloud, William A. and, Robert J. Mallouf

1996   Aboriginal Material Culture. In *Archeological Reconnaissance on Big Bend Ranch State Park: Presidio and Brewster Counties, Texas, 1988–1994*, by J. David Ing, Sheron Smith-Savage, William A. Cloud, and Robert J. Mallouf, pp. 170–194. Texas Parks and Wildlife Department, Texas Historical Commission and Sul Ross State University and Center for Big Bend Studies, Alpine, Texas.

Cloud, William A., and Jennifer C. Piehl

2008   *The Millington Site: Archaeological and Human Osteological Investigations, Presidio County, Texas.* Papers of the Trans-Pecos Archaeological Program 4, Center for Big Bend Studies, Sul Ross State University, Alpine, Texas.

266 | References Cited

Coleman, Shawn, Glen L. Evans, and Thomas R. Hester
2000   An Overview of the Archeology at Montell Rockshelter, Uvalde County, Texas. *TARL Research Notes* 7:121–131.

Colette, James
1993   Archeological Site Data Form for Site 41VV890. Curated in the Val Verde County Files at the Texas Archeological Research Laboratory, Austin.

Collins, Michael B.
2004   Archeology in Central Texas. In *The Prehistory of Texas*, edited by Timothy K. Perttula, pp. 101–126. Texas A&M University Press, College Station.

Collins, Michael B., and Jason M. Fenwick
1974   Heat Treating of Chert: Methods of Interpretation and Their Application. *Plains Anthropologist* 19(64):131–145.

Collins, Michael B., and Karen S. Collins
1990   A Metal Arrowpoint Found Embedded in the Moore-Hancock Log House (41TV105), Travis County, Texas. *La Tierra* 17(3):13–19.

Cook, Harold J.
1927   New Geological and Paleontological Evidence Bearing on the Antiquity of Mankind in America. *American Antiquity* 27(3):240–247.

Corbin, James E.
1963   Archaeological Materials from the Northern Shore of Corpus Christi Bay, Texas. *Bulletin of the Texas Archeological Society* 34:5–30.
1974   A Model for Cultural Succession for the Coastal Bend Area of Texas. *Bulletin of the Texas Archeological Society* 45:29–54.

Corbin, James E., Heather A. Brown, Mary G. Canavan, and Sharon Toups
1990   *Mission Dolores de los Ais (41SA25): San Augustine County, Texas.* Papers in Anthropology 5. Stephen F. Austin State University, Nacogdoches.

Corliss, David W.
1972   *Neck Width of Projectile Points: An Index of Culture Continuity and Change.* Occasional Papers of the Idaho State University Museum 29, Pocatello.

Corrick, Donald W.
2000   The Manufacture and Age of Toyah Arrow Points from Big Bend National Park, Texas. *Journal of Big Bend Studies* 12:1–12.

Costa, August G., and Amy Fox
2016   An Experimental Evaluation of Gar Scale Arrow Points. *The Journal* 136:23–31. Houston Archeological Society.

Cox, Kim A., and Herman A. Smith
1989   Perdiz Point Damage Analysis. *Bulletin of the Texas Archeological Society* 30:283–302.

References Cited | 267

Creel, Darrell G.

1990 *Excavations at 41TG91, Tom Green County, Texas 1978*. Publications in Archeology, Report No. 38. Texas State Department of Highways and Public Transportation, Austin.

Crook, Wilson W., III

1985 The Branch #2 Site: A Northeast Texas Puebloan Intrusive Contact. *Texas Archeology* 29(3):9–11.

2008–09 An Unusual Late Prehistoric Projectile Point Concentration from the Upper Farmersville Site (41COL34), Collin County, Texas. *The Journal* 132:21–36. Houston Archeological Society.

2011 The Gilkey Hill Site (41DL406): A Large Late Prehistoric Occupation in Dallas County, Texas. *Archeological Journal of the Texas Prairie-Savannah* 1(1):9–17.

2013 Puebloan Intrusive Artifacts in Archeological Sites along the East Fork. *Archeological Journal of the Texas Prairie Savannah* 3(1):36–43.

2016 X-Ray Fluorescence Re-Analysis of Five Obsidian Arrow Points from the Branch Site (41COL9), Collin County, Texas. *Archeological Journal of the Texas Prairie-Savannah* 1(1):27–33.

2017 Interpreting Arrow Point Damage from Late Prehistoric Sites along the East Fork of the Trinity River and Its Tributaries. *The Journal* 137:51–66. Houston Archeological Society.

Crook, Wilson W., III, and Mark D. Hughston

2009a A Unique Cache of Edwards Chert from Rockwall County, Texas. *Archeological Journal of the Texas Prairie-Savannah* 1(1):57–61.

2009b The Upper Farmersville Site (41COL34): A Large Late Prehistoric Occupation in Collin County, Texas. *The Record* 56(1):25–46. Dallas Archeological Society.

2015a *The East Fork Late Prehistoric: A Redefinition of Cultural Concepts along the East Fork of the Trinity River, North Central Texas*. CreateSpace, a DBA of On-Demand Publishing (an Amazon Company), Charleston, South Carolina.

2015b Three New Radiocarbon Dates from the East Fork. *The Journal* 135:31–40. Houston Archeological Society.

Davis, Clint, David O. Brown, and Thomas R. Hester

n.d. Ojo Zarco: A New Obsidian Source in the Eastern Bajio of Guanajuato, Mexico, and Its Occurrence in Southern Texas. Manuscript on file with the junior author.

Davis, Dan R., Jr.

1995 *Prehistoric Artifacts of the Texas Indians: An Identification and Reference Guide*. Pecos Publishing, Fort Sumner, New Mexico.

268 | **References Cited**

Davis, W. R.

1983   *Points and Tools of the Texas Indians*. Published by L. Davis.

Davis, Mike, and Jack Skiles (with contributions by Dan Potter and James Collett)

1999   Archeological Data on Cultural Features at Sites 41VV740 and 41VV890 Near Langtry, Texas. In *The Steward*, a publication of the Texas Archeological Stewardship Network, Daniel R. Potter and Helen Simons, editors, pp. 49–69.

Densmore, Julie A.

2007   A Detailed Analysis of the Variation in Morphology of the Gary Dart Point. *Lithic Technology* 32(1):7–16.

Dickens, William A.

1993a   Tool Types, Reduction Strategies, and Local Gravel: Analysis of Lithic Artifacts. *The Brazos Valley Slopes Archaeological Project: Cultural Resource Assessments for the Texas A&M University Animal Science Teaching and Research Complex, Brazos County, Texas*. Alston V. Thoms, editor, pp. 113–144. Reports of Investigations No. 14, Archaeological Research Laboratory, Texas A&M University, College Station.

1993b   Lithic Analysis. In *Archaeological Investigations in Bull Branch: Results of the 1990 Archaeological Field School*, David L. Carlson, editor, pp. 79–116. United States Army, Fort Hood Archaeological Resource Management Series, Research Report No. 19.

1993c   Lithic Artifact Analysis. In *Archaeological Investigations in Spicewood Creek: Results of the 1991 Summer Archaeological Field School*, David L. Carlson, editor, pp. 75–112. United States Army, Fort Hood Archaeological Resource Management Series, Research Report No. 12.

1995   Identification and Prehistoric Exploitation of Chert from Fort Hood, Bell and Coryell Counties, Texas. Unpublished master's thesis, Department of Anthropology, Texas A&M University, College Station.

1997   Lithic Artifact Analysis. In *Archaeological Investigations along Owl Creek: Results of the 1992 Summer Archaeological Field School*, David L. Carlson, editor, pp. 45–61. United States Army, Fort Hood Archaeological Resource Management Series, Research Report No. 29.

Dickens, William A., and John Dockall

1993   Lithic Analysis. In *Archaeological Site Testing and Evaluation on the Henson Mountain Helicopter Range AWSS Project Area, Fort Hood, Texas*. David L. Carlson, editor, pp. 61–82. United States Army Fort Hood Archaeological Resource Management Series, Research Report No. 26.

Dockall, John E.

1997   Wear Traces and Projectile Impact: A Review of the Experimental and Archaeological Evidence on JSTOR. *Journal of Field Archaeology* 24(3):321–331.

References Cited | 269

Duffield, Lathel L.

1961   The Limerick Site at Iron Bridge Reservoir, Rains County, Texas. *Bulletin of the Texas Archeological Society* 30:51–116.

1963   The Wolfshead Site: An Archaic Neo-American Site in San Augustine County, Texas. *Bulletin of the Texas Archeological Society* 34:83–14.

Duncan, Marjorie, Larry Neal, Don Shockey, Don Wykoff, Michael Sullivan, and L. M. Sullivan

2007   *Southern Plains Lithics: The Small Points.* Special Bulletin 26. Oklahoma Anthropological Society, Norman.

Ellis, C.

1997   Factors Influencing the Use of Stone Projectile Tips: An Ethnographic Perspective. In *Projectile Technology*, edited by H. Knecht, pp. 37–74. Plenum Press, New York.

Evans, Oren

1957   Probable Use of Stone Projectile Points. *American Antiquity* 23(1):83–84.

1961   The Development of the Atlatl and the Bow. *Bulletin of the Texas Archeological Society* 30:159–162.

Fenenga, Franklin

1953   The Weights of Chipped Stone Points: A Clue to Their Functions. *Southwestern Journal of Anthropology* 9:309–323.

Fields, Ross C.

1988   *Cultural Resources Investigations along Whiteoak Bayou, Harris County, Texas.* Reports of Investigations 62, Prewitt & Associates, Inc.

1995   The Archeology of the Post Oak Savannah of East Central Texas. *Bulletin of the Texas Archeological Society* 66:301–330.

2004   The Archeology of the Post Oak Savannah of East Central Texas. In *The Prehistory of Texas*, Timothy K. Perttula, editor, pp. 347–369. Texas A&M University Press, College Station.

Figgins, Jesse Dade

1927   The Antiquity of Man in America. *Natural History* 27(3):229–239.

Flinn, Richard, and Judy Flinn

1968   The High Bluff Site on the Clear Fork of the Brazos River. *Bulletin of the Texas Archeological Society* 38:93–125.

Ford, James A.

1951   Greenhouse: A Troyville-Coles Creek Period Site in Avoyelles Parish, Louisiana. *Anthropological Papers of the American Museum of Natural History* 44(3).

1952   Measurements of Some Prehistoric Design Developments in the Southeastern States. *Anthropological Papers of the American Museum of Natural History* 44(3):Part 3.

270 | References Cited

Ford, James A., and Gordon R. Willey
1940   Crooks Site, A Marksville Period Burial Mound in LaSalle Parish, Louisiana. *Department of Conservation, Louisiana Geological Survey, Anthropological Study No. 3*, New Orleans.

Forrester, Robert E.
1951   A Series of Eighteen Indian Skeletons Excavated in Shackelford County, Texas. *Bulletin of the Texas Archeological and Paleontological Society* 22:132–143.

1987a   The Moran Point from North-Central Texas. *Bulletin of the Oklahoma Anthropological Society* 36:131–136.

1987b   Pestles for Boat-Shaped Mortars in Texas. Unpublished manuscript on file at the Texas Archeological Research Laboratory, Austin.

Foster, Michael S.
1993   *Archaeological Investigations at Pueblo Sin Casas (FB6273), a Multicomponent Site in the Hueco Basin, Fort Bliss, Texas.* Historic and Natural Resources Report No. 7, Cultural Resources Branch, Environmental Management Division, Directorate of Environment, United States Army Air Defense Artillery Center, Fort Bliss, Texas, with contributions by Ronna Jane Bradley and Lorna Lee Scarbrough.

Fowler, Don D., Jr., and John F. Matley
1979   *Material Culture of the Numa: The John Wesley Powell Collection, 1867–1880.* Smithsonian Contributions to Anthropology, No. 26. Smithsonian Institution Press, Smithsonian Institution, Washington, DC.

Fox, Anne A., and Steve A. Tomka
2006   Excavations at Presidio Nuestra Señora de Loreto de la Bahía del Espíritu Santo. *Bulletin of the Texas Archeological Society* 77:33–160.

Fox, Daniel E.
1979   *The Lithic Artifacts of Indians at the Spanish Colonial Missions, San Antonio, Texas.* Center for Archaeological Research, Special Report No. 8, University of Texas at San Antonio.

1983   *Traces of Texas History: Archeological Evidence of the Past 450 Years.* Corona Publishing Company, San Antonio.

Frederick, Charles D., Michael D. Glasscock, Hector Neff,
and Christopher M. Stevenson
1994   *Evaluation of Chert Patination as a Dating Technique: A Case Study from Fort Hood, Texas.* United States Army, Fort Hood Archeological Research Management Series, Research Report No. 32.

Frederick, Charles D., and Christopher Ringstaff
1994   Lithic Resources at Fort Hood: Further Investigations. In *Archeological Investigations on 571 Prehistoric Sites at Fort Hood, Bell and Coryell Counties, Texas*, W. Nicholas Trierweiler, editor, pp. 125–181. Fort Hood Archeological Research Management Series, Research Report No. 31.

Gadus, Eloise F., Marie E. Blake, and Ross C. Fields

1997   *The Archeology and History of Cooper Lake, Texas.* United States Army Corps of Engineers, Fort Worth, Texas.

Gadus, E. Frances, Ross C. Fields, and Karl W. Kibler

2006   *Data Recovery Excavations at the J. B. White site (41MM341), Milam County, Texas.* Report of Investigations 145, Prewitt & Associates, Inc. and Archeological Studies Program Report 87, Environmental Affairs Division, Texas Department of Transportation, Austin.

Galindo, Mary Jo

1998   Analysis of the Riley Projectile Point Collection from Mier, Tamaulipas. Unpublished manuscript on file at the Texas Archeological Research Laboratory, Austin.

Galloway, William E., and William R. Kaiser

1980   *Catahoula Formation of the Texas Coastal Plain: Origin, Geochemical Evolution, and Characteristics of Uranium Deposit.* University of Texas at Austin, Bureau of Economic Geology, Report of Investigations No. 100.

Geno, Kirk R.

1984   *Origin and Distribution of Chert in the Edwards Limestone (Lower Cretaceous), Central Texas.* Unpublished bachelor of science thesis, Baylor University, Waco.

Gibson, Jon L., and Hiram F. Gregory

1992   Dr. Webb. *Bulletin of the Louisiana Archeological Society* 19 (entire volume).

Glasgow, Marvin

2011   Metal Points from Site 41PR92, Parker County, Texas. *Archeological Journal of the Texas Prairie-Savannah* 1(1):47–48.

Glasrud, Bruce A., and Robert J. Mallouf (editors)

2013   *Big Bend's Ancient and Modern Past.* Texas A&M University Press, College Station.

Goebel, Patsy, Robert Goebel, and Jimmy L. Mitchell

1987   Notes on a Metal Arrow Point from McCulloch County, Texas. *La Tierra* 14(1):32–35.

Goldschmidt, Walter R.

1935   A Report on the Archeology of Titus County. *Bulletin of the Texas Archeological and Paleontological Society* 7:89–99.

Gonzalez, Juan L., James R. Hinthorne, Russell K. Skowronek, Thomas Eubanks, and Don Kumpe

2014   Characteristics and Genesis of El Sauz Chert, an Important Prehistoric Lithic Resource in South Texas. *Lithic Technology* 39(3):151–161.

272 | References Cited

González, Juan L., James R. Hinthorne, Russell K. Skowronek,
Roseann Bacha-Garza, Christopher L. Miller, and Sarah M. Hardage
2024   Social Legacy and Geoheritage Significance of the Largely Overlooked
Catahoula Volcanic Ash of South Texas. *Geological Society of London,
Special Publication*, Bath, United Kingdom. https://doi.org/10.1144
/SP543-2022-253.

Green, F. Earl
1962   The Lubbock Reservoir Site. *Museum Journal* 6:83–123.

Green, F. Earl, and Jane Holden Kelley
1960   Comments on Alibates Flint. *American Antiquity* 25:413–414.

Greengo, R. E.
1964   Issaquena: An Archaeological Phase in the Yazoo Basin of the Lower
Mississippi Valley. Society for American Archaeology, *Memoir* 18.

Greer, John W.
1967   *A Description of the Stratigraphy, Features, and Artifacts from an Archeological Excavation at the Alamo*. Archeological Program, Report No. 3.
State Building Commission, Austin.
1968a   Excavations at a Midden Circle Site in El Paso, Texas. *Bulletin of the Texas
Archeological Society* 39:111–132.
1968b   Notes on Excavated Ring Midden Sites, 1963–1968. *Bulletin of the Texas
Archeological Society* 38:39–44.

Gregory, Hiram F. (editor)
1980   Excavations: 1979—*Presidio de Nuestra Señora del Pilar de Zaragoza de
los Adaes*. Report published by the Office of State Parks, Department of
Culture, Recreation, and Tourism. Baton Rouge.
1982   *Excavations: 1981-82, Presidio de Nuestra Señora del Pilar de Zaragoza de
los Adaes*. Report in Fulfillment of a Contract for the Office of the State
Parks, State Department of Culture, Recreation, and Tourism, Baton
Rouge.

Grinnell, George B.
1962   *The Cheyenne Indians: Their History and Ways of Life*. Vol. 1. Cooper
Square Publishers, New York.

Gunter, Rita R.
1985   The Ben Bickham Collection from North Padre Island, Texas. *La Tierra*
12(1):6–17.

Hafernik, David
1984   Descriptive Analysis of Surface Collected Lithic Artifacts from Jim Wells
County, Texas, and Vicinity. Unpublished Manuscript on File at the Center for Archaeological Research, University of Texas at San Antonio.

References Cited | 273

Hall, Grant D.
1981 *Allen's Creek: A Study in the Cultural Prehistory of the Lower Brazos River Valley, Texas.* Texas Archeological Survey, Research Report No. 61. University of Texas at Austin.

Hall, Grant D., Stephen L. Black, and C. Graves
1982 *Archaeological Investigations at Choke Canyon Reservoir, South Texas: The Phase I Findings.* Center for Archaeological Research, University of Texas at San Antonio, Choke Canyon Series, No. 5.

Hall, Grant D., Thomas R. Hester, and Stephen L. Black
1986 *The Prehistoric Sites at Choke Canyon Reservoir, South Texas: Results of the Phase II Archaeological Investigations.* Center for Archaeological Research, University of Texas at San Antonio, Choke Canyon Series, Vol. 10.

Hamilton, T. M.
1982 *Native American Bows,* 2nd ed., Special Publications 5, Missouri Archaeological Society, Columbia.

Harris, Adam Duncan
2013 *George Catlin's American Buffalo.* Giles, Ltd., Lewes, United Kingdom.

Harris, R. King, and Curtis D. Tunnell
1966 Miscellaneous European Goods. *Bulletin of the Texas Archeological Society* 36:105–111.

Harris, R. King, Inus Marie Harris, and J. Ned Woodall
1967 Tools. In *The Gilbert Site: A Norteño Focus Site in Northeastern Texas,* edited by Edward B. Jelks, pp. 18–32. *Bulletin of the Texas Archeological Society* 37 (entire volume).

Harris, R. King, Inus Marie Harris, Jay C. Blaine, and Jerry Lee Blaine
1965 A Preliminary Archeological and Documentary Study of the Womack Site, Lamar County, Texas. *Bulletin of the Texas Archeological Society* 36:287–365.

Hedrick, John A.
1975 Archaeological Survey of the Plateau Complex, Culberson County, Texas. *The Artifact* 13(4):45–82.
1986 Five Arrowpoint Types from the Plateau Complex, Van Horn, Texas. *Transactions of the Twenty-Second Regional Archeological Symposium for Southeastern New Mexico and Western Texas,* pp. 15–27. El Paso Archaeological Society, El Paso.
1989 A Preliminary Report on Archeological Resources in Southern Culberson County in the Vicinity of Van Horn, Texas. *Bulletin of the Texas Archeological Society* 59:129–156.
1993 A Felsite Quarry in the Van Horn Mountains, Culberson County, Texas. *The Cache* 1:3–8.

274 | References Cited

Heinrich, Paul V.
1984 Lithic Resources in Western Louisiana. *Louisiana Archaeology* 11:165–190.
Henderson, Jerry
2001 *Excavations at the Rainey Site (41BN33), A Late Prehistoric Sinkhole in Bandera County, Texas.* Texas Department of Transportation, Archeological Studies Program, Report 5, Austin.
Hester, Thomas R.
1986 Notes on South Texas Archaeology: The Texas-Idaho Connection. *La Tierra* 13(2):1–5.
1968 Notes on Some Historic Indian Artifacts Found Near Ozona, Texas. *Newsletter of the Midland Archeological Society* June issue, pp. 3–5.
1969 *Archeological Investigations in Kenedy and Kleberg Counties, Texas, August 1967.* Archeological Program Report 15. State Building Commission, Austin.
1970a Metal Projectile Points from Southern Texas. *The Record* 27(1):9–11.
1970b Notes on the Edwards Arrow Point Type. *The Record: Journal of the Dallas Archeological Society* 26(2):17–18.
1971 Archeological Investigations at the La Jita Site, Uvalde County, Texas. *Bulletin of the Texas Archeological Society* 42:51–148.
1977 The Lithic Technology of Mission Indians in Texas and Northeastern Mexico. *Lithic Technology* 6(1–2):9–13.
1978 Notes on the Edwards Arrow Point Type. *La Tierra* 5(4):21–22.
1980 *Digging into South Texas Prehistory: A Guide for Amateur Archaeologists.* Corona Publishing Company, San Antonio.
1988 Paleo Obsidian Artifacts in Texas: A Review. *Current Research in the Pleistocene* 5:27–29.
1989 Perspectives on the Material Culture of the Mission Indians on the Texas-Northeastern Borderlands. In *Columbian Consequences*, edited by D. H. Thomas, pp. 213–230, Vol. 1. Smithsonian Institution Press, Washington, DC.
1995 The Prehistory of South Texas. *Bulletin of the Texas Archeological Society* 66:427–460.
2004 The Prehistory of South Texas. In *The Prehistory of Texas*, edited by Timothy K. Perttula, pp. 127–154. Texas A&M University Press, College Station.
Hester, Thomas R., and Jack D. Eaton
1983 Middle-Lower Rio Grande Archaeology. In *Borderlands Sourcebook: A Guide to the Literature on Northern Mexico and the American Southwest*, edited by E. Stoddard, R. Nostrand, and J. West, pp. 70–74, University of Oklahoma Press, Norman.

References Cited | 275

Hester, Thomas R., and Charles M. Whatley
1992   Notes on South Texas Archaeology 1992-3: Chipped Stone Artifacts from Site 41DM59. *La Tierra* 19(3):1–7.
1997   Archaeological Materials from the Middle Rio Grande, Southern Texas, and Coahuila. *La Tierra* 24(2):3–12.

Hester, Thomas R., J. W. House, Robert N. Jack, and Fred H. Stross
1975   X-Ray Fluorescence Analysis of Obsidian Artifacts of the Rio Grande Plain, Southern Texas. *Texas Journal of Science* 26:286–289.

Hester, Thomas R., Frank Asaro, Helen Michel, Fred H. Stross, and Fred W. Nelson
1986   Appendix V: Trace Element and Geological Sources Studies of an Obsidian Artifact from 41LK51, Live Oak County, Texas. Center for Archaeological Research, University of Texas at San Antonio, Choke Canyon Series, Vol. 10.

Hester, Thomas R., Frank Asaro, Fred H. Stross, and Helen Michael
1991   An Overview of the Results of the Texas Obsidian Project. *La Tierra* 18(1):4–7.

Hester, Thomas R., Frank Asaro, Fred H. Stross, and Robert Giaugue
1992   On the Beach: Trace Element Analysis of an Obsidian Artifact from Site 41JF50, Upper Texas Coast. *La Tierra* 19(2):2–5.

Hester, Thomas R., James R. Boyd, Frank Asaro, Fred H. Stross, Robert Giaugue, Don Kumpe, and Jacob Bourbon
1996   Mesoamerican Obsidian at Sites in the Falcon Reservoir and Lower Rio Grande Area of Southern Texas and Northeastern Mexico. *La Tierra* 23(3):2–6.

Hester, Thomas R., Frank Asaro, Fred H. Stross, Robert D. Giaugue, and Mike Krzywonki
1999   Geological Source Analysis of Obsidian Artifacts from the Rio Grande Delta, Texas and Tamaulipas. *La Tierra* 26(4):1–5.

Hildebrandt, William R., and Jerome H. King
2012   Distinguishing between Darts and Arrows in the Archaeological Record: Implications for Technological Change in the American West. *American Antiquity* 77(4):789–799.

Hill, T. C., and Thomas R. Hester
1971   Isolated Late Prehistoric and Archaic Components at the Honeymoon Site (44IZV34), Southern Texas. *Plains Anthropologist* 15(54):52–59.

Holden, W. C.
1938   Blue Mountain Rock Shelter. *Bulletin of the Texas Archeological Society* 10:208–221.

Hoffman, Michael
1971   A Partial Archaeological Sequence for the Little River Region, Arkansas. Unpublished thesis, Department of Anthropology, Harvard University, Cambridge, Massachusetts.

276 | References Cited

Hudgins, Joe D.
1982   Historic Indian Sites in Wharton County, Texas. *Houston Archeological Society Journal* 74:2–7.
1984   A Historic Indian Site in Wharton County, Texas. *Bulletin of the Texas Archeological Society* 55:29–51.

Hughes, Jack T.
1942   An Archaeological Report on the Harrell Site of North Central Texas. PhD dissertation, Department of Anthropology, University of Texas at Austin.

Hughes, Jack T., and Patrick S. Willey
1978   *Archeology at Mackenzie Reservoir.* Texas Historical Commission, Office of the State Archeologist, Archeological Survey Report 24, Austin.

Hughes, Richard E.
1988a   The Coso Volcanic Field Reexamined: Implications for Obsidian Sourcing and Hydration Dating. *Research in Geoarchaeology* 3:253–265.
1988b   Notes on Obsidian from the Fort Hood Area of Central Texas. *Bulletin of the Texas Archeological Society* 59:193–199.

Hughes, Richard E., and Thomas R. Hester
2009   Geochemical Evidence for a Mexican Source of Origin for an Obsidian Artifact from South Central Texas. *Bulletin of the Texas Archeological Society* 80:77–84.

Imlay, Ralph W.
1931   Geology of the Sierra de Cruillas, Tamaulipas, Mexico. PhD dissertation, University of Michigan.

Ing, J. David, Sheron Smith-Savage, William A. Cloud, and Robert J. Mallouf
1996   *Archeological Reconnaissance of Big Bend Ranch State Park, Presidio and Brewster Counties, Texas, 1988-1994.* Center for Big Bend Studies, Occasional Papers 1. Sul Ross State University and Texas and Parks Wildlife Department, Austin.

Inman, Betty
1999   The Lithic Artifacts of the Native Americans at the Spanish Colonial Missions at Guerrero, Coahuila, Mexico. *Bulletin of the Texas Archeological Society* 70:363–384.

Jarvis, R. Whitby, and Daymond D. Crawford
1974   *Archaeological Excavations on Interstate Highway 10, Sutton County, Texas.* Highway Design Division, Publications in Archaeology, Report No. 4. Texas State Department of Highways and Public Transportation, Austin.

Jelks, Edward B.
1953   Excavations at the Blum Rockshelter. *Bulletin of the Texas Archeological Society* 24:189–207.

1962	*The Kyle Site: A Stratified Central Aspect Site in Hill County, Texas.* Department of Anthropology, Archeology Series No. 5. University of Texas at Austin.
1967	The Gilbert Site: A Norteño Focus Site in Northwestern Texas. *Bulletin of the Texas Archeological Society* 37 (entire volume).
1993	Observations on the Distributions of Certain Arrow Point Types in Texas and Adjacent Regions. *Lithic Technology* 18(1–2):9–15.

Jelks, Edward B., and Juliet C. Jelks (editors)

| 1988 | *Historical Dictionary of North American Archaeology.* Greenwood Press, New York. |

Johnson, Eileen, Vance T. Holliday, Michael J. Kaczor, and Robert Stuckenrath

| 1977 | The Garza Occupation at the Lubbock Lake Site. *Bulletin of the Texas Archeological Society* 48:83–110. |

Johnson, LeRoy, Jr.

| 1964 | *The Devil's Mouth Site: A Stratified Campsite at Amistad Reservoir, Val Verde County, Texas.* University of Texas at Austin, Department of Anthropology, Archaeology Series No. 6, Austin. |
| 1967 | *Toward a Statistical Overview of the Archaic Cultures of Central and Southwestern Texas.* Bulletin 12 of the Texas Memorial Museum, Austin. |

Johnson, LeRoy, Jr., Dee Ann Suhm, and Curtis D. Tunnell

| 1962 | *Salvage Archeology of Canyon Reservoir: The Wuderlich, Footbridge, and Oblate Sites.* Texas Memorial Museum, Bulletin No. 5, Austin. |

Johnson, Malcom L.

1987	Two Metal Points from Osage, Colorado County, Texas. *La Tierra* 14(1):36–39.
1994	*The Life and Times of the Toyah Folk Culture: The Buckhollow Encampment, Site 41IKM16, Kimble, County, Texas.* Office of the State Archeologist, Report 38. Texas Department of Transportation and Texas Historical Commission, Austin.
2000	Colors and Sources of the Chert. In *Life and Death as Seen at the Bessie Kruze Site (41WM13) on the Blackland Prairie of Williamson County, Texas,* by LeRoy Johnson, pp. 113–119. Texas Department of Transportation, Environmental Affairs Division, Archeology Studies Program, Report 22, Austin.

Jones, William K.

| 1969 | *Notes on the History and Material Culture of the Tonkawa Indians.* Smithsonian Contributions to Anthropology, Vol. 2, no. 5, Smithsonian Institution Press. Washington, DC. |

278 | References Cited

Justice, Noel D.

1987 *Stone Age Spear and Arrow Points of the Midcontinental and Eastern United States.* Indiana University Press, Bloomington.

2002 *Stone Age Spear and Arrow Points of the Southwestern United States.* Indiana University Press, Bloomington.

Katz, Paul R.

1978 *An Inventory and Assessment of Archaeological Sites in the High Country of Guadalupe Mountains National Park, Texas.* Center for Archaeological Research, Survey Report 36. University of Texas at San Antonio.

Katz, Paul R., and Paul D. Lukowski

1981 Results of Archaeological Survey in the Salt Flat Locality of Northern Hudspeth County, Texas. In *Five Archeological Investigations in the Trans-Pecos Region of Texas*, pp. 1–26. Texas Antiquities Committee, Permit Series 6. Texas Antiquities Committee, Austin.

Katz, Susanna R., and Paul R. Katz

1974 *An Inventory and Interpretation of Prehistoric Resources in Guadalupe Mountains National Park, Texas.* Department of Anthropology, Texas Tech University, Lubbock.

Kehoe, Thomas F.

1966 The Small Side-Notched Point System of the Northern Plains. *American Antiquity* 31(6):827–841.

Keller, John E., and Frank A. Weir

1979 *Excavations at the Strawberry Hill Site, San Jacinto County, Texas.* Texas Publications in Archaeology, Report 13. Department of Highways and Public Transportation, Austin.

Kelley, J. Charles

1947a The Cultural Affiliations and Chronological Positions of the Clear Fork Focus. *American Antiquity* 13(2):97–109.

1947b The Lehman Rock: A Stratified Site of the Toyah, Uvalde, and Round Rock Foci. *Bulletin of the Texas Archeological and Paleontological Society* 18:115–128.

1957 The Livermore Focus: A Clarification. *El Palacio* 64(1–2) 44–52.

Kelley, J. Charles, T. N. Campbell, and Donald J. Lehmer

1940 The Association of Archaeological Materials with Geological Deposits in the Big Bend Region of Texas. *West Texas Historical and Scientific Society* 21(3).

Kelly, Thomas C.

1963 Archeological Investigations at Roark Cave, Brewster County, Texas. *Bulletin of the Texas Archeological Society* 33:191–228.

Kelly, Thomas C., and C. Graves

1980   *The El Sauz Project: Archaeological Testing of Selected Sites in the Arroyo Los Olmos Watershed, Starr County, Texas.* Center for Archaeological Research, Archaeological Survey Report 88. University of Texas at San Antonio.

Kennard, Don (editor)

1975   Canadian Breaks: A Natural Area Survey, Part VII of VIII. Division of Natural Resources and Environment, University of Texas at Austin.

Kennedy, Skip, and Jimmy L. Mitchell

1988   Metal Arrow Points from the Vicinity of Fort Lipantitlan (41NU14), Nueces County, Texas. *La Tierra* 15(1):26–34.

Kenmotsu, Nancy A., and Timothy K. Perttula

1993   *Archeology in the Eastern Planning Region, Texas: A Planning Document.* Department of Antiquities Protection, Cultural Resource Management Report 3. Department of Antiquities Protection, Austin.

Kenmotsu, Nancy A., and Douglas K. Boyd (editors)

2012   *The Toyah Phase of Central Texas: Late Prehistoric Economic and Social Processes.* Anthropology Series, Texas A&M University Press, College Station.

Kilman, Ed

1959   *Cannibal Coast.* Naylor, San Antonio.

Kindall, Sheldon M., and Leland W. Patterson

1986   The Andy Kyle Archeological Collection, Southeast Texas. *The Journal, Houston Archeological Society* 86(14–21).

King, Kevin, and Mike Turner

1993   The West Island Site (41MX65). *Notes on Northeast Texas Archaeology* 1:25–33.

Krieger, Alex D.

1944   The Typological Concept. In *American Antiquity* 9(3):271–288.

1946   *Culture Complexes and Chronology in Northern Texas with Extension of Puebloan Datings to the Mississippi Valley.* Publication 4640. University of Texas at Austin.

Krone, Milton F.

1976   The Ahumada Point: A Projectile Point from Northern Chihuahua, Mexico. *The Artifact* 14(2):41–43.

Kumpe, Don

1993   Site Form for 41ZP154. On File at the Texas Archeological Research Laboratory on the Campus of the University of Texas at Austin.

Kumpe, Don, and Richard J. McReynolds

2017   Unidentified Projectile Point and Tool Forms from Falcon Reservoir, Zapata County, Texas. *La Tierra* 42(1):43–52.

280 | References Cited

Kumpe, Don, Richard J. McReynolds, and C. K. Chandler
2000   A Highly Serrated Arrow Point from Starr and Zapata Counties, Texas. *La Tierra* 27(1):33–45.

Kumpe, Don, and M. Kryzwonski
2009   El Sauz Chert, a Distinctive Lithic Resource on the Lower Rio Grande. *La Tierra* 36(1):33–39.

Lemley, Harry J.
1936   Discoveries Indicating a Pre-Caddo Culture on Red River in Arkansas. *Bulletin of the Texas Archeological and Paleontological Society* 8:25–55.

Leo, R. F.
1975   Silification of Wood. PhD dissertation, Harvard University, Cambridge, Massachusetts.

Leslie, Robert H.
1978   Projectile Point Types and Sequence of the Eastern Jornada-Mogollon, Extreme Southeastern New Mexico. In *Transactions of the 13th Regional Archeological Symposium for Southeastern New Mexico and Western Texas*, pp. 81–157. Dawson County Archeological Society, Lamesa, Texas.

Lintz, Christopher
1981   Prehistoric Perishable Hunting Implements from the Oklahoma Panhandle. *Oklahoma Anthropological Society Newsletter* 29(8):6–10.
1998   The Occurrence and Prehistoric Aboriginal Utilization of Opalite in the Palo Duro Creek Vicinity of the Texas Panhandle. *Bulletin of the Oklahoma Anthropological Society* 46:107–126.
2009   Avian Procurement and Use by Middle Ceramic Period People on the Southern High Plains: A Design for Investigations. *Bulletin of the Texas Archeological Society* 80:85–131.

Lintz, Christopher, and Leon George Zabawa
1984   Analysis of Cordage, Mats, Sandals, and Baskets from 34Ci50, Kenton, Oklahoma. Unpublished manuscript, on file with the primary author.

Lohse, Jon C.
1999   Lithics from the San Antonio de Valero Mission: Analysis from 1979. *Bulletin of the Texas Archeological Society* 70:265–280.

Lucas, Spencer G., and Karl Krainer
2002   Permian Stratigraphy in the Jarilla Mountains, Otero County, New Mexico. In *Geology of White Sands*, edited by Virgil Lueth, Katherine A. Giles, Spencer G. Lucas, Barry S. Kues, Robert G. Myers, and Dana Ulmer-Scholle. New Mexico Geological Society, 53rd Annual Fall Field Conference Guidebook, Socorro, New Mexico.

Luedtke, Barbara E.
1978   Chert Sources and Trace-Element Analysis. *American Antiquity* 43(3):413–423.

References Cited | 281

1992   *An Archaeologist's Guide to Chert and Flint*. Archaeological Research Tools 7. Institute of Archaeology, University of California, Los Angles.

Lukowski, Paul D.

1987   *Archaeological Investigations at 41BX1, Bexar County, Texas*. Center for Archaeological Research, Archaeological Survey Report 126, University of Texas at San Antonio.

MacNeish, Richard S.

1958   Preliminary Archaeological Investigations in the Sierra de Tamaulipas, Mexico. *Transactions of the American Philosophical Society* 4(6):1–210.

Mallouf, Robert J.

1976   *Archeological Investigations at Proposed Big Pine Lake, 1974–75, Lamar and Red River Counties, Texas*. Office of the State Archeologist, Survey Report No. 18. Texas Historical Commission, Austin.

1985a   The John Z. and Exa Means Cache: New Discovery Yields Insights into Big Bend's Prehistoric Indians. *La Vista de la Frontera* 20:1–3.

1985b   A Synthesis of Eastern Trans-Pecos Prehistory. Master's thesis, University of Texas at Austin.

1987   *Las Haciendas: A Cairn-Burial Assemblage from Northeastern Chihuahua, Mexico*. Office of the State Archeologist, Report 35. Texas Historical Commission, Austin.

2009   *Alazán: An Arrow Point Type from the Eastern Trans-Pecos and Big Bend Region of Texas*. Center for Big Bend Studies, Sul Ross University, Alpine, Texas.

2012   Some New and Revised Projectile Point Classifications for the Eastern Trans-Pecos and Big Bend Region of Texas. *La Tierra* 39:5–22.

2013   Some New and Revised Projectile Point Classifications for the Eastern Trans-Pecos and Big Bend Region of Texas. In *Archaeological Explorations of the Eastern Trans-Pecos and Big Bend: Collected Papers*, Vol. 1, edited by Pat Dasch and Robert J. Mallouf. Center for Big Bend Studies, Sul Ross State University, Alpine, Texas.

Mallouf, Robert J., Barbara J. Baskin, and K. L. Killen

1977   *A Predictive Assessment of Cultural Resources in Hidalgo and Willacy Counties, Texas*. Office of the State Archeologist, Survey Report 25. Texas Historical Commission, Austin.

Mallouf, Robert J., and Anthony Zavaleta

1979   *The Unland Site: A Prehistoric Group Burial from Laguna Atascosa National Wildlife Refuge, Cameron County, Texas*. Office of the State Archeologist, Special Report No. 35. Texas Historical Commission, Austin.

Mallouf, Robert J., and Virginia A. Wulfkuhle

1989   An Archeological Reconnaissance in the Rosillos Mountains, Brewster County, Texas. *Journal of Big Bend Studies* 1:1–34.

282 | References Cited

Marmaduke, William S.

1978　Prehistoric Culture in Trans-Pecos Texas: An Ecological Explanation. PhD dissertation, Department of Anthropology, University of Texas at Austin.

Martin, George Castor

1930　Two Sites on the Callo Del Oso, Nueces County, Texas. *Bulletin of the Texas Archeological and Paleontological Society* 2:7–17.

Martin, William A.

1990　*Archeological Bibliography for the Northeastern Region of Texas.* Department of Archeological Planning and Review, Cultural Resource Management Report 1, and Office of the State Archeologist, Special Report 32. Texas Historical Commission, Austin. With the assistance of Dee Ann Story, Timothy K. Perttula, Janice A. Guy, and Deborah Smith.

Mauldin, Raymond P.

1993　*The DIVAD Archaeological Project.* Historic and Natural Resources Report No. 8, Cultural Resources Branch, Environmental Management Division, Directorate of Environment, United States Army Air Defense Artillery Center, Fort Bliss, Texas.

Mauldin, Raymond P., Steve A. Tomka, and Harry J. Shafer

2004　*Millican Bench (41TV163): A Multicomponent Site in Travis County, Texas.* Center for Archaeological Research, Archaeological Survey Report 351. University of Texas at San Antonio.

McBride, F. E., and A. Thompson

1970　The Caballos Novaculite, Marathon Region, Texas. Geological Society of America, Special Paper 122. Boulder, Colorado.

McClurkan, Burney B.

1966　The Archaeology of Cueva de la Zona de Derrumbes, a Rockshelter in Nueva Leon, Mexico. Master's thesis, Department of Anthropology, University of Texas at Austin.

1968　*Livingston Reservoir 1965–1966: Late Archaic and Neo-American Occupations.* Papers of the Texas Archeological Salvage Project No. 12. University of Texas at Austin.

McCormick, Olin F., III

1973　*The Archeological Resources in the Lake Monticello Area of Titus County, Texas.* Southern Methodist University Contributions in Anthropology No. 8. Southern Methodist University, Department of Anthropology, Dallas.

McCrocklin, Claude

1993　Chipped Glass, Ceramics, and Axe Handles. *Notes on Northeast Texas Archaeology* 2(8–13).

McGahey, Samuel O.

2000　*Mississippi. Projectile Point Guide.* Mississippi Department of Archives and History, Archaeological Report No. 31, Jackson.

McGregor, Daniel E.

1987a　Lithic Artifacts. In *The Bird Island and Adams Ranch Sites: Methodological and Theoretical Contributions to North Central Texas Archaeology*, edited by James E. Bruseth and William A. Martin. Vol. 2. Archaeology Research Program, Institute for the Study of Earth and Man, Southern Methodist University, Dallas.

1987b　Lithic Raw Material Utilization. In *The Bird Island and Adams Ranch Sites: Methodological and Theoretical Contributions to North Central Texas Archaeology*, edited by Daniel E. McGregor and James E. Bruseth, pp. 185–196. Richland Creek Technical Series, Vol. 2. Archaeology Research Program, Institute for the Study of Earth and Man, Southern Methodist University, Dallas.

1995　"Lithic Resource Availability in the Upper Trinity Region: The Evidence from Joe Pool Lake." In *Advances in Texas Archeology: Contributions from Cultural Research Management*, edited by James E. Bruseth and Timothy K. Perttula, pp. 187–202, Texas Historical Commission, Austin.

McReynolds, Richard L.

1982　An Iron Projectile Point from Gillespie County, Texas. *La Tierra* 9(2):30–32.

McReynolds, Richard L., and Don Kumpe

2008　Metal Points from a Cast Metal Pot: A Cache from the Rio Alamo in Northern Tamaulipas, Mexico. *La Tierra* 35(1&2):53–60.

Mentzer, F, J., and Bob H. Slaughter

1971　Upland Gravels in Dallas County and Their Bearing on the Former Extent of the High Plains Physiographic Province. *Texas Journal of Science* 22(2–3):217–222.

Mercado-Allinger, Patricia A.

2004　The Hackberry Cache (41RB95): An Alibates Cache from the Northeastern Texas Panhandle. *Bulletin of the Texas Archeological Society* 75:105–118.

Mercado-Allinger, Patricia A., Nancy A. Kenmotsu, and Timothy K. Perttula

1996　*Archeology in the Central and Southern Planning Region, Texas: A Planning Document.* Office of the State Archeologist, Special Report 35, and the Department of Antiquities Protection, Cultural Resource Management Report 7. Department of Antiquities Protection, Austin.

Metcalf, George

1963　Star Village: A Fortified Historic Arikara Site in Mercer County, North Dakota. River Basin Surveys Papers No. 27. Smithsonian Institution, Bureau of American Ethnology, Bulletin 185:57–122.

284 | References Cited

Miller, E. O., and Edward B. Jelks
1952   Archaeological Investigations at the Belton Reservoir, Coryell County, Texas. *Bulletin of the Texas Archeological and Paleontological Society* 23:168–217.

Mitchell, Jimmy L.
1974   Notes on Metal Projectile Points from Southern Texas. *Journal of South Texas* 1:47–51.
1980   Brief Notes on the Archaeology of Mission San Juan de Capistrano. *La Tierra* 7(4):18–26.
1982   The Sabinal Point. *La Tierra* 9(4):1–6.

Mitchell, Jimmy L., and Lynn Highley
1982   Notes on a Metal Projectile Point from Southern Texas: The Brom Cooper Collection. *La Tierra* 9(1):21–23.

Mitchell, Jimmy L., and Shirley Van der Veer
1983   Late Prehistoric Projectile Points from the Vicinity of the Dan Baker Site, 41CM104, Comal County, Texas. *La Tierra* 10(3):11–16.

Mitchell, Jimmy L., and William E. Moore
1984   *An Annotated Index of La Tierra* (1974–1983). Southern Texas Archaeological Association, Special Publication No. 3, San Antonio.

Mitchell, Jimmy L., Thomas R. Hester, Frank Asaro, and Fred H. Stross
1980   Notes on Trace Element Analysis of Obsidian from Hutchinson and Roberts Counties in the Texas Panhandle. *Bulletin of the Texas Archeological Society* 51:302–308.

Middlebrook, Tom, and Timothy K. Perttula
1997   The Middle Caddoan Period in East Texas: A Summary of the Findings of the East Texas Caddoan Research Group. In *Journal of Northeast Texas Archaeology*, edited by Timothy K. Perttula, No. 9, pp. 1–8. Friends of Northeast Texas Archaeology, Austin and Pittsburg, Texas.

Mokry, E. R., Jr.
1977   Preliminary Report on Investigations of a Multicomponent Archaeological Site, 41NU33. *La Tierra* 4(1):2–16.

Moore, Clarence B.
1912   Some Aboriginal Sites on Red River. *Journal of the Natural Sciences of Philadelphia* 14, Part 4, pp. 526–636.

Moore, William E. (Bill)
1976   An Archeological Survey of Walker County, Texas. Unpublished manuscript on file with the author and the Texas Archeological Research Laboratory, Austin.
1985   Analysis of Artifacts from a *Rangia Cunneta* Shell Midden (41HR133) on Peggy Lake, Harris County, Texas. *The Journal* 81:2734. Houston Archeological Society.

1986	Louisiana Archaeology: An Index to the First Ten Years. *Louisiana Archaeology* 10:337366.
1988a	Analysis of SurfaceCollected Materials from 41GL19, a Late Prehistoric Site in Gillespie County, Texas. *La Tierra* 15(2):2126.
1988b	*A Bibliography of Archaeological Reports Prepared by the Contract Laboratory, Texas A&M University.* Bibliographies in Archaeology, No. 1. Brazos Valley Research Associates, Bryan, Texas.
1990	*Abstracts in Texas Contract Archeology 1988.* Department of Antiquities Protection, Abstracts in Texas Contract Archeology 1. Texas Historical Commission, Austin. With the assistance of Janice Murray and William A. Martin.
1991a	*Abstracts in Texas Contract Archeology 1987.* Department of Archeological Planning and Review, Abstracts in Texas Contract Archeology 2. Texas Historical Commission, Austin. With the assistance of Janice Murray and William A. Martin.
1991b	*An Archaeological Survey of the Glen Rose Country Club Project, Somervell County, Texas.* BVRA Contract Report No. 11. Brazos Valley Research Associates, Bryan, Texas.
1992a	*Abstracts in Texas Contract Archeology 1990.* Department of Archeological Planning and Review, Abstracts in Texas Contract Archeology 3. Texas Historical Commission, Austin. With the assistance of William A. Martin and Stephanie Stoermer Strickland.
1992b	*Abstracts in Texas Contract Archeology 1991.* Department of Antiquities Protection, Abstracts in Texas Contract Archeology 4. Texas Historical Commission, Austin. With the assistance of William A. Martin.
1993a	*Abstracts in Texas Contract Archeology 1989.* Department of Antiquities Protection, Abstracts in Texas Contract Archeology 5. Texas Historical Commission, Austin. With the assistance of William A. Martin.
1993b	*The Technical Bulletin Series Published by the Texas Archeological Research Laboratory, 1971–1987: A Bibliography.* Texas Archeological Research Laboratory, Technical Series 34. University of Texas at Austin.
1994	*Abstracts in Texas Contract Archeology 1992.* Department of Antiquities Protection, Abstracts in Texas Contract Archeology 6. Texas Historical Commission, Austin. With the assistance of William A. Martin.
2013	A Report on Four Sites in Madison County, Texas (41MA27–41MA30). Brazos Valley Research Associates, Contributions in Archaeology, No. 3. Bryan, Texas.
2015	An Index to the Houston Archeological Society Newsletters and Journals: 1959–2015. Brazos Valley Research Associates, Contributions in Archaeology, No. 4. Bryan, Texas.

286 | References Cited

Moore, William E., and Roger G. Moore
1982 An Annotated Bibliography of Texas Related Articles in the Plains Anthropologist (1947–1981). *La Tierra* 9(1):2438.
1986 *Historical Archaeology in Texas: A Bibliography.* Center for Archaeological Research, University of Texas at San Antonio, Guidebooks in Archaeology, No. 2.

Moore, William E., and Michael R. Bradle
1986 An Annotated Index to the First Ten Volumes of the Bulletin of the Central Texas. *Bulletin of the Texas Archeological Society* 55:189212.

Moore, William E., and Helen Simons
1989 *Archeological Bibliography for the Southeastern Region of Texas.* Office of the State Archeologist, Special Report 31, Texas Historical Commission, Austin. With contributions by Paul V. Heinrich, Lynne Biesaart Mallouf, Leland W. Patterson, Helen Simons, and Lisa Clinton Spotts.

Moore, William E., Linda Wootan Ellis, and John E. Dockall
1990 Archaeological Testing at the Derrick Adams Site (41WA100): A Late Prehistoric Site in Walker County, Texas. Brazos Valley Research Associates. Contributions in Archaeology, No. 1. Bryan, Texas.

Moore, William E., Michael R. Bradle, Michael A. Nash, and Lee C. Nordt
1997 Phase II and III Evaluations of Site 41NV670 to be Impacted by the Construction of the Gabion Chute M4 Flood Control Structure on Mill Creek in Navarro County, Texas. Brazos Valley Research Associates, Contract Report No. 48. Bryan, Texas.

Mounger, Maria A.
1959 Mission Espíritu Santo of Coastal Texas: An Example of Historic Site Archeology. Master's thesis, Department of Anthropology, University of Texas at Austin.

Nelson, Larry Lee
1968 The Effect of Annealing on the Properties of Edwards Plateau Flint. Master's thesis, University of Denver.

Newell, H. Perry, and Alex D. Krieger
1949 The George C. Davis Site, Cherokee County, Texas. *Memoirs of the Society for American Archaeology* 5:1–255. Reprint 2002.

Newton, Milton B., Jr.
1968 The Distribution and Character of Sites, Arroyo Los Olmos, Starr County, Texas. *Bulletin of the Texas Archeological Society* 38:18–24.

Olds, Doris L.
1965 Report on Materials from Brawley's Cave, Bosque County, Texas. *Bulletin of the Texas Archeological Society* 36:111–152.

Olsen, S. J.

1968   Fish, Amphibians, and Reptile Remains from Archaeological Sites, Part 1, Southeastern and Southwestern United States. *Papers of the Peabody Museum of Archaeology and Ethnology* 56(2).

Opler, Morris Edward

1996   *An Apache Life Way: The Economic, Social, and Religious Institutions of the Chiricahua Indians.* University of Nebraska Press, Lincoln. Reprint of original published in 1941.

Parker, Wayne

1983   Three Metal Projectile Points from a Historic Indian Workshop Site. *La Tierra* 10(1):39–42.

Parsons, Mark L.

1967   *Archeological Investigations in Crosby and Dickens Counties, Texas during the Winter 1966-1967.* Archeological Program Report 7. State Building Commission, Austin.

Patterson, Leland W.

1976   The Catahoula Point: A Distributional Study. *Louisiana Archaeology* 3:217–234.

1982   Initial Employment of the Bow and Arrow. *La Tierra* 9(2):18–26.

1987   The Catahoula Perforator, A Possible New Artifact Type. *Houston Archeological Society Journal* 88:19–21.

1989a   An Archeological Data Base for the Southeastern Texas Coastal Margin. Houston Archeological Society Report 7, Houston.

1989b   Bibliography for the Prehistory of the Upper Texas Coast. Houston Archeological Society, Special Report 7, Houston.

1989c   A Data Base for Inland South Texas Archeology. Houston Archeological Society Report 6, Houston.

1992   Current Data on the Early Use of the Bow and Arrow in Southern North America. *La Tierra* 19(4):15–16.

1994a   Gar Scale Arrow Points. *Houston Archeological Society Journal* 109:13–15.

1994b   Identification of Unifacial Arrow Points. *Houston Archeological Society Journal* 108:19–24.

1995   Prewitt's Projectile Point Type Distributions, as Seen from Southeast Texas. *Houston Archeological Society Journal* 112:20–22.

2001   Current Data on Gar Scale Arrow Points in Southeast Texas. *Houston Archeological Society Journal* 127:7–8.

Pearce, James Edwin

1936   Destructive Activities of Unscientific Explorers in Archaeological Sites. *Bulletin of the Central Texas Archeological Society* 2:44–48.

288 | References Cited

Perino, Gregory H.

1968   *Guide to the Identification of Certain American Indian Projectile Points.* Special Bulletin No. 3. Oklahoma Anthropological Society, Norman.

1971   *Guide to the Identification of Certain American Indian Projectile Points.* Special Bulletin No. 4. Oklahoma Anthropological Society, Norman.

1985   *Selected Preforms, Points, and Knives of the North American Indians,* Vol. 1. Privately published by Gregory H. Perino.

1991   *Selected Preforms, Points, and Knives of the North American Indians,* Vol. 2. Privately published by Gregory H. Perino.

1995   The Dan Holdeman Site (41RR11): Red River County, Texas. In *Journal of Northeast Texas Archaeology,* No. 6, edited by Timothy K. Perttula, pp. 3–65. Friends of Northeast Texas Archaeology, Austin and Pittsburg, Texas.

2002   *Selected Preforms, Points, and Knives of the North American Indians,* Vol. 3. Privately published by Gregory H. Perino.

Perttula, Timothy K.

1997   The Archaeology of the Middle Caddoan Period in the Middle Red River Valley of Northeast Texas. *Journal of Northeast Texas Archaeology* 10:47–51, Austin and Pittsburg, Texas.

2004   *The Prehistory of Texas.* Texas A&M University Press, College Station.

2020   *Archeological Investigations in the Upper Trinity River Basin in Parker County.* Friends of Northeast Texas Archaeology, Special Publication 1. North Texas Archeological Society, Austin and Pittsburg, Texas.

Perttula, Timothy K., Bob D. Skiles, Michael B. Collins, Margaret C. Trachte, and Fred Valdez Jr.

1986   This Everlasting Sand Bed: Cultural Resources Investigations at the Texas Big Sandy Project, Wood and Upton Counties, Prewitt & Associates, Inc. Reports of Investigations, No. 52, Austin.

Perttula, Timothy K., and J. Brett Cruse

1997   The Caddoan Archaeology of Sabine River Basin during the Middle Caddoan Period. In *Journal of Northeast Texas Archaeology,* edited by Timothy K. Perttula, No. 9, pp. 30–37. Friends of Northeast Texas Archaeology, Austin and Pittsburg, Texas.

Perttula, Timothy K., and James E. Bruseth

1998   *The Native History of the Caddo: Their Place in Southeastern Archeology and Ethnohistory.* Studies in Archeology 30, Texas Archeological Research Laboratory, University of Texas at Austin.

Perttula, Timothy K., and Thomas R. Hester

2016   Obsidian Artifacts from East Texas Sites. *Journal of Northeast Texas Archaeology* 66:85–90. Index of Texas Archaeology: Open Access Gray Literature from the Lone Star State: Vol. 2016, Article 37. https://doi.org/10.21112/.ita.2016.1.37. ISSN: 2475–9333. Available at: https://scholarworks.sfasu.edu/ita/vol2016/iss1/37.

References Cited | 289

Perttula, Timothy K., and Paul Marceaux

2018 *The Lithic and Ceramic Artifacts from the Spradley Site (41NA206), Nacogdoches County, Texas.* Special Publication No. 50, Friends of Northeast Texas Archaeology, Austin and Pittsburg, Texas.

Perttula, Timothy K., Bo Nelson, and Mark Walters

2009 Caddo Ceramic and Lithic Artifacts from the Washington Square Mound Site (41NA49) in Nacogdoches County, Texas: 1985 Texas Archeological Society Field School Investigations. *Bulletin of the Texas Archeological Society* 80:145–193.

Pevny, Charlotte D.

2014 Twin Bird Islands (16CD118): A Late Paleoindian–Early Archaic Site in Caddo Parish, Louisiana. *Louisiana Archaeology* 37:108–141.

Phelps, Alan L.

1964 *Cultural Analysis of Pre-Historic Indian Sites of Northern Chihuahua, Mexico.* Special Report No. 2. El Paso Archaeological Society.

1966 *Cruciform: An Unusual Artifact of the El Paso Southwest.* Special Report No. 5. El Paso Archaeological Society.

Pittman, J. S.

1959 Silica in the Edwards Limestone. In *Silica in Sediments*, edited by H. A. Ireland, pp. 121–134. Society of Economic Paleontologists and Mineralogists, Tulsa, Oklahoma.

Pope, Saxton

1918 Yahi Archery. *University of California, Publications in Archaeology and Ethnography* 13(3):103–152.

1923 A Study of Bows and Arrows. *University of California, Publications in Archaeology and Ethnography* 13(9):195–212.

Prewitt, Elton R.

1981 Cultural Chronology in Central Texas. *Bulletin of the Texas Archeological Society* 52:65–89.

1995 Distributions of Typed Projectile Points in Texas. *Bulletin of the Texas Archeological Society* 66:83–174.

Prewitt, Elton R., Susan V. Lisk, and Margaret Ann Howard

1987 *National Register Assessments of the Swan Lake Site, 41AS16, on Copano Bay, Aransas County, Texas.* Reports of Investigation, No. 56. Prewitt & Associates, Inc., Austin.

Prikryl, Daniel J.

1987 A Synthesis of the Prehistory of the Lower Elm Fork of the Trinity River. Master's thesis, University of Texas at Austin.

1993 Introduction. In *Archeology in the Eastern Planning Region, Texas: A Planning Document*, edited by Nancy Adele Kenmotsu and Timothy K. Perttula, pp. 191–204. Department of Antiquities Protection Cultural Resources Report 3. Texas Historical Commission, Austin.

290 | References Cited

Pyszczyk, Heinz W.
1999   Historic Period Metal Points and Arrows, Alberta, Canada: A Theory
        for Aboriginal Arrow Design on the Great Plains. *Plains Anthropologist*
        44(168):163–187.
Quigg, J. Michael, Christopher Lintz, Fred M. Oglesby, Amy C. Earls,
Charles D. Frederick, W. Nicholas Trierweiler, Karl Kibler, and Douglas Owsley
1993   *Historic and Prehistoric Data Recovery at Palo Duro Reservoir, Hansford
        County, Texas.* Technical Report 495. Mariah Associates, Inc., Austin.
Quigg, J. Michael, Matthew T. Boulanger, and Michael D. Glascock
2011   Geochemical Characterization of Tecovas and Alibates Source Samples.
        Plains Anthropologist 56(219):121–141.
Quimby, George I., Jr.
1957   Bayou Goula Site, Iberville Parish, Louisiana. *Fieldiana Anthropology*
        47(2):89–170.
Randall, Mark E.
1970   The Archeology of the Lamb County, Texas Area. Lower Plains Archeo-
        logical Society Bulletin No. 1, pp. 43–53.
2010   Data Recovery at the McGloin Bluff Site (41SP11): A Late Prehistoric Rock-
        port Phase Fishing Camp on Corpus Christi Bay. *Current Archeology in
        Texas* 12(2):8–15.
Ray, Cyrus E.
1929   A Differentiation of the Prehistoric Cultures of the Abilene Section. *Bulle-
        tin of the Texas Archeological and Paleontological Society* 1:7–22.
1930   Report on Some Recent Archaeological Researches in the Abilene Section.
        Bulletin of the Texas Archeological and Paleontological Society 2:45–58.
Reger, Brandi, Juan L. González, and Russell K. Skowronek
2020   Lithic Raw Materials in the Lower Rio Grande Valley, South Texas and
        Northeast Mexico. *Lithic Technology* 45(3):184–196.
Riches, Susan M.
1976   Prehistoric Utilization of the Environment of the Eastern Slopes of the
        Guadalupe Mountains, Southeastern New Mexico. PhD dissertation,
        Department of Anthropology, University of Wisconsin, Madison.
Ricklis, Robert A.
1994   *Aboriginal Life and Culture on the Upper Texas Coast: Archaeology at the
        Mitchell Ridge Site (41GV66), Galveston Island.* Coastal Archaeological
        Research, Inc., Corpus Christi.
1995   Prehistoric Occupations of the Central and Lower Coast: A Regional
        Overview. *Bulletin of the Texas Archeological Society* 66:265–300.
2000   *Archaeological Testing at the Spanish Colonial Mission Sites of Espíritu
        Santo (41GD1) and Nuestra Senora del Rosario, Goliad County, Texas.*
        Coastal Archaeological Research, Corpus Christi.

2010   Data Recovery at the McGloin Bluff Site (41SP11): A Late Prehistoric Rock-port Phase Fishing Camp on Corpus Christi Bay. *Current Archeology in Texas* 12(2):8–15.

Ricklis, Robert A., and Michael B. Collins

1994   *Archaic and Late Prehistoric Human Ecology in the Middle Onion Creek Valley, Hays County, Texas.* Vol. 1. Studies in Archeology 19, Texas Archeological Research Laboratory. University of Texas at Austin.

Roberts Tim, and Luis Alvarado

2011   *Terminal Archaic/Late Prehistoric Cooking Technology in the Lower Pecos: Excavation of the Lost Midden Site (41VV1991), Seminole Canyon State Park and Historic Site, Val Verde County, Texas.* Texas Parks and Wildlife Department, Cultural Resource Program, Austin.

Robinson, W. S.

1951   A Method for Chronologically Ordering Archaeological Deposits. *American Antiquity* 16(3):239–301.

Roney, John R.

1985   Prehistory of the Guadalupe Mountains. Thesis, Department of Anthropology, Eastern New Mexico State University, Portales.

Ross, Richard E.

1966   The Upper Rockwall and Glen Hill Sites, Forney Reservoir, Texas. Papers of the Texas Archeological Salvage Project No. 9, Austin.

Runkles, Frank A.

1964   The Garza Site: A Neo-American Campsite Near Post, Texas. *Bulletin of the Texas Archeological Society* 35:101–125.

1982   Metal Project Points. Wayne Parker (1983) cites this source as an unpublished manuscript but does not say where it can be found.

Runkles, Frank A., and E. D. Dorchester

1986   The Lott Site (41GR56): A Late Prehistoric Site in Garza County, Texas. *Bulletin of the Texas Archeological Society* 57:83–115.

Russell, Carl P.

1967   *Firearms, Tools, and Traps of the Mountain Men.* Alfred Knopf, New York.

Saner, Bryant, Jr., Kay Woodward, and Woody Woodward

2004   Four Metal Projectile Points from the Hill Country of South Central, Texas. *Ancient Echoes* 2:17–24.

Saner, Bryant, Jr., Kay Woodward, Woody Woodward, and John Benedict

2019   Archeological Investigations of Site 41KR600 on Quinlan Creek, Kerr County, Texas. *Ancient Echoes* 8:53–68.

Saunders, John T., and Elaine L. Saunders

1978   A Ranch Survey in the Upper Isabella Watershed, Webb County, Texas. *La Tierra* 5(1):2–18.

292 | References Cited

Saunders, R. K.
1985   Recovery of Drowned Rio Grande River Artifacts. *La Tierra* 12(2):6–20.
Saunders, R. K., and Thomas R. Hester
1993   A Typological Study of Side-Notched Arrow Points from the Falcon Lake
Region of Texas and Mexico. *La Tierra* 20(2):22–31.
Sayles, Edwin B.
1935   Unpublished notes on file at the Texas Archeological Research Laboratory
on the campus of the University of Texas at Austin.
Scarbrough, Lorna Lee, and Michael S. Foster
1993   Chipped Stone Artifacts. In *Archaeological Investigations at Pueblo Sin
Casas (FB6273), a Multicomponent Site in the Hueco Basin, Fort Bliss,
Texas*. Historic and Natural Resources Report No. 7, pp. 17–37, Cultural
Resources Branch, Environmental Management Division, Directorate
of Environment, United States Army Air Defense Artillery Center, Fort
Bliss, Texas.
Schmiedlin, E. H.
1993   Investigations of a Toyah Horizon Site in Karnes County, Texas. *The
Cache*, Vol. 1, pp. 33–45.
Schmiedlin, Smitty
1997   Preliminary Report on Salvage Operations at 41VT38, a Multiple-
Component Site in Victoria County. In *The Steward*, edited by Daniel R.
Potter and Hellen Simons, Vol. 4, pp. 51–55.
Schiffer, Michael B., and John H. House
1975   *The Cache River Archaeological Project: An Experiment in Contract Ar-
chaeology*. Arkansas Archaeological Survey Publications in Archaeology,
Research Series 8.
Schneider, Fred
1966   The Harrell Point: A Discussion. *University of Oklahoma Papers in An-
thropology* 7:33–45.
Schoch, Werner H., Gerlinde Bigga, Utz Böhner, Pascale Richter,
and Thomas Terberger
2015   New Insights on the Wooden Weapons from the Paleolithic Site of
Schöningen. *Journal of Human Evolution*, xxx, 1–12.
Schuetz, Mardith K.
1956   An Analysis of Val Verde County Cave Material. *Bulletin of the Texas
Archeological and Paleontological Society* 27:129–160.
1961   An Analysis of Val Verde County Cave Material: Part II. *Bulletin of the
Texas Archeological and Paleontological Society* 31:166–205.
1963   An Analysis of Val Verde County Cave Material: Part III. *Bulletin of the
Texas Archeological and Paleontological Society* 33:131–166.

References Cited | 293

1969   *History and Archeology of San Juan Capistrano, San Antonio, Texas, Volume II.* Archeological Program, Report 11. State Building Commission, Austin.

Seebach, John D.

2007   *Late Prehistory along the Rimrock, Pinto Canyon Ranch.* Papers of the Trans-Pecos Archaeological Program Vol. 3. Center for Big Bend Studies, Sul Ross State University, Alpine, Texas.

Selden, Robert Z., Jr., John E. Dockall, C. Britt Bousman, and Timothy K. Perttula

2021   Shape as a Function of Time + Raw Material + Burial Context? An Exploratory Analysis of Perdiz Arrow Points from the Ancestral Caddo Area of the American Southeast. *Journal of Archaeological Science: Reports,* pp. 1–14.

Selden, Robert Z., Jr., and John E. Dockall

2023   Perdiz Arrow Points from Caddo Burial Contexts Aid in Defining Discrete Behavioral Regions. *Southeastern Archaeology* 42(2):122–135.

Sellards, Elias Howard, Walter S. Adkins, and Frederick B. Plummer

1954   *The Geology of Texas, Vol. I: Stratigraphy.* Bureau of Economic Geology, Bulletin 3232. University of Texas at Austin.

Shackelford, William J.

1955   Excavations at the Polvo Site in Western Texas. *American Antiquity* 20(3):256–262.

Shafer, Harry J.

1968   *Archeological Excavations in the San Jacinto River Basin, Montgomery County, Texas.* Papers of the Texas Archeological Salvage Project 13, University of Texas at Austin.

1969   *Archeological Investigations in the Robert Lee Reservoir Basin, West Central Texas.* Papers of the Texas Archeological Salvage Project 17, University of Texas at Austin.

1973   Lithic Technology at the George C. Davis Site, Cherokee County, Texas. PhD dissertation, University of Texas at Austin.

1981   Archeological Investigations at the Attaway Site, Henderson County, Texas. *Bulletin of the Texas Archeological Society* 52:142–178.

2006   *People of the Prairie: A Possible Connection to the Davis Site Caddo.* Module prepared for the Archeological Studies Program, Texas Department of Transportation and Prewitt and Associates, Inc.

Shafer, Harry J., Dee Ann Suhm, and J. Dan Scurlock

1964   An Investigation and Appraisal of the Archeological Resources of Belton Reservoir, Bell and Coryell Counties, Texas: 1962. Texas Archeological Salvage Project Papers No. 1, University of Texas at Austin.

294 | References Cited

Shafer, Harry J., and Thomas B. Stearns
1975   Archeological Investigations at the Scott's Ridge Site (41MQ41), Montgomery County, Texas. Anthropology Laboratory, Report No. 17, Texas A&M University, College Station.

Shafer, Harry J., John E. Dockall, and Robbie L. Brewington
1999   Archaeology of the Ojasen (41EO289) and Gobernadora (41EP321) Sites, El Paso County, Texas. A Joint Publication of the Center for Ecological Archaeology, Texas A&M University, Reports of Investigations No. 2 (College Station) and the Texas Department of Transportation, Environmental Affairs Division, Archeology Studies Program, Report 13 (Austin). Texas Antiquities Permit No. 292.

Shawn, Ronnie A.
1975   The Blue Hill Site Excavations. *Transactions of the Tenth Regional Archeological Symposium for Southeastern New Mexico and Western Texas.* South Plains Archeological Society, pp. 1–47.

Shiner, Joel L.
1983   Archeology of the Sheldon Site. *Bulletin of the Texas Archeological Society* 54:309–318.

Shott, Michael J.
1993   Spears, Darts, and Arrows: Late Woodland Hunting Techniques in the Upper Ohio Valley. *American Antiquity* 62:86–101.
1997   Stones and Shafts Redux: The Metric Discrimination of Prehistoric Dart and Arrow Points. *American Antiquity* 58:425–443.
2021   *Prehistoric Quarries and Terranes: The Modena and Tempiute Obsidian Sources of the American Great Basin.* University of Utah Press, Salt Lake City.

Simons, Helen
1988   *Archeological Bibliography for the Northern Panhandle Region of Texas.* Office of the State Archeologist, Special Report 30, Texas Historical Commission, Austin.

Simons, Helen, and William E. Moore
1997   *Archeological Bibliography for the Central Region of Texas.* Office of the State Archeologist, Special Report 36, Texas Historical Commission, Austin. With contributions by Norman A. Flaigg and Patricia Mercado-Allinger.

Skinner, S. Alan, R. King Harris, and Keith M. Anderson (editors)
1969   Archeological Excavations at the Sam Kaufman Site, Red River County, Texas. Southern Methodist University, Contributions in Anthropology No. 5. Dallas.

Smith, Clinton, and Jefferson D. Smith
2002   *The Boy Captives.* San Saba Printing, San Antonio. Reprint of the first edition published in 1927.

References Cited | 295

Smith, Ray
1984   Notes on Three Iron Projectile Points from South Texas. *La Tierra* 11(3):28–390.

Smyers, Cindy, R. Smyers, and David Calame Sr.
2019   The Esquivel Burial Cache (41CR33), Crane County, Texas. *La Tierra* 43:65–72.

Sollberger, J. B.
1967?   A New Type of Arrow Point with Speculations as to Its Origin. *The Record* 23(3):12–22.

1970   The Rockwall Point. *Newsletter of the Oklahoma Anthropological Society* 18(2):3–5.

1978   A New Type of Arrow Point with Speculations as to Its Origin. *La Tierra* 5(4):13–20.

Sorrow, William M.
1966   The Pecan Springs Site, Bardwell Reservoir, Texas. Texas Archeological Salvage Project Papers No. 10, University of Texas at Austin.

Spier, Leslie
1978   *Yuman Tribes of the Gila River.* Dover Press, New York.

Steele, D. Gentry, and E. R. Mokry Jr.
1983   Archeological Investigations of Seven Prehistoric Sites along Oso Creek, Nueces County, Texas. *Bulletin of the Texas Archeological Society* 54:287–308.

Steely, James Wright
1984   *A Catalog of Texas Properties in the National Register of Historic Places.* Texas Historical Commission, Austin.

Stephenson, Robert L.
1952   The Hogge Bridge Site and the Wylie Focus. *American Antiquity* 17(4):299–312.

Stillwell, Barbara
2011   Archaeology of Rough Enough Rockshelter, Val Verde, Texas: The 2000–2006 Excavations. *La Tierra* 38:1–48.

1981   Archeological Investigations at the George C. Davis Site, Cherokee County, Texas: Summers of 1979 and 1980. Texas Archeological Research Laboratory, Occasional Papers No. 1, University of Texas at Austin.

Story, Dee Ann
1965   The Archeology of Cedar Creek Reservoir, Henderson and Kaufman Counties, Texas. *Bulletin of the Texas Archeological Society* 36:263–257/.

Suhm, Dee Ann, and Alex D. Krieger
1954   An Introductory Handbook of Texas Archeology. *Bulletin of the Texas Archeological Society* 25. With a contribution by Edward B. Jelks.

296 | References Cited

Suhm, Dee Ann, and Edward B. Jelks
1962   *Handbook of Texas Archeology: Type Descriptions.* Texas Archeological Society, Special Publication Number. One and the Texas Memorial Museum, Bulletin No. 4.

Taylor, A. J.
1989   A Preliminary Study of Arrow Points. Unpublished manuscript on file at TARL.

Taylor, Walter W.
1966   Archaic Cultures Adjacent to the Northeastern Frontiers of Mesoamerica. In *Handbook of Middle American Indians* (Vol. 4), edited by Gordon F. Ekholm and Gordon R. Willey, pp. 59–94. University of Texas Press, Austin.

Thomas, David Hurst
1978   Arrowheads and Atlatl Darts: How the Stones Got the Shaft. *American Antiquity* 43(3):461–472.

Thoms, Alston V. (editor)
1993.   *The Brazos Valley Slopes Archaeological Project: Cultural Resource Assessments for the Texas A&M University Animal Science Teaching and Research Complex, Brazos County, Texas.* Reports of Investigations No. 14, Archaeological Research Laboratory, Texas A&M University, College Station. With contributions by Barry W. Baker, Shawn B. Carlson, Patricia A. Clabaugh, J. Phillip Dering, William A. Dickens, D. K. Kloetzer, Ben W. Olive, and Michael R. Waters.

Thurmond, J. Peter
1985   Late Caddoan Social Group Identifications and Sociopolitical Organization in the Upper Cypress Basin and Vicinity. *Bulletin of the Texas Archeological Society* 54:185–200.

Tomka, Steve A.
2016   Guerrero Arrow Points: Patterns of Distribution and Archeological Investigations. *Bulletin of the Texas Archeological Society* 87:101–122.

Thompson, Mark
1980   A Survey of Aboriginal Metal Points from the Apacheria. *The Artifact* 18(1):1–10.

Tully, L. N.
1986   *Flint Blades and Projectile Points of the North American Indians.* Collector Books, A Division of Schroeder Publishing Company, Paducah, Kentucky.

Tunnell, Curtis B.
1962   Oblate: A Rockshelter Site. In *Salvage Archeology of Canyon Reservoir: The Wunderlich, Footbridge, and Oblate Sites,* edited by LeRoy Johnson, Jr., Dee Ann Suhm, and Curtis D. Tunnell, pp. 77–116. Texas Memorial Museum Bulletin No. 5, University of Texas at Austin.

References Cited | 297

Tunnell, Curtis D., and W. W. Newcomb Jr.
1969   *A Lipan Apache Mission: San Lorenzo de la Santa Cruz, 1762-1771*. Bulletin of the Texas Memorial Museum 14, University of Texas at Austin.

Tunnell, Curtis D., Thomas R. Hester, and Gail L. Bailey
1998   *Chapters in the History of Texas Archeology: Selected Papers by E. Mott Davis*. Texas Archeological Research Laboratory, University of Texas at Austin.

Tunnell, John W., Jr, and Jace W. Tunnell
2015   *The Pape-Tunnell Collection*. Texas A&M University Press, College Station.

Turnbull, C. M.
1965   *Wayward Servants: The Two Worlds of the African Pygmies*. Eyre & Spottiswoode, London.

Turner, Ellen Sue, and Thomas R. Hester
1985   *A Field Guide to Stone Artifacts of Texas Indians*. Texas Monthly Press, Austin.
1993   *A Field Guide to Stone Artifacts of Texas Indians*. Texas Monthly Press. Austin.
1999   *A Field Guide to Stone Artifacts of Texas Indians*. Texas Monthly Press. Austin.

Turner, Ellen Sue, Thomas R. Hester, and Richard J. McReynolds
2011   *Stone Artifacts of Texas Indians*. Taylor Trade Publishing, Lanham, Maryland.

Turpin, Solveig A.
1998   Wroe Ranch: Small Shelter Occupancy on the Edge of the Trans-Pecos. Cultural Resource Report 3. Borderlands Archeological Research Unit, University of Texas at Austin.

Udden, Johan A., Charles Lawrence Baker, and E. Boise
1916   Texas University Bureau of Economics and Technology, Bulletin 44, p. 39, Lubbock.

Waguespack, Nicole M., Todd A. Surovell, Allen Denoyer, Alice Dallow, Adam Savage, Jamie Hyneman, and Dan Tapster
2009   Making a Point: Wood- versus Stone-Tipped Projectiles. *American Antiquity* 83:786–800.

Walters, E., and R. M. Rogers
1975   Notes on Presence of Indians of Historic Period in Pecos County and Iraan, Texas Area. *Transactions of the Tenth Regional Archeological Symposium for Southeastern New Mexico and Western Texas*. South Plains Archeological Society, pp. 89–100.

Watt, Frank H.
1935   Stone Implements of Central Texas. *Central Texas Archeologist* 1:16–19.
1967   Lookout Point, Lake Waco. *Central Texas Archeologist* 9:27–39.

298 | References Cited

Webb, Clarence H.
1948   Caddoan Prehistory, the Bossier Focus. *Bulletin of the Texas Archeological and Paleontological Society* 19:1–47.
1959   *The Belcher Mound: A Stratified Caddoan Site in Caddo Parish, Louisiana.* Memoirs for the Society of American Archaeology No. 16.
1963   The Smithport Landing Site: An Alto Focus Component in DeSoto Parish, Louisiana. *Bulletin of the Texas Archeological Society* 34:143–187.
1976   Typical Projectile Points. *Newsletter of the Louisiana Archaeological Society* 3(2):4–5.
1981   *Stone Points and Tools of Northwestern Louisiana.* Special Publication No. 1, Louisiana Archaeological Society, Lafayette.
2000   *Stone Points and Tools of Northwestern Louisiana.* Louisiana Archaeological Society, Lafayette.

Webb, Clarence H., and Monroe Dodd Jr.
1939   Bone "Gorget" from a Caddoan Mound Burial. *American Antiquity* 4:265–268.

Webb, Clarence H., and Ralph R. McKinney
1975   Mounds Plantation (16CD12), Caddo Parish, Louisiana. *Louisiana Archaeology* 2:39–127.

Weinstein, R. A.
2002   *Archaeological Investigations at the Guadalupe Bay Site (41CL2): Late Archaic through Historic Occupation along the Channel to Victoria, Calhoun County, Texas.* 2 vols. Coastal Environments, Inc., Baton Rouge. Submitted to Galveston District, US Army Corps of Engineers.

Weir, Frank
1956   Surface Artifacts from La Perdida, Starr County, Texas. *Bulletin of the Texas Archeological Society* 26:59–78.

Weir, Frank A., and Glen H. Doran
1980   The Anthon Site (41UV60). *La Tierra* 7(3):17–23.

Wesolowsky, A. B., Thomas R. Hester, and Douglas R. Brown
1976   Archeological Investigations at the Jetta Court Site (41TV151), Travis County, Texas. *Bulletin of the Texas Archeological Society* 47:25–87.

Wheat, Joe B.
1947   Notes on the W. A. Myatt Site. *Bulletin of the Texas Archeological and Paleontological Society* 18:87–93.
1953   An Archeological Survey of the Addicks Dam Basin: A Preliminary Report. *Bulletin of the Bureau of American Ethnology,* Washington, DC.

Wheat, Patricia, and Richard L. Gregg (editors)
1988   A Collection of Papers Reviewing the Archeology of Southeast Texas. Report No. 5, Houston Archeological Society.

References Cited | 299

Wheaton, Gene

2009 Investigations at 41CU658. In *Archaeological Investigations for the AT&T Nexgen/Core Project: Texas Segment: Part 2: Site Descriptions.* Western Cultural Resource Management, Inc., Farmington, New Mexico.

Wheeler, Richard P.

1954 Selected Projectile Point Types of the United States. *Bulletin of the Oklahoma Anthropological Society* 2(1–6).

White, A. M., Lewis R. Binford, and M. L. Papworth

1963 Miscellaneous Studies in Typology and Classification. Anthropological Papers No.19. Museum of Anthropology, University of Michigan, Ann Arbor.

Willey, Patrick S., and Jack T. Hughes

1978 *Archeology at Mackenzie Reservoir.* Texas Historical Commission and Office of the State Archeologist, Archeological Survey Report No. 24.

Williams, Stephen, and Jeffrey P. Brain

1983 *Excavations at the Lake George Site, Yazoo County, Mississippi, 1958–1960.* Papers of the Peabody Museum of Archaeology and Ethnology 74.

Wilson, D. E., and Thomas R. Hester

1996 *Salvage of Prehistoric Skeletal Remains from 41ZP7, the Beacon Harbor Lodge Site, Zapata County, Texas.* Technical Bulletin 45, Texas Archeological Research Laboratory, University of Texas at Austin.

Wiseman, Regge N.

1971 The Neff Site, a Ceramic Period Lithic Manufacture Site on the Rio Felix, Southeastern New Mexico (LA 5863). *The Artifact* 9(1):1–30.

Wood, W. Raymond

1963 Two New Projectile Points: Homan and Agee Points. *Arkansas Archeologist* 4(2):1–16.

Word, James H.

1971 The Dunlap Complex in Eastern Central Crockett County, Texas. *Bulletin of the Texas Archeological Society* 42:271–318.

Word, James H., and T. N. Campbell

1962 Metal Projectile Points from Floyd County, Texas. *Texas Archeology* 6(2):8–9.

Word, James H., and Charles L. Douglas

1970 Excavations at Baker Cave, Val Verde County, Texas. Texas Memorial Museum, Bulletin 16, Austin.

Wormington, H. Marie

1957 *Ancient Man in North America.* Denver Museum of Natural History, Popular Series No. 4.

300 | References Cited

Yang, Wen, Bernd Gludovatz, Elizabeth A. Zimmermann, Hrishikesh A. Bale, Robert O. Ritchie, and Marc A. Meyers

2013   Structure and Fracture Resistance of Alligator Gar (*Artactosteus spatula*) Armored Fish Scales. *Acta Biomaterialia* 9(4):5876–5889.

Young, Wayne C.

1981a   *Investigations at the Squawteat Peak Site, Pecos County, Texas.* Texas State Department of Highways and Public Transportation, Highway Design Division, Publications in Archaeology No. 20, Austin.

1981b   *Test Excavations at the Tankersley Creek Site, Titus County, Texas.* Texas State Department of Highways and Public Transportation, Highway Design Division Publications in Archaeology, Report No. 22, Austin.

1982a   *Archaeological Excavations at Site 41BT6, Burnet County, Texas.* Texas State Department of Highways and Public Transportation, Highway Design Division Publications in Archaeology, Report No. 28, Austin.

1982b   *Excavations at the Ram's Head Site (41PC35), Pecos County, Texas.* Texas State Department of Highways and Public Transportation. Highway Design Division, Publications in Archaeology, Report No. 23, Austin.

Yu, Pei-Lin

2006   From Atlatl to Bow and Arrow: Implicating Projectile Technology in Changing Systems of Hunter-Gatherer Mobility. In *Archaeology and Ethnoarchaeology of Mobility*, edited by Frederic Sellet, Russel Greaves, and Pei-Lin Yu, pp. 201–220. University Press of Florida, Gainesville.

Index

agate, 25, 29, 30, 32, 130, 139, 198
Agee point type, 75–77
Ahumada point type, 78–79
Alazán point type, 80–83
Alba point type, 83–88
Alibates agate, 32, 130
Alibates chert, 25, 32–33, 46, 118, 152, 212, 230
Alibates Flint Quarries, 32
Anagua point type, 89–90
archeological planning regions, 59–67
arrowhead, defined, 13–24
atlatl, 13–14, 16–17, 236

basalt, 25, 33, 41
Bassett point type, 90–93
Bayou Goula point type, 93–94
Benton point type, 172–73
bird points, 18
black banded metamorphic rock, 33–34
black chert, 33
black marine chert, 33
Bonham point type, 95–97
Boomerang point type, 125–27
Bulbar Stemmed point type, 97–99
Burrow Mesa chert, 28

Caballos novaculite, 38
Cameron point type, 99–101
Canyon chert, 38
Caracara point type, 102–4
Catahoula point type, 104–8
Catahoula sedimentary quartzite, 35

Central and Southern Planning Region, 63–66
Central Coastal Plains subregion, 64
Central Texas subregion, 64–65
Chadbourne point type, 108–9
chalcedony, 25, 29, 30, 32, 38
chert: Alibates, 25, 32–33, 46, 118, 152, 212, 230; black, 33; black marine, 33; Burrow Mesa, 28; Canyon, 38; Cowhouse White, 27; Eagle Hill, 35; Edwards Plateau, 26, 34–35; El Sauz, 25, 27, 35; Fleming Gravel, 35; Fort Hood Gray, 27; Fort Hood Tan, 27; Georgetown Flint/Blue, 25, 36; gravel, 35; Heiner Lake, 27; intercalated, 34; Jarilla, 36; Maravillas/Maravillas Gap, 38; Owl Creek Black, 27, 38; Pisgah Ridge, 36–37; Potter, 43–44; Purple-Tan, 30; Rancheria, 41, 44; Round Rock, 45
Claremore point type, 172
Cliffton point type, 110–12
Colbert point type, 112–14
Cowhouse White chert, 27
Cuney point type, 114–16

Deadman's point type, 117–19
Diablo point type, 119–23
dolomite, 25, 32

Eagle Hill chert, 35
Eastern Planning Region, 61–63
Edwards Plateau chert, 26, 34–35

302 | Index

Edwards point type, 123–25
El Sauz chert, 25, 27, 35

feldspar, 34
felsite, 30, 35–36
Fillinger point type, 172, 173–74, 182
Fleming Gravel chert, 35
Fleming opal, 35
flint, 25. *See also* chert
Form 2 point type, 125–27
Fort Hood Gray chert, 27
Fort Hood Tan chert, 27
Fresno point type, 127–31
Friley point type, 131–34

Gar Scales point type, 25, 134–36
Garza point type, 137–40
gastroliths, 25
Georgetown Flint/Blue chert, 25, 36
glass points, 25, 71, 140–42
Granbury point type, 143–45
gravel chert, 35
Guadalupe point type, 145–47
Guerrero point type, 5, 147–49

Harbison point type, 172, 173, 182
Harrell point type, 150–52
Haskell point type, 6
Hayes point type, 153–55
Heiner Lake chert, 27
Homan point type, 155–57
hornstone, 25
Howard point type, 55–56
Huffaker point type, 55

intercalated chert, 34

Jarilla chert, 36
jasper, 25, 30, 43, 46

Kobs Triangular point type, 157–58

Lipantitlan point type, 172, 174, 181
Livermore point type, 159–61
Lott point type, 161–63
Lower Pecos subregion, 65
Lozenge point type, 163–65

Manning Fused Glass, 25, 37–39, 87
Maravillas/Maravillas Gap chert, 38
Maud point type, 167–69
McGloin point type, 165–67
Means point type, 169–71
metal points, 18–19, 21–25, 172–87
Moran point type, 187–89
Morris point type, 189–91

Navasot Beveled point type, 50
Northeast Texas subregion, 63
Northern Panhandle subregion, 66–67
notched point types, 50
novaculite, 25, 27, 38

obsidian, 24, 25, 33–34, 37, 38–43
opalite, 43
Owl Creek Black chert, 27, 38

Padre point type, 191–93
Perdiz point type, 193–200
Pinwah point type, 200–201
Pisgah Ridge chert, 36–37
Plains Planning Region, 66–67
planning regions, 59–67
Potter chert, 43–44
Prairie Savanna subregion, 61–62
Purple-Tan chert, 30

quartz, 34, 46
quartz arenite, 30
quartzite, 25, 31, 35, 41, 43–44, 46–47

Rancheria chert, 41, 44
raw materials, 25–47; agate, 25, 29, 30,

32, 130, 139, 198; basalt, 25, 33, 41; black banded metamorphic, 33–34; felsite, 30, 36; Georgetown flint, 25, 36; glass, 25, 71, 140–42; hornstone, 25; jasper, 25, 30, 43, 46; Manning Fused Glass, 25, 37–39, 87; novaculite, 25, 27, 38; obsidian, 24, 25, 33–34, 37, 39–43; opalite, 43; quartz, 34, 46; quartz arenite, 30; quartzite, 25, 31, 35, 41, 43–44, 46–47; rhyolite, 25, 29, 41, 44–45; shell, 214–15; silicified wood, 25, 35, 45–47; Tecovas Jasper, 46; Uvalde gravels, 46–47. *See also* chert

Ray point type, 202–3

rectanguloid stem point types, 52

Revilla point type, 203–5

rhyolite, 25, 29, 41, 44–45

Rio Grande Plains subregion, 65–66

Rockwall point type, 205–6

Round Rock chert/flint, 45

Sabinal point type, 207–9

Scallorn point type, 209–13

shell points, 214–15

silicified palm, 46

silicified wood, 25, 35, 45–47

Southeast Texas subregion, 62–63

Southern Coastal Corridor subregion, 65

Starr point type, 216–17

Steiner point type, 218–20

stemmed point types, 51–52

Talco point type, 220–22

Tecovas Jasper, 46

Toyah point type, 223–25

Trans-Pecos Planning Region, 53, 67

trinomial archeological site identification, 6

Turner point type, 226–27

Turney point type, 227–29

type sites, 5–6

Unnamed Region, 67

unnotched point types, 52

Uvalde gravels, 46–47

Washita point type, 229–31

Watson point type, 172

Young point type, 231–33

Zapata point type, 233–35

Zavala point type, 235–37